It has been fashionable for many years for science—medicine in particular and psychiatry explicitly—to reduce the human experience to biology, chemistry, and physics. For many, this has left the landscape of the healing arts ultimately barren and desolate. But thanks be to God, into this very landscape comes *The Opposite of Depression*, and with it our trusted guide Dr. David Carreon. Here we find the accessible, practical— and, above all, *hopeful*—words of one who knows his craft, who loves God, and whose mission is to bring help and healing to those of us who are willing to listen. Read this beautiful rendition of how to meaningfully respond to depression and discover the beauty of life in ways you might never have imagined.

CURT THOMPSON, MD
Author of *The Soul of Desire* and *Anatomy of the Soul*

The Opposite of Depression is far more than a book about mental health (though it's that too); it brilliantly inverts the contours of depression to reveal the way to a flourishing life. Bursting with insights on contemporary challenges from trauma to weariness to loneliness, it provides both a concrete way forward and the hope to inspire perseverance. If you're depressed, read this book. If you're not depressed, read this book.

JOHN ORTBERG
Founder of Become New and author of *Eternity Is Now in Session*

David Carreon is an outstanding young psychiatrist who truly understands the importance of addressing not only the mind, but also the body and the soul when it comes to living a life of meaning and fulfillment. Anyone who struggles with depression or is just weary of life-as-usual will find this book extremely helpful in pointing them in the direction of flourishing.

JEFFREY M. SCHWARTZ, MD
Coauthor of *You Are Not Your Brain*, *The Mind and the Brain*, and *The Wise Advocate*

The Opposite of Depression

DAVID M. CARREON, MD

THE

OPPOSITE

—— OF ——

DEPRESSION

What My Work with Suicidal Patients
Has Taught Me about Life, Hope,
and How to Flourish

TYNDALE
REFRESH®

Think Well. Live Well. Be Well.

For information about special discounts for bulk purchases, please contact Tyndale House Publishers at csresponse@tyndale.com, or call 1-855-277-9400.

Library of Congress Cataloging-in-Publication Data

A catalog record for this book is available from the Library of Congress.

ISBN 978-1-4964-5535-2 (hc)
ISBN 978-1-4964-5536-9 (sc)

Printed in the United States of America

30	29	28	27	26	25	24
7	6	5	4	3	2	1

To my wife, Abigail

Contents

Introduction

There's a well-known story about a farmer who went out to sow seeds in his field. As he broadcast the seed, some fell on the pathway and was quickly devoured by the birds. Other seed fell on rocky soil, where it sprouted quickly but just as quickly wilted under the hot sun. Still other seed fell among thorns, which grew up alongside the tender plants and eventually choked them out. But some seed fell on good, fertile soil, where the plants were able to put down deep roots and *flourish*, producing an abundant crop up to a hundred times what had been planted.[1]

This book is about how to flourish in life. It's about expanding and growing your overall sense of well-being—especially if you are struggling with a nagging sense of dissatisfaction or weariness, or if you're depressed. And who hasn't felt that way at some point? Life throws us challenges that test us physically, emotionally, mentally, and spiritually. If it hasn't happened to you yet, there's a chance it will someday, and a very good chance it will happen to someone you care about. But whatever your situation, and whatever your life circumstances, my hope is that this book will show you how to experience the fullness of life, health, and purpose.

My profession has given me a helpful vantage point for observing people who flourish and people who don't. As a psychiatrist specializing in treating major depression, I have witnessed the suffering of my patients firsthand and listened to their distress. Patients come to my clinic precisely because they are *not* flourishing. Their depression has robbed them of much of what makes life feel satisfying, purposeful, and worthwhile. But in the course of my practice, I have also seen that it's possible for someone to move from a crippling state of misery, weariness, and disappointment to a life of thriving.

Being depressed feels bad—very bad. But in my years of battling on behalf of and alongside patients with depression, I've learned that this misery-maker can serve a hidden and useful purpose: It gives us important clues about how to flourish instead.

As I'll explain in the chapters to come, the opposite of depression is not necessarily happiness or the complete absence of suffering. Even under the best of circumstances, life can be difficult, and we can't control everything that happens to us. But we can make *choices* and develop good *habits* that will give us greater contentment in our lives. We can discover a sense of meaning and purpose. We can feel all the emotions we're meant to feel. We can live out our deepest values more consistently. We can have the energy to pursue activities that give us joy. We can bring our best selves to our family, friends, and coworkers.

A key assumption of this book is that there are habits of well-being, just as there are habits of depression. Often, the habits of depression are exactly the opposite of the habits of flourishing. We will look at both sets of habits, and I will offer some practical steps you can take to start moving your life in a healthier and more satisfying direction.

The way you approach these action steps may differ from others, depending on your starting point—whether you're simply feeling weary or are downright depressed. (In the next chapter, we will explore the difference between dissatisfaction and depression.) If you're suffering from major depression, you don't have the energy right now to implement all the habits of flourishing we will discuss. That's okay. As we'll see, changing even one small pattern or practice can generate some positive momentum—something you can build on. I'll show you how to choose a practice and start changing your life—even if, at first, it's only a microstep at a time. Any positive step is progress, and progress leads to more progress. In other words, there's *hope*.

Another key assumption is that, as humans, we have inherent value and purpose. I'm writing as a Stanford-trained psychiatrist who is also a

Christian, and thus I have a high view of human flourishing. As you read, it will become clear that my faith is an important part of my worldview. It should also be clear that I don't assume my readers (or my patients) share my faith or my worldview. Most of what I've written is based on my clinical experience and the latest scientific knowledge, but I will also refer occasionally to spiritual wisdom, including stories and images from the Bible. These stories are part of our collective consciousness. They have endured, not least because of how deeply they have resonated with people. During the many centuries when scribes were rare and parchment was an audacious expense, countless good-but-not-great stories were likely lost. The stories in the book we now call the Bible were among the ones that made it through. You don't have to share my faith to find value in them.

My worldview also shapes the structure of this book, which is divided into three sections. The first section is about the *mind*, exploring the role of thoughts and feelings in depression and how we can train and use these capacities to build a better, more flourishing life. The second section shows how the *body* affects depression and depression affects the body, and how to transform the physical habits of depression into patterns that help us become healthier and more productive. The final section looks at the capacities of the *soul*, showing how we experience transcendent aspects of reality and how to lead a life of purpose and meaning.

Whether or not you share my worldview, I think you'll find that applying the habits of flourishing will help you move past much of what's keeping you stuck in your depression, dissatisfaction, or weariness. In the chapters to come, you'll learn how to recognize unhealthy patterns that can drag you down, and how to flip the script on those patterns so you can move toward greater well-being.

If even the thought of embarking on this journey feels a bit daunting or exhausting right now, I understand. And I want to encourage you. I believe every person is created in the image of God—and as such, is innately valuable. *You* are valuable. You are worthy of care. What's more, you are designed to flourish in mind, body, and soul. If you're ready to see new life blooming in your heart and mind, let's get started.

1

DEPRESSION'S SURPRISING GIFT

Out of the night that covers me,
Black as the pit from pole to pole,
I thank whatever gods may be
For my unconquerable soul.

WILLIAM HENLEY, "Invictus"

In a sense, a life of flourishing can be described very simply: It is the *opposite* of depression. Though you may be familiar with what depression feels like and how debilitating it can be, you may be surprised at how exceptionally common it is in our society.

In 2020, the National Institute of Mental Health estimated that 8.4 percent of adults in the United States had experienced a major depressive disorder in the previous year.[1] Add to that all the people with bipolar depression, subclinical depression, and dysthymia—a less severe but more persistent and longer-lasting form of depression—and we're talking about a substantial segment of the population, including many of our friends, family members, and coworkers. I'm sure you know many people living with depression. Maybe you're one of them.

As a psychiatrist, I have focused my career on combating major depressive disorder—and let me tell you, I *hate* depression. It is a pernicious and tenacious enemy. Not only is depression both common and debilitating, but it is also *pervasive*. Unlike most other medical conditions, which may affect one or more parts or systems in the body but leave the mind intact, depression impinges on *every* aspect of a person: body, mind, and soul (that aspect of ourselves that relates to the supernatural or transcendent).

Severe depression may cause altered moods, disordered sleep, changes in weight, an inability to concentrate, sexual dysfunction, and many other incapacitating symptoms. In fact, depression's reach goes even deeper than our physical and mental selves. Whereas cancer may metastasize within the body but leave our cognition and personality intact, depression metastasizes throughout our entire being—affecting our deepest sense of identity, our sense of purpose, our faith in God, and our hopes for this life and the next.

People with depression don't just feel like a more limited version of themselves; they don't feel like themselves *at all*. Understandably, this can make them question the value of their existence. Depression is one of the worst states of disease a person can experience, and it has been found to be the second leading cause of disability worldwide.[2] The authors of a 2015 research study that sought to quantify all medical suffering on a scale from 0.0 to 1.0 found that enduring a day with severe depression (0.66) was even worse than a day when a person has a nonfatal heart attack (0.43) or a day living with unrelieved terminal cancer (0.57). In short, depression was found to be more debilitating than nearly every illness covered in the survey.[3]

Though the researchers defined *death* as the extreme end of the spectrum (1.0), some of my patients have told me they would prefer death. These people are not being overly dramatic; sadly, it's simply a common feeling.

Depression has afflicted the human race for a very long time. One gut-wrenching illustration of the despair that often accompanies depression is found in the story of Job, one of the most ancient stories recorded in the Bible. It's a story passed down by people with souls like ours; people whose storytelling may have gone a long way toward making us who we are.

As the story unfolds, Job loses all his wealth, his ten children are killed, and he is saddled with a chronic illness and emotionally abandoned by his wife. Finally, as if all that weren't enough, Job is falsely accused by his closest friends of causing his own suffering.[4] In the midst of his agony, he cries out,

When I lie down I think, "How long before I get up?"
The night drags on, and I toss and turn until dawn. . . .
My days are swifter than a weaver's shuttle,
and they come to an end without hope. . . .
I prefer strangling and death,
rather than this body of mine.

JOB 7:4, 6, 15, NIV

Like many of my patients, Job had manifold symptoms, and everything together produced a desire for death. But that's not the end of the story. Fortunately, there's hope. Understanding the miserable details of depression can be useful, not only to create empathy in others for those who suffer, but also to help us see what the *good life*—the opposite of depression—looks like. For that, it's helpful to look at what happens when depressed people get well.

In the course of my clinical work, I see both the suffering caused by depression and the relief that comes when people are healed of their depression. It is truly awe-inspiring to witness, not unlike a resurrection. And it has important lessons to teach every one of us.

ARISE, O SLEEPER

I run a clinic in Silicon Valley called Acacia Mental Health. We provide holistic care—including psychotherapy and traditional medication management—for the most hopelessly depressed. But when other therapies don't work, we also have a secret weapon: a treatment called *transcranial magnetic stimulation* (TMS).

TMS has been around since 1985 and has been FDA cleared since 2008 as a safe, effective, noninvasive treatment for major depression.[5] TMS activates or deactivate parts of the brain, restoring the brain to normal patterns. Typically, TMS is administered through a monthslong course of treatment, but Acacia is one of only a few clinics in the world to apply TMS in an accelerated manner, compressing the entire treatment into five consecutive days. As of this writing, we're also one of only a very few clinics using a patient's individual brain activity, measured by functional magnetic resonance imaging (fMRI), to target treatment. This allows us to stimulate the exact part of the brain most likely to alleviate depression. We also integrate other aspects of treatment (such as therapy and chaplaincy) to care for the person's soul, through a process we call HOPE—Holistic, Optimized, Personalized, Expedited—TMS. In short, we can radically change people's brain activity in a matter of a few days, restoring them to mental health.

I love my job because I regularly get to see people who have lost all hope walk into our clinic on Monday and walk out on Friday with their depression gone. I often receive comments such as these: "I feel quiet inside . . . like I used to be" and "I feel like I have my life back." Sometimes friends and family who don't know that the patient has gotten the treatment will notice positive changes in the color of their face, their posture, or how they walk.

Following up with psychotherapy and adjustments to medication, we have helped many people escape from truly terrible depressions. But what's most relevant for our purposes here is that the *speed* of this new treatment has provided amazing insights into the nature of depression.

When I practiced traditional psychiatry, change was typically slow—often almost imperceptible. After meeting with depressed patients for session after session with little tangible improvement, it was easy to start believing that the morose people sitting in my office had always been that way; depression felt much more like a permanent personality than an acquired condition. When recovery occurred, it was usually gradual and thus the changes were often difficult to notice from one session to the next. But with accelerated TMS, the improvements that occur during the compressed, five-day treatment course are readily apparent and often quite remarkable.

It's almost as if our patients *wake up* from their depression. When they first come in, they haven't been feeling like themselves for a very long time—in some cases, for more than a decade—and that's because they *weren't* like themselves. I understand this now because, after successful HOPE TMS treatment, I can see who they really are. One of the great joys of my job is being able to meet the real person underneath all the despair and hopelessness.

I remember one patient who came to me on a Monday for a five-day treatment. What she didn't tell me until a year later was that she'd had supplies in her car to kill herself on Saturday if the treatment hadn't worked by Friday. But it *did* work. By the end of the week, she was free of any thoughts of suicide, and they had not returned by a year later.

As I began observing these rapid and remarkable changes, it gradually dawned on me that a bright and shining gift lay hidden within the terrifying package of depression: *Because depression is practically the definition of a life that disappoints, discourages, and debilitates, its opposite must be a unique and powerful representation of the good life.*

Depression can hold us down in so many domains of life, but without depression we are free to pursue wellness in all those same domains. Sometimes it's hard to see our desired life up ahead on the horizon. Sometimes the only way to find the right direction is by walking away from the coldness and chaos of despair, by doing something—*anything*—that moves us in a positive direction.

I soon found, however, that taking away the biological *symptoms* of depression doesn't necessarily take away the *habits* of depression: lack of exercise, poor diet, isolation, poor sleep patterns, ignoring beauty, avoiding church and community activities, unhealthy thought patterns, neglecting to serve others, and so on. These people were undepressed, but they weren't *thriving*; their lives were not flourishing. Depression isn't just a painful emotion, and the opposite of depression is not just the absence of depressive symptoms or just feeling good emotionally. Depression is an actual illness that affects every aspect of our lives. But the reverse is also true: Every aspect of our lives can have an effect on our depression. What we've learned by temporarily reversing depression using tools such as rapid TMS is that people will not achieve true flourishing unless they start adopting habits of well-being. The good news is that there are several different entry points into flourishing and we can pick a place to start.

Once the depression lifts, people need to learn some new habits—healthy habits—that support a life of meaning and purpose. This can be done even when suffering is still part of their lives. Though it's neither possible nor desirable to avoid all emotional pain, it's almost always possible for someone to adopt at least some patterns of a flourishing life, and to experience more contentment than they would have otherwise.

Here's an analogy you might find helpful: Learning new life habits after recovering from depression is similar to doing physical therapy after surgery. The surgeon can replace a bad knee, but physical therapy is still needed to restore optimal function. Moreover, learning how to move appropriately will help to prolong the benefits of the surgery and possibly prevent further damage.

Likewise, if you're in the grip of depression, there are therapies available to help you feel like your true self again. That's where you want to start. But once the disease of depression has been successfully treated and you're ready to pursue a more flourishing life, you will still need to recognize and unlearn the *habits* of depression and replace them with the habits of flourishing. What you will find in the remainder of this book are practical and proven ways to do just that—to start moving toward the *opposite* of depression.

WHAT DOES IT MEAN TO FLOURISH?

Though I will share many insights in these pages about the disorder of depression (where I think they can be helpful), depression is ultimately not what this book is about.[6] While I believe the practices in this book, along with professional treatment, can help a depressed person heal, my primary focus is on how to live life to the full—that is, to *flourish*.

Flourishing means living a life that develops as it should—just as an acorn will flourish by growing into a healthy oak tree if not hindered by drought, disease, or weeds. People who flourish grow into a more developed version of themselves, without the hindrance of mental illness, bad habits, or unedifying relationships. Flourishing people have good habits of body, not slowed down by unnecessary sugar crashes or sleep deprivation. Flourishing people have activities that are meaningful, relationships that are full of love, and a relationship with God or the transcendent that pulls them forward into the future.

Flourishing doesn't just mean *happiness*—which many people assume is the opposite of depression. Recovery from depression doesn't merely mean feeling happy again. It's about feeling a *full range* of emotions. Depression often paints a monochromatic gray over its victims' emotions, regardless of their actual circumstances, but recovery helps people experience a variety of *appropriate* emotions. Sometimes that emotion is happiness, but if one's circumstances are objectively bad, then the appropriate feeling might be sadness, anger, grief, or some other seemingly negative emotion. Flourishing means being able to respond appropriately to our circumstances and take meaningful steps to improve the quality of our lives—in every aspect.

Mood is only one part of the picture. Depression involves so many other dimensions of a person's life. What if we could actively seek depression's opposite in all those areas, or at least the ones that are most important to us? What if we could see new life sprouting up everywhere?

I strongly believe that, by understanding how depression affects every major domain of a person's life, we can learn how to flourish in those same areas. By pursuing the opposite of depression, we have the beginning of a pathway toward physical health, mental calmness, interpersonal connection, and ultimate meaning.

Flourishing will not look the same for everyone. Tolstoy said, "All happy families are like one another; each unhappy family is unhappy in its own way,"[7] but it seems to me the opposite is true of people with depression. Though depression can be somewhat monotonous in the type of misery it produces, every flourishing person flourishes in a unique way. The fascinating variety of human traits, characteristics, and interests that emerge is a beautiful thing. God seems to love diversity, be it of heavenly bodies, each separate in its brilliance; of animals, each different in its appearance and habits; or of humans, in the multitude of diverse ways we express our true selves when unhindered by depression, oppression, or distraction.

What kind of flourishing have you been dreaming about? What deficiencies in your life will cause you regret if you don't deal with them? These are the areas where you can concentrate on learning to flourish.

ARE YOU DEPRESSED OR ARE YOU JUST WEARY?

This book is for anyone who wants greater well-being, but especially for two broad groups of readers: those who are *depressed* and those who are *weary*. As I provide descriptions of these two groups, I invite you to think about which one fits you best. Your identity as either depressed or weary can affect which information in this book will be most helpful to you, which goals you will settle on, and how quickly you can expect change to occur.

In this section, I will describe the symptoms of depression. But before I do, a quick word of caution: *A book cannot diagnose depression.* There is no substitute for professional evaluation; wisdom and experience are required to appropriately apply general criteria or descriptions to real people. Though this book can be a helpful complement to professional treatment, you will get the most out of it once your depression has improved. To deal with your depression, see a doctor or therapist, and then move on to the opposite of depression with the help of this book.

According to the *Diagnostic and Statistical Manual of Mental Disorders* (DSM), in my role as a physician I may diagnose a person with major depressive disorder if he or she has had at least five of the following nine symptoms for at least two weeks and these symptoms are causing social or occupational impairment:

1. Depressed mood most of the day, nearly every day, as indicated by subjective report (e.g., feeling sad, empty, hopeless) or observation made by others (e.g., appears tearful).
2. Markedly diminished interest or pleasure in all, or almost all, activities most of the day, nearly every day (as indicated by either subjective account or observation).
3. Significant weight loss when not dieting, or weight gain (e.g., a change of more than 5 percent of body weight in a month), or decrease or increase in appetite nearly every day. (In children, this can manifest as failure to make expected weight gains.)
4. Insomnia or hypersomnia nearly every day.
5. Psychomotor agitation (e.g., fidgeting, pacing, tapping, rapid talking) or impairment (e.g., trouble with walking, daily activities, or communication) nearly every day (observable by others, not merely subjective feelings of restlessness or being slowed down).
6. Fatigue or loss of energy nearly every day.
7. Feelings of worthlessness or excessive or inappropriate guilt (which may be delusional) nearly every day (not merely self-reproach or guilt about being sick).

8. Diminished ability to think or concentrate, or indecisiveness, nearly every day (either by subjective account or as observed by others).

9. Recurrent thoughts of death (not just fear of dying), recurrent suicidal ideation without a specific plan, or a suicide attempt or a specific plan for dying by suicide.[8]

Those are the formal criteria, and they often play out in the following ways:

- You lose your appetite and neglect good nutrition.
- Your movements are curtailed and sluggish.
- You can't sleep, and when you do it doesn't feel restorative.
- You feel despondent and despairing every hour of every day.
- Nothing in your life feels good; pleasure is a distant memory that feels as if it happened to someone else, or else it's a shadow of what it once was.
- Your attention and focus are all over the board, driven by the hurricane winds of emotion and circumstance.
- You have limited ability to take action; your depression might as well be physical chains holding you down on your bed, or a physical weight you carry everywhere.
- You are racked with guilt, beating yourself up for sins, both real and imagined.
- Your past haunts you, destroying current relationships and experiences that would otherwise be shelters in the storm.
- Whatever action you take feels meaningless; you can't imagine anything you could do that would matter.
- Your mind sends you deceptive messages throughout the day— like propaganda from a hostile radio station. You believe what you're hearing, feeling powerless to rebut the arguments.
- Many of your relationships have faded away because of neglect or conflict; those that remain feel flat.
- The world appears gray, with no beauty or transcendence.
- You are convinced that nothing will ever change. You feel that any choices you make will be pointless or futile.

Depression can feel like fighting for your life in a chaotic sea—like you must swim with all your might merely to keep your head above water and survive.

WEARINESS

But what if you're not actually depressed? What if your burdens aren't as heavy as those associated with clinical depression, yet the inordinate weight of daily existence is pulling you down and wearing you out? Maybe you've fallen prey to the ennui so pervasive in our culture—that dull sense of dissatisfaction that afflicts so many in Western society today. There's nothing exactly *wrong*, but in a way, that's the problem. You're disappointed with the direction of your life but feel powerless to change it. I refer to those in this state as people who are *weary*. Weariness is not a mental illness, per se. It doesn't have criteria listed in the DSM. But it's something I often see in a professional capacity as people emerge from episodes of major depressive disorder, or hear about ever more commonly, even apart from those who've had a formal diagnosis.

Do you feel relief when someone cancels their plans with you? Do you feel as if you barely make it through the day, often feeling tired? Are you often sad? Do you feel distracted and unable to focus and do deep work? Do you have a hard time believing that what you're doing really matters? Do you feel bored when you're not working? Do you feel a bit detached or lukewarm toward friends or family? Do you beat yourself up about minor mistakes you've made? Do you rarely feel a sense of transcendence?

If you answered yes to several of the above, you might be weary. That's the catchall word I've chosen to use here, but there are many other labels that describe similar states: *burned out, melancholy, glum, morose, dissatisfied.* If this describes you, you're not depressed. In fact, you're probably pretty typical. You probably don't need to see a doctor. Prozac wouldn't help you. However, you're not fully free. You are carrying invisible weights that make everything harder. You can still move and change, but it takes extra effort and vision that may be hard to conjure up. Life is hard for everyone, but if you're in that in-between space—somewhere between depression and flourishing—the difficulties of life seem to weigh heavier. But again, there's hope.

FIRST STEPS FOR THOSE WHO ARE DEPRESSED

So where do we begin in our efforts to turn a life of depression into a life of flourishing?

First, remember that you are worthy of care. You have a truly devastating condition that affects your body, mind, and soul. You ought to be provided with mental health care that addresses your entire being. This may include treatments such as psychotherapy, medication, or brain stimulation.

Second, it's important for you to know that treatment *works*. Psychotherapy works. Medications work. Brain stimulation works. Like any medical treatment, there are exceptions to the rule, but most people who get treatment find relief. If you have tried all of this and it hasn't helped—which is when most of my patients come to me—you are the exception. But you should know that psychiatry is rapidly advancing, and we may well have new treatments soon.

Third, in combination with treatment, there are steps you can take to move against your burdens. While there's no guarantee you'll ever be fully free of all symptoms of depression in this life, there is value in fighting the disease regardless. You are meant to thrive, and it is worth the effort to pursue a return to full health.

So, how do you fight? Where do you start?

We will explore a range of action steps you can take in different areas of your life. If you are dealing with depression, you may need to begin with the simpler ones. There's nothing wrong with that. Quite the opposite! As you start to improve, you may be able to choose more ambitious goals. In any case, it's likely your suffering is only temporary. Medical and other treatments may provide relief from your depression, perhaps sooner than you imagine.

Some people describe themselves as "depressive," as if depression itself is an inseparable part of their being. But I want you to know that your depression can be fully separated from who you are, restoring you to a healed and complete person. Your suffering is not essentially who you are; it is a condition that can often be successfully treated. Not unlike a resurrection, you can be "brought back to life," free of the disease you once had.

The best way to start moving toward a reality characterized by freedom from depression is by *fighting* the disease. Look for positive things you can do that you're not doing now, or for negative things you're doing that you should stop. Take one step at a time and believe that it's worth it, even if it feels futile. Step by step, you may be able to find your way out of the dark forest of depression and keep going—not just back to "normal" but on to flourishing.

FIRST STEPS FOR THOSE WHO ARE WEARY

If you're not clinically depressed but you're weary, let the soul-draining dissatisfaction you feel drive you to change. Let it be the annoyance that prompts you to take off your shoe and shake out the pebble. There's a lot you can do to turn your life in a more positive direction. Though you may not be brimming with motivation right now, you have enough energy to start reworking habits and attitudes that are not serving you well. Where to begin? Anywhere you like! All positive movement is movement toward a more flourishing outlook on life. The peak toward which you are navigating is the same as for those who are depressed, but you're closer to it and have more resources at your disposal to complete the journey.

Whether you *feel* it or not, you are in an incredibly good position. Though it's not always the case for someone who is clinically depressed that making lifestyle changes alone will lead to a lifting of the depression, most people who are weary, burned out, or dissatisfied will find that even small changes in the right direction can kick-start a virtuous cycle. Every positive change leads to a greater ability to make more positive changes. The more success you have, the more you will be able to change. It's easier to get from weariness to flourishing, because you're both closer to your goal and have more capacity to make changes.

A LIFE IN BLOOM

In the course of providing rapid TMS treatments to depressed people, I have come to believe that depression uniquely incapacitates the core faculties of the human experience. But with successful treatment, many patients can learn to exhibit a delightful variety of ways to flourish. What depression teaches us about ourselves provides valuable information for making progress toward our desires, whether we are depressed or merely languishing in our dissatisfaction with the status quo. This truth informs the remainder of this book.

STEPS TOWARD FLOURISHING

If you are suffering from depression or if you are weary, burned out, or dissatisfied with your life, the first thing you need to know is that there is *hope* for a better day. You may need to receive treatment or therapy (if you are depressed) and/or learn and apply the habits of flourishing, but life *can* be better than what you're experiencing now. You can start by internalizing three fundamental truths: (1) You are worthy of care, (2) treatment *works*, and (3) there are steps you can take to be free from your burdens.

Part 1

MIND

2

MOOD: FEELINGS AND EMOTIONS

Jesus wept.
JOHN 11:35

Blessed are those who mourn,
for they shall be comforted.
MATTHEW 5:4

What is the human mind? To materialists, our bodies are all we are. Many materialists doubt whether the mind has any reality that cannot be reduced to the physical properties of the brain. Perhaps the most succinct summary of this viewpoint comes from Francis Crick, the codiscoverer of DNA:

> "You," your joys and your sorrows, your memories and your ambitions, your sense of personal identity and free will, are in fact no more than the behavior of a vast assembly of nerve cells and their associated molecules. . . . You're nothing but a pack of neurons.[1]

Dr. Jeffrey M. Schwartz, an acclaimed neuroscientist at UCLA, and also my colleague and mentor, declares a contrary view in the title of his book *You Are Not Your Brain*. Dr. Schwartz draws an important distinction between the human *brain* and the *mind*:

The brain receives inputs and generates the *passive* side of experience, whereas the mind is *active*, focusing attention, and making decisions. . . .

The brain receives information from the environment, including images, verbal communication from others, emotional reactions, bodily sensations, and so on, and then processes that information in an automatic and rote way . . . [and] presents the information to our conscious awareness. . . .

The mind has the ability to determine whether it wants to focus either on that information coming from the brain or on something else. . . .

In essence, the mind is the agent that ensures you are following the path to achieving your goals as defined by your true self . . . using insight, awareness, morals, and values to guide your responses and empower you to make choices that are in your long-term best interest. . . .

The brain and the mind work together, as a team. Neither is "better" than the other.[2]

I'm on Dr. Schwartz's side. I believe that, as humans, we have a mind that is closely associated with the brain but can be meaningfully discussed as not merely the firing of neurons. Undoubtedly, there is mystery and uncertainty about the properties of the mind; but I believe there is much we already understand about it that we can use to pursue our vision of the good life.

The mind has many capacities and abilities—including the capacity to feel the tragedy of a loved one's death, and to see right and wrong. It has the ability to experience sadness and happiness; to focus attention and reprogram the brain; to drive us toward our goals; to recall the past and tune the brain to be prepared for future situations.

Although depression can affect all of these capacities and abilities, the mind is nevertheless a crucial avenue for healing a person from depression.

What is the emotional context that your mind is providing for your life? If you're stuck in mostly negative thoughts—sadness, bitterness, and hopelessness, for example—you're not likely to make much progress toward the kind of future you'd like to have for yourself. But "looking on the bright side" or "putting on a smile" isn't the answer either. What we'll discover through looking at depression is that having a rich life in an imperfect world requires us to experience feelings that are appropriate to each situation.

AMONG THE MELANCHOLY

The first topic in our discussion of the mind will be *mood*, which is usually the first thing we think of when it comes to defining depression. A depressed mood is the most blatant of depressive symptoms. In fact, many people think of depression simply as being sad. But if you've never been clinically depressed, it's difficult to appreciate just how deep that well of sadness goes. Many would even object to my calling it sadness, because the depression experience is qualitatively different. The truth is, many depressed people have been *terribly* sad for a *very long* time. It's worse than what most undepressed people experience during even the most difficult times of their lives. People may say they feel "low" from time to time, but a depressed patient's feelings can create a deep valley or bottomless gorge in their emotional landscape.

When I began treating seriously depressed people, I quickly came to realize that their sadness could be palpable—as if their moods emanated gravity like a heat lamp emanates warmth.

The other notable thing about depression is how *persistent* it can be. The sadness doesn't come and go; it mostly comes and stays. By formal definition, a depressed person's mood is down at least half the day, nearly every day. For most people with depression, there's little variance in how bad they feel. Even worse is when they don't feel anything at all.

For some people who are depressed, things start out sad or blue, perhaps with weeping and crying. But when the depression gets worse, that blue turns to black—a void, a vacancy, a hopelessness that isn't just sadness; a despair that isn't just weeping. It's around this time that the tears dry up and the person becomes emotionally numb. For many, this experience feels worse than even the terrible sadness.

Problems bring real pain, and the resulting sorrow (perhaps even mild or periodic depression) may have a serious effect on our lives. When our emotions are inappropriate—when they don't align with our circumstances in scope or intensity—they can hinder our progress or even paralyze us. Emotions are inappropriate when they are maladaptive and they keep us from achieving our goals or living flourishing lives. We can't eliminate every sadness-causing circumstance in our lives, but if we want to move forward toward the good life, we must learn what to do with our emotions, particularly the negative ones.

WHY DO WE HAVE EMOTIONS?

You might ask, Why do we have emotions in the first place? What is their purpose? Though there's no easy or short definition of human emotion, we can point to several things that are clear about what emotions are and what they do.

Perhaps the most important thing that healthy emotions do for us is help to *direct our attention*. Suppose you received some sad, but not devastating, news. Perhaps a cousin you knew but weren't particularly close to has passed away. When you attend the funeral, you feel sadness, and in this state your attention is directed away from the problem at work you were thinking about and toward other losses in your life. Maybe you were thinking about a conflict with a colleague, but then you realize there are ways in which you haven't done all you could to resolve conflict in your own family. In the sorrow of the moment, memories of your cousin begin to bubble up. You focus on your own mortality and reflect on the ways you haven't been living in light of your inevitable death. The appropriate emotion of sadness shifts your attention toward thoughts, memories, and ideas that would otherwise be displaced by workaday concerns. Thus, attending the funeral, and the strong emotion of sadness that results, directs your attention toward ultimate concerns. In the wise words of King Solomon:

> It is better to go to the house of mourning
>   than to go to the house of feasting,
> for this is the end of all mankind,
>   and the living will lay it to heart.
> Sorrow is better than laughter,

for by sadness of face the heart is made glad.
The heart of the wise is in the house of mourning,
   but the heart of fools is in the house of mirth.[3]

Different emotions draw our attention to different types of things—for example, sadness to loss; or anger to trespass or injustice. Emotions are like a special type of vision. Just as soldiers sometimes use thermal goggles to see heat signatures that would otherwise be invisible to the naked eye, emotions are the thermal goggles of our daily experience. We have the ability to turn on special kinds of vision that vary with our emotions. Like a background color, emotions help to highlight the kind of environment we're in. Is this a sad scene or a happy one? An anxious moment or an angry one?

Emotions can also shift our metabolism and physiology. They help our bodies adapt to our current circumstances. Does blood need to go to our digestive system or our muscles? Does our heart need to beat faster or slower? Emotions highlight things psychologically, but they also affect the optics of our eyeballs. When we're angry, our pupils dilate, creating a shallower depth of field so that one thing is in focus and the background is blurred. Our physical vision is focused on our opponent. When we're calm again, our pupils constrict, creating a deeper depth of field.

Emotions help us shift our psychological energy as well. Some emotions are useful for increasing our energy, others for decreasing our energy—again, to enable us to respond appropriately.

Emotions are also a *lightning-fast calculator.* Here's how it works: We'll have a microflash of emotion, say, about a word or an image to which we're exposed. Then—sometimes even before we can consciously process the word or image—it affects our emotions, which in turn influences our actions. If this is a good word or a bad word, an angry word or a sad word, we get micro-experiences that prime us to respond accordingly.

But respond *how?*

We have certain sets of emotions built in from birth. The ability to be angry or frightened when in pain, for example, is common to both humans and animals. But we can also be conditioned by our culture to respond in certain ways. In one study, researchers flashed a country's flag to participants for 16 milliseconds, too fast to be consciously perceived. Nevertheless, it affected how participants answered questions afterward. As the researchers summarized their findings, "subtle reminders of one's nationality significantly influence political thought and overt political behavior."[4]

This is quite useful, as the process of making every decision rationally and deliberatively would be exhausting. Being able to navigate nearly every decision because we've trained our emotions to be in line with our higher values allows us to focus our attention on the really hard decisions.

Emotions also help us *communicate with others*—in everything from facial expressions to tone of voice to cadence of speech. When we're sad, for example, it shows on our face and in our body language. The same goes for other emotions, such as being fearful, angry, or elated. People can pick up on our emotions without our saying a word. And they can react accordingly.

Imagine you've stopped by a friend's home. You show up with a smile on your face, expecting a friendly greeting and some happy chatter and laughter. But when your friend opens the door, she is wearing a frown and her shoulders are drooping. You know immediately that your friend is unhappy, and your own face quickly loses its brightness. You say, "Oh no, what's wrong?" Your friend hasn't said a word yet, but you're already prepared to respond to her in an appropriate way.

The communication created by our emotions is not always straightforward; it can be more like the mood in a piece of music than like an explicit description of feelings. Nonetheless, our interest is piqued and we look closer to try to figure out what is going on.

ARE EMOTIONS GOOD?

So are our emotions actually good? Some say we should just seek the positive and avoid the negative. But that's a naive perspective—at least in a finite and imperfect world. Proper sadness is an appropriate response to loss. Proper anger is an appropriate response to trespass or injustice. Proper anxiety is an appropriate response to uncertainty or threat. As long as such things as loss, injustice, and threat are part of this world, these emotions will be as well.

As long as we are here on earth, negative emotions are appropriate. As I tell my fellow Christians, Jesus himself felt frustration, anguish, anger, and sorrow, so there must be times when those emotions are suitable for us as well.[5]

Feeling some degree of sadness isn't what's so problematic about a depressed mood. A bigger problem for those who are depressed is the inability to experience a full range of emotions because they feel *nothing but* sadness much of the time, or else just numbness. They aren't reacting to the reality around them in appropriate ways—they aren't able to. And for the rest of us who periodically get stuck in sadness or other negative emotions, we're experiencing the same limitation, even if we don't realize it.

Emotions are valuable in shaping how we view the world. We must be able to experience our emotions appropriately in order to benefit from them.

ERRANT EMOTIONS

It's not uncommon to hear that we shouldn't *judge* our emotions. Emotions aren't right or wrong, the thinking goes. They simply *are*. This is an almost universal opinion among my colleagues, but it's *erroneous*. Not every emotion is good.

To suggest such a thing is blasphemy in many circles. For some, authentic emotion is the ground truth of reality and experience, the holy flame that must be guarded against all attempts to change or alter it. Yet there are many ways in which emotions can be bad. For one thing, we can say from a behavioral perspective that a particular emotion isn't *useful*. For example, the all-pervading despair of depression serves no good purpose. We can also say that an emotion isn't *seemly*. It doesn't fit the context. Think of a jealous person who scowls at their best friend's wedding, or someone who laughs at an enemy's funeral.

These small examples point to a deeper reality: Emotions that are out of line with the good, the true, and the beautiful are bad. They may be understandable, they may need to be explored, and they are not the person's fault for experiencing them, but they are bad nonetheless. Some emotions, or patterns of emotions, hinder us from becoming the fully flourishing, fully integrated humans that God intends for us to be.

Perhaps a better way to say it is that we shouldn't *pre*judge our emotions. We ought to allow our emotions to arise and then observe them and understand what they are trying to tell us. For example, imagine a quiet morning when you're sitting in a comfortable chair and sipping your coffee, and you suddenly feel a pang of anxiety. It's an unwanted emotion because it is interrupting an otherwise peaceful morning, so you redirect your attention back to your delicious cup of coffee. Fifteen minutes later, you hear the trash truck rumbling past your house. *You forgot to put the bin out on the street!* That pang of anxiety you felt was your subconscious wordlessly trying to remind you of your error, but you wouldn't listen.

This is a trivial example, of course, but it makes the broader point: Sometimes our subconscious knows something that it wants our conscious self to attend to. We don't want to dismiss an emotion and thereby overlook something important in our marriage, family, or career.

We should pay attention to our emotions with curiosity. Many people have problems because they won't allow themselves to experience their emotions. They engage in what's sometimes called *suppression*, where they push down the emotion or avoid it so they don't consciously feel it. This might help them avoid some pain—temporarily. But because our emotions are a means for making us aware of something, suppressing those emotions only serves to blind us.

Suppression isn't a foolproof means of protection, anyway. If we try to prevent important emotions from entering our consciousness, our subconscious will try even harder to break into our awareness.

After we've taken stock of our emotions, a crucial second step involves our *cognition*. Using our minds, we can consider to what degree an emotion is good. Some emotions, though understandable, do not contribute to our becoming our best selves. Knowing or recognizing that an emotional response is less than ideal isn't easy. It's an error-prone process that requires repetition. And the further step of training our emotions differently is an even more difficult task. Just because we're able to flag an emotion as inappropriate doesn't mean there's a direct pathway to reforming it—which would be the immediate next step. But I believe that many mental health leaders have gone overboard in their zeal to fight emotional suppression, and their advice that encourages the embracing of all emotions ought to be reworked.

VIEWS FROM THE COGNITIVE LENS

We have all experienced strong emotions that seem to have a life of their own, without foundation or explanation. One school of thought—the cognitive model—asserts that even these emotions have a foundation in an underlying thought. We may not be consciously aware of that thought, but deep within us is a belief that has led to this particular emotion. For example, in people with depression, a common but perhaps not consciously recognized belief is that *I am worthless*. Of course, believing in one's own worthlessness might lead to the emotion of sadness or despair that the person has not been able to account for. And thus the cognitive model of therapy says, "If we can address those underlying beliefs, we can undercut the foundation of depression."

Other schools of thought, especially psychodynamic schools, tend to de-emphasize the importance of explicit beliefs and emphasize the *felt sense* of worthiness that may emerge in relationship with the therapist.

Regardless of approach or perspective, there is broad agreement that the process of putting into words the seemingly infinite complexity of our emotions is somehow healing. In fact, "Putting Feelings into Words" is the title of one of the most influential (and dare I say it, best-titled) scientific papers on the subject.[6]

A team led by Matthew Lieberman put people in an fMRI scanner, showed them pictures of faces showing different emotions, and took note of which part of the brain responded. Predictably, in the control condition, a deep emotional part of the brain called the amygdala activated when presented with emotional faces (e.g., angry, sad). They then asked the people to label the emotions. The external stimulus didn't change, but when the participants had to think of a word that matched the face they were seeing, their brains reacted differently. When they put their feelings into words, the more rational parts of their brain activated and the amygdala calmed down.

It seems there are many pathways to recovery from depression without directly changing a person's thought processes. For some patients, I address depression using only medication and brain stimulation. For many people, these biological solutions bring full remission to their depression without directly addressing their distorted thoughts, perceptions, or beliefs. I find it astonishing when patients who have declined psychotherapy but received TMS report a sudden change in beliefs about themselves. It seems like these beliefs exist in a brain network and I may be, at least in part, "changing their minds" by changing their brains. Nonetheless, it has almost universally been found in psychiatry that biological treatments work better when combined with psychotherapy; this is indeed my very strong recommendation to my patients.

In any case, we should pay attention to our emotions and take them seriously, but also subject them to analysis to decide whether they are appropriate and what we should do with them.

INSIGHTS FROM MEDICATION

Although my clinic's signature treatment is accelerated TMS, we also prescribe psychoactive medications. One of the most common classes of medications I prescribe is called *selective serotonin reuptake inhibitors* (SSRIs), such as fluoxetine (Prozac) and escitalopram (Lexapro). These medications have been around for decades and are effective at treating depression. For patients who have not taken an SSRI before, about one-third will go into full remission, essentially symptom-free. Usually, people see me after having tried several medications, but sometimes I get the privilege of starting a patient on their first one and watching as it helps the patient hit a home run.

When this treatment approach works, it really is a marvel of modern medicine. For as little as three dollars a month, a person who felt as if he or she would rather be dead sometimes feels fully recovered. Furthermore, these medications have minimal side effects, certainly compared to many things we prescribe in other areas of medicine.

What can we learn about the human condition from these medications? Is serotonin the happy chemical and do we just need more of it? Why shouldn't everybody be on Prozac?

First, let's talk about how they work.

You may have heard that depression is caused by a chemical imbalance and that medications such as SSRIs correct the imbalance. However, a 2022 umbrella review consolidating the results of seventeen earlier serotonin studies found "no convincing evidence that depression is associated with, or caused by, lower serotonin concentrations or activity."[7] Further, there was no correlation found between changes in serotonin level and improvements in mood. In other words, having high levels of serotonin, or increasing one's serotonin, is not necessarily going to make any difference to a person's mood. I was well into my medical school training when I first found this out; I remember where I was standing and who told me. This was a game changer for me.

So, what *is* happening?

The theory I find most compelling is that some *regions* in the brain have high levels of serotonin receptors. It turns out that one such serotonin receptor–rich region, the subgenual anterior cingulate cortex (sgACC), is hyperactive in depression. Thus, the sgACC garnered a lot of attention when it became possible to look at depression using magnetic resonance imaging (MRI).[8]

The sgACC is the same region of the brain that is active in a healthy person who is thinking about a sad event. It consistently comes up in searches for regions that are hyperactive in depression, and it returns to normal when a person responds to medication. Interestingly, the spot also returns to normal if the person gets better through a non-medication option such as cognitive behavioral therapy. So here we have a plausible place where both medication and psychotherapy might be acting.

It seems that depression is not a matter of low serotonin in general, but of *hyperactivity* of a particular region. Specifically, when there is hyperactivity in a serotonin-rich region, increasing the serotonin across the brain interrupts the signaling of that particular region more than in other places.

Then there's the issue of the speed at which SSRIs work. A patient must use these medications for a full month before he or she *starts* to experience the benefits. This onset delay is thought to occur because the medication has to modify not only the serotonin level but also the ability for those receptors to be present on the neurons. In other words, an increased presence of serotonin may decrease the number of serotonin receptors a neuron puts out. The medication acts almost as a jammer, like putting static into a radio channel. The body responds by "turning down the volume" on the serotonin station, but it takes a month or two for that to happen. This may also explain why some people get emotional flattening as a side effect.

SSRIs not only reduce extreme sadness and despair, but also help with extreme anxiety, such as panic attacks and generalized anxiety disorder, and extreme anger, such as intermittent explosive disorder. In fact, SSRIs moderate extreme negative emotions across the board.

It's worth noting that SSRIs may work by changing a patient's personality. In the parlance of the Five Factor Model for human personality—*openness, conscientiousness, extraversion, agreeableness,* and *emotional stability* (sometimes referred to by its opposite, *neuroticism,* in older studies), SSRIs seem to work by increasing emotional stability and extraversion.[9] It seems the medication works as a kind of tourniquet, cutting off or reducing negative emotion in order to save the whole person. When the patient takes the medication, it often narrows the emotional spectrum, along with dramatically reducing the bottom extreme.[10] For someone who comes to me with major depressive disorder, this is often a winning exchange.

One of the more intriguing and unanticipated side effects of the medication was discovered in a study on healthy controls.[11] (Healthy controls are people used in a study who do not have the disease or disorder being studied.) The healthy controls were given an SSRI (citalopram in this case) and asked to play the Ultimatum Game.

The Ultimatum Game was developed by behavioral economists and has a proud history as part of the proof that humans are not fully rational. (This work was awarded the Nobel Prize in 1994. In non-economics circles, the existence of human irrationality was identified considerably earlier.) In the game, player A is given a sum of money, such as ten dollars, and is allowed to give any amount of it to player B. Player B then has a choice to either accept the offer or burn all the money in the game. In other words, player B can choose to get richer or to make both players walk away with nothing. If player A gives player B five dollars, player B almost always accepts the offer. But when given one dollar (which means player A intends to keep nine dollars), player B almost always rejects the offer, choosing to burn everything instead.

The "rational" person would say, "One dollar is greater than zero dollars. I don't care who gets whatever else; I'd be happy to accept the dollar." Some people play that way (without medications involved), but most people don't.

Researchers found that when healthy controls were given the SSRI citalopram, they were more willing to accept unfair offers. In other words, the SSRI made them more "rational" than they otherwise would have been.

Now, from one perspective, we might say this is wonderful: People are more rational and less vindictive—great! But think about it some more. Is "rationality" always good? After all, "rationality" probably isn't as useful in negotiating for a fair wage, launching a revolution, or wooing a partner. Maybe boosting "rationality" by chemical means has unforeseen consequences.

SSRIs are effective; but like everything, the benefit comes with a cost. There's no such thing as a free lunch, certainly not when tweaking the brain. In the case of SSRIs, the cost helps us to understand what the emotions are in the first place and how they can be useful when properly ordered.

INSIGHTS FROM TMS

When we're treating depressed people with TMS, especially accelerated TMS, one of the most incredible things to see is emotion flooding back in. During the accelerated treatment days, it's not uncommon for people to cry for no apparent reason. Some start smiling, and others start feeling negative emotions for the first time in a while.

I had one patient who had been involved in something that had deeply violated his personal values. While he was depressed, he didn't feel bad about it. The depression had numbed him. With successful treatment, his despair and suicidal thoughts improved, but he began to weep and mourn over past decisions he'd made.

The return of emotion suggests that, in depression, the parts of the brain are working fine, but they're not properly connected. Successful treatment restores the brain to a normal firing pattern, and we can see emotions rush back in.

Flatness of emotion is a distortion of the way the system is designed to work. Our emotions are not supposed to be unchanging. Emotions are helpful only if they vary. Our baseline emotions should change in response to our circumstances and experiences. The problem with depression is that patients often feel bad even though their life circumstances are good. For most patients, remission from depression means a return of happiness. But for the patient who had violated his own values, successful treatment restored his ability to feel happy, but it also restored the healthy emotions of guilt and remorse. His depression had been preventing him from appropriate remorse.

Healthy emotions are variable by design, helping us prepare for and respond to situations appropriately.

KNOW YOUR HEART

This next section is about ways you can explore and appreciate the role that emotion plays in your life. The goal of these exercises is to explore the impact and presence of emotion. If emotion is not an area that you struggle with, you may want to prioritize the applications in other chapters. But if you find that your emotions are particularly challenging for you, you should consider getting professional support.

As I approach the how-to material in this chapter (and future chapters), I suggest that you evaluate how important it is to you to change a particular area of your life, and how much energy you have to make those changes. Each chapter will present some things you can do that are relatively easy, and others that may be medium or hard changes for you. Regardless of whether you are depressed or simply weary, burned out, melancholy, glum, morose, or dissatisfied, making even small changes can be a big step in the right direction. As you grow stronger and more confident in your pursuit of a flourishing life, you'll be able to make bigger changes, which will have an even greater effect on how you're feeling.

Track your strong emotions

The first thing you can do to move toward healthier emotions is to start paying attention when you have a particularly strong emotion. Not just a minor annoyance or a temporary sadness, but a *strong* emotion—such as intense dislike for someone or something, sustained anger, or an intensified sense of confident pride. You can also do this exercise with a problematic behavior driven by emotion. For example, maybe you snapped at your partner or shut down in a conversation with your boss.

One way to explore your strong emotions is by committing to spend a few minutes near the end of your day reflecting on the emotions you felt that day. It's best to approach this exercise methodically and not just mentally. Take out a pen or record a note on your smartphone.

1. Write down an event that occurred during the day that sparked a strong emotion.
2. Write down all the *feeling* words you can think of that are connected to it. If you have difficulty finding words to describe your emotions, maybe look online for a list of emotion words to prompt you. Sometimes you may feel only a single emotion; at other times it might be many. Emotions have a way of blending together like that.
3. Write down things that led up to the emotion you felt. Were there any influences on that emotion? For example, maybe you were hungry or lonely or were thinking about something else.
4. Consider the consequences of that emotion. Where did it go? How long did it last? How did it affect other things in your life?

The primary benefit of this exercise is that by simply putting feelings into words you will have a better understanding of yourself and your emotions. Also, by considering the causes and consequences of an emotion, you may discover different behavior patterns that serve you and others better. For example, if you realized that you snapped at your partner at 11:00 a.m. but also that you'd skipped breakfast and stayed up late the night before, you could decide to be more intentional about eating and sleeping. Or maybe you snapped at your partner at 11:00 a.m. because you were still holding on to something that happened at 11:00 p.m. the night before.

Work through a self-help book

A moderately difficult but potentially quite helpful step would be to systematically explore your emotions by working through a cognitive behavioral therapy (CBT) self-help book. And by "working through," I mean it literally: Get a pen or pencil and complete the written exercises in the book. Classics in the area of cognitive behavioral therapy include *Feeling Good* and *Feeling Great* by David Burns, and *You Are Not Your Brain* by Jeffrey M. Schwartz and Rebecca Gladding.

Explore your emotions in conversation

Another effective strategy is to talk with someone about your strong emotions. You can do this with a trusted friend, or if necessary, a professional therapist. Initially, this might be a single or occasional conversation, but if you find it helpful, you may wish to make it a more regular practice. Maybe you already have a robust community in which to explore your emotions. If not, you may have to risk the awkward feeling of asking a friend—who would probably be more than willing to help if asked. If you need a framework for your conversations, try doing the previous exercise and then discuss the results with your friend.

What would Jesus feel?

In the Christian faith, we believe God made us in his own image, as beings with emotions. The Bible describes God as one who experiences a full range of emotions, including sorrow, anger, compassion, and love.[12] Christians also believe that God became a human, Jesus. While on earth, he demonstrated a full range of emotions that we can emulate.[13] Jesus is the epitome of emotional health, and his emotions appropriately match the circumstances.

Healthy people will also have a full range of emotions. As it says in the book of Ecclesiastes, "For everything there is a season, and a time for every matter under heaven . . . a time to weep, and a time to laugh; a time to mourn, and a time to dance."[14] We are healthy—not just undepressed but flourishing—when we are able to feel appropriate deep sadness. We'll also be able to feel anger at injustice and anxiety when threatened. Our emotions are tuned to help us accurately see the situations we are in and prepare us to respond appropriately.

Spend some time reflecting on your current situation, and ask yourself: *Am I feeling the same emotions that Jesus would feel in these circumstances?* By identifying where your feelings are at variance with God's, you can see areas in your life where you need to make changes. If you're feeling bitter toward someone who hurt you, for example, maybe you need to work toward forgiveness.

JOY COMES WITH THE MORNING

The famed English writer G. K. Chesterton once said,

> Everything human must have in it both joy and sorrow; the only matter of interest is the manner in which the two things are balanced or divided. . . . Man is more himself, man is more manlike, when joy is the fundamental thing in him, and grief the superficial. Melancholy should be an innocent interlude, a tender and fugitive frame of mind; praise should be the permanent pulsation of the soul. Pessimism is at best an emotional half-holiday; joy is the uproarious labour by which all things live.[15]

Depression is an unvarying low mood. The opposite of depression is a dynamically appropriate mood. Chesterton used the word *joy*—not a superficial happiness, but a deep, settled feeling of contentment and satisfaction that pervades the soul. Sad things are still sad and must be given their due, but with joy comes buoyancy that brings us back to a positive state of mind, even in the midst of difficult circumstances. A joyful person is like a well-built ship, which can endure all manner of wind and waves but in the end stays well above the water.

One of my favorite reports from patients is not "I feel *good*," but "I feel *normal*." Even patients who had been depressed as far back as they could remember have told me they recognized "normal" even if they had never felt it before. Just as people with chronic pain can recognize the absence of it, so too those with depression can rebuild their lives on a foundation of joy when the depression is removed.

The world is a good place. The mere fact of existence is good. Horrors and evil still happen, but that doesn't make them foundational to life. In my experience, such a pessimistic outlook is most often a symptom of a disease. When people receive adequate treatment, it severs the root of depression, and the weed of pessimism withers.

Some might argue that pessimism is a perfectly reasonable conclusion, given the vicissitudes of life, and that joy is not "the fundamental thing" defined by Chesterton. There are certainly respected intellectual approaches that describe the world as a dark place or say that all joy is ephemeral because the world was born in darkness and is going to darkness. I must admit this philosophy has never been tempting to me personally, but my clinical experience makes it even more implausible. It's like telling an orthopedic surgeon that walking is fundamentally painful. For a doctor whose job is fixing broken legs, who routinely hears from patients after surgery and recovery that they can walk again "like normal" and without pain, the theory that "all walking is pain" doesn't resonate.

It isn't always possible to live in perpetual joy, and the brain disorders I treat often prevent people from doing so. And to give the (literal) devil his due, philosophical pessimism apart from that caused by brain disease deserves more space than we can give it here. Let me simply reiterate that I agree with Chesterton that joy is the state for which we are all designed.

STEPS TOWARD FLOURISHING

When we are living flourishing lives, we will experience a dynamic range of emotions. As emotions arise, we don't prejudge them, but rather welcome them and explore them. We reform or dismiss those emotions that are not in line with truth or goodness; the rest we embrace and experience in their fullness. We mourn when there is tragedy and feel anger when there is injustice. Otherwise, we feel joy often, and sometimes without a specific catalyst.

3

PLEASURE: THE PATHWAY OF ENJOYMENT

O God! God!
How weary, stale, flat, and unprofitable
Seem to me all the uses of this world!
WILLIAM SHAKESPEARE, *Hamlet*

The goal towards which the pleasure-principle impels us—of becoming
happy—is not attainable; yet we may not—nay, cannot—give up the
effort to come nearer to realization of it by some means or other.
SIGMUND FREUD, *Civilization and Its Discontents*

The more a thing is perfect, the more it feels pleasure and likewise pain.
DANTE ALIGHIERI, *The Inferno*

Why do we do the things we do? Given two options, how do we decide?

This is one of the more interesting and possibly fruitful debates in the history of philosophy.

Some would say the primary motivating force is survival and reproduction. The Darwinist or neo-Darwinist case is that these two interwoven drives are behind every bacterium swimming toward food, every mating call bellowed on the wind, every grand war fought, every opera performed, and even every tax form completed. Richard Dawkins, the well-known evolutionary biologist and atheist, summarizes this perspective when he says, "We are survival machines—robot vehicles blindly programmed to preserve the selfish molecules known as genes. This is a truth which still fills me with astonishment."[1]

Others argue that survival may be only a common manifestation of something deeper. Friedrich Nietzsche said that humans all do what they do because of a will to power: "Physiologists should think twice before positioning the drive for self-preservation as the cardinal drive of an organic being. Above all, a living thing wants to *discharge* its strength—life itself is will to power: self-preservation is only one of the indirect and most frequent *consequences* of this."[2]

A third idea is that we do things to maximize our overall pleasure. Aristotle summarizes this idea nicely: "Pleasure and pain are . . . the standards by which we all, in a greater or less degree, regulate our actions."[3]

This last idea is perhaps the most plausible mechanism psychologically. Why did I choose that job? Because I thought in the end it would make me happy. Why did I seek the promotion? Why did I have a child? Why did I pick vanilla ice cream over chocolate?

Whether *pleasure* is the only motivator is something of an article of faith. One cannot finally prove that I chose vanilla because it would maximize my fitness in the struggle for survival and reproduction, or that it was an expression of my will to power. The satisfying of my desire was the end in itself. Regardless, the conscious experience of all of these pathways seems to include pleasure as a final common motivator.

Human flourishing involves moving toward pleasure and away from pain. But it's not a simple and obvious choice—because, as we'll see, hedonism ultimately disappoints. Still, finding the opposite of depression involves understanding what gives us pleasure, and when and how to pursue it, because depression is a state of being that is devoid of pleasure.

PLEASURE LANDSCAPE

Imagine a "pleasure landscape" in which elevation represents degrees of pleasure. Mountain peaks are moments of extreme pleasure; valleys are periods of pain.

How would you navigate?

You might see a mountain or a high plateau and navigate toward it. You might be willing to go through a painful valley if you saw beyond it a place you wanted to be.

What is the topography of a depression landscape? It's all pain, all the time. Imagine that a depressed traveler looks around for a mountain to navigate toward. It's no good. A thick fog obscures the heights in all directions. Perhaps the traveler can move in the nearest uphill direction. That plan also fails. The valley is perfectly level. There is no indication of which direction will lead from pain into pleasure.

The pleasure topography of depression is mostly flat. In severe depression, even the micro-pleasures of completing our daily routines are gone.

In a healthy, flourishing environment, we receive little rewards to fuel us and propel us forward. Brushing our teeth? It feels good (reward) to do something we're used to doing and we know is good for us. Greet our neighbor on the way to work? It's enjoyable (reward) to make a friendly social connection. Pay attention to an interesting podcast? It's pleasurable (reward) to learn something new and hear a familiar voice. We're like thirsty marathon runners cheered on every mile and given little cups of refreshing water by our brain as we go throughout our day. Depressed people are forced to try running the marathon without water.

Without felt pleasure, the number of things that draw on our limited store of conscious energy can be exhausting, even if we started the day with a full tank. Nothing feels good. Nothing is different from anything else. The pleasure of connecting with loved ones is gone. The deep emotions that come with being with a parent, a child, or a spouse are not there. These emotions, rightly or wrongly, are a major source of identity and value for many people, and losing touch with them is often the single most painful symptom of depression. The once-loving father feels nothing at all about his previously beloved son. The wife looks at her husband and feels no different than she would toward a friendly stranger. Even the memory of how things used to feel is forgotten or overwritten by the present numbness.

This emotional flattening is a symptom that often leads patients to consider suicide, especially those who explicitly believe that their life is about maximizing their enjoyment (in contrast to those who may be seeking tranquility of mind, holiness, or salvation as a final end). With their depression saying, *It will always be like this, and you'll never enjoy things again*, people can come to believe that life is not worth living. Of course, apart from these mental distortions, life *is* worth living; but for people who are depressed, this is hard to see.

VIRTUE AT THE CENTER

One of the most foundational questions is, How do we know the upright, moral, or ethical thing to do? How do we tell good from bad? How do we make decisions when there is ambiguity?

Imagine that you're standing on a sidewalk and you see a trolley hurtling down a hill. It seems as if the brakes are out and the conductor has lost control. Looking ahead, you see a group of five unsuspecting people crossing the tracks. They will surely die if the trolley can't be stopped, and it's too late to shout a warning. Right in front of you, you notice there's a lever. You know that if you pull it, it will switch the trolley to another track, saving the lives of the five people. But then you see a lone person on the other track, who would become the unfortunate victim of the trolley accident. Either five people are going to die or one person will. It's up to you. Do you pull the lever?

The trolley problem and its countless variants have been the subject of nearly ten thousand scholarly publications.[4] It's a good theoretical problem because it breaks down the two dominant ideas we have about how to do the right thing. Some would say (following Immanuel Kant) that ethical duties are dominant: We shouldn't kill people, and by pulling the lever, we'd be responsible for killing someone. Utilitarians, on the other hand, would see that death is inevitable here and would argue for the greatest good for the greatest number. Thus, we should pull the lever to save five lives at the cost of one. Most people agree with the utilitarians, at least until we make a presumably minor modification to the story.

Imagine the same trolley is heading for the same five people, except this time there is no lever to pull. Instead, there is an enormously heavy man sitting on a bridge who could be pushed into the path of the trolley, bringing it to a somewhat gruesome stop. (You might be willing to jump to your own death to save the five, but you know your weight is simply insufficient.) Given this scenario, the average person changes his or her mind and thinks it's wrong to kill one person even if it would save five.

Why are we talking about trolleys? And what's the answer? My answer is that it's an interesting, but ultimately inappropriate, debate. Knowledge of right and wrong is not primarily found by arguing about it. It's about becoming the kind of person who would naturally do the right thing. This position is called *virtue ethics*.

We often know exactly the right thing to do, but there are ten thousand ways we fail to do it. The question about exactly what is the right thing to do is rarely the hard part, because doing the right thing is much more like learning to ride a horse than it is like trying to solve an algebra problem. It's a thing that takes practice and that is highly dependent on circumstance, but in which it is nonetheless easy to see the difference between experts and novices.

Aristotle describes the good life as having *eudaimonia*, which could be rendered literally as "good spirit." The emphasis is not on accumulation of material goods or physical pleasure, but on the cultivation of a type of life that includes such things as virtue and friendship. As described by theologian N. T. Wright, "for Aristotle, the goal was the ideal of a fully flourishing human being. Think of someone who has lived up to his or her full potential, displaying a complete, rounded, wise, and thoroughly formed character."[5] Like skills, these virtues take attention and repetition to develop.

Aristotle also had a radical idea: If being a good person doesn't make you happy, you're not a good person yet. You're only on your way to becoming a good person. If abstaining from overeating doesn't itself give you pleasure, you're not temperate. For Aristotle, a person becomes virtuous only when his pleasures have aligned with virtuous action: "He who stands his ground against things that are terrible and delights in this or at least is not pained is brave, while the man who is pained is a coward. For moral excellence is concerned with pleasures and pains; it is on account of the pleasure that we do bad things, and on account of the pain that we abstain from noble ones."[6]

Wright conveys similar ideas in his own framework of Christian virtue. He writes, "The New Testament's vision of Christian behavior has to do, not with struggling to keep a bunch of ancient and apparently arbitrary rules, nor with 'going with the flow' or 'doing what comes naturally,' but with the learning of the language, in the present, which will equip us to speak it fluently in God's new world."[7] The apostle Paul undoubtedly would have been aware of Aristotle and those who followed him. So perhaps, while not necessarily disagreeing with the framework of virtue ethics,

Paul replaced Greek virtues such as magnanimity with Christian virtues like *agape* (love).

So, from a mental healing standpoint, is living a life of *eudaimonia* good for your mental health? What about a life of positive emotion?

The concept of flourishing includes several aspects that have been taken up only relatively recently by researchers. One key study looked at "six dimensions of psychological well-being: self-acceptance, positive relationships with others, personal growth, purpose in life, environmental mastery, and autonomy."[8] Based on participant responses in these areas, the researcher separated people into four groups: *depressed, languishing, moderately healthy*, and *flourishing*. The study found that "the risk of a major depressive episode was two times more likely among languishing than moderately mentally healthy adults, and nearly six times greater among languishing than flourishing adults."[9] In other words, living out a life of *eudaimonia* results in robust protection against depression. Or to state it conversely, failing to live virtuously does to your mind what smoking does to your lungs.

Another team of researchers looked at direct measures of *hedonic well-being* (which comprises emotional well-being, including happiness and life-satisfaction), along with a report of what they called *eudaimonic well-being* (psychological and social well-being), both of which they associated with "the comprehensive state of flourishing."[10] Results showed that those who were flourishing had a 28 percent lower risk of developing depression and a 53 percent lower risk of developing anxiety. What was astonishing was that the benefit held even if a person had only one of the two indicators (hedonic or eudaimonic well-being). In other words, a person who lacked positive emotions but had meaningful activities and relationships would be protected against depression, as would a person who lacked eudaimonia but had positive emotion. It was the people who lacked both that were at higher risk.

PSYCHOLOGICAL WELL-BEING AND DEPRESSION

Some people think about mood like points on a scale. Typically, a minus ten is very sad and a plus ten is very happy. Though this is often how it feels and is sometimes a workable approximation, happiness is not just the opposite of sadness. Happiness and sadness can't be captured in a single dimension; they are two perpendicular lines, like the axes on a graph. A multidimensional approach is more useful in depicting the seasons of life, or single moments of mingled happiness and tragedy. However, psychiatry has focused a lot of attention on the "sadness scale" while largely neglecting the dimension of happiness.

An extreme demonstration of this can be seen in people with bipolar disorder, who may experience incredibly deep depressions followed by periods of extremely elevated moods with grandiose levels of self-esteem. (One of my patients, during a manic episode, believed he had "invented nuclear fission," and another went to visit his friend Elon Musk: "But security at Tesla wouldn't let me in to see him.") People with bipolar disorder also have dramatic reductions in the need to sleep, intense productivity, and increased risk taking. Sometimes a person will experience depression and mania at the same time. Imagine all the energy and disinhibition of mania with the despair and self-loathing of depression. These mixed states are exceptionally dangerous, but they are important in showing that these two seeming opposites can sometimes exist simultaneously in the same brain.

Under normal conditions, we, too, can feel sadness and joy simultaneously. In the Pixar movie *Inside Out*, the climax of the movie (spoiler alert!) is when the protagonist learns that Sadness and Joy can come together in a moment to form a new "core memory." Every embrace through sad tears has that aspect of the grief of loss mingled with the joy of connection.

Positive emotion is *not* the opposite of negative emotion. Living a balanced and flourishing life may mean embracing joyous moments at times, tragic moments at other times, and allowing the two to mingle if the music of life blends the two themes. Seeking pleasure wisely doesn't mean eliminating sadness. Some of the most profound moments in life come with mixed emotions.

TAKING THE MEASURE OF PLEASURE

Typically, the fear associated with pleasure is that too much will lead to vice. Though this may definitely be a risk for some, the problem for people who are depressed or languishing is *too little* pleasure, not too much. If that describes your situation, I suggest finding things you can do that you *enjoy* that are also good and noble (or at least morally neutral), even if the degree is very small. Depression predicts that any enjoyment you might gain from an activity will be zero and thus not worth it. In reality, for all but those in the worst states, there is still some small pleasure possible.

Of course, pleasure is not the be-all and end-all of life, nor will it give you definitive information about what you should be doing with yourself. But it can be a guide to better understanding how God made you and what changes might open up a more valuable future for you.

The following action steps, moving from easier to more difficult, revolve around systematically doing things you find enjoyable or pleasurable.

Plan your pleasure

Consider scheduling pleasurable activities as you would anything else on your to-do list. Often, practical concerns crowd out the things we enjoy, or we get out of the habit of having fun. So while scheduling enjoyment may seem odd at first, it's actually an easy—and very helpful—way to get pleasure back into your life.

Go to your calendar. As you think ahead to the next day or week, write down some things you will do that you think will be enjoyable. For example, you might allot an hour or two each day for a hobby, or for reading a book or listening to a podcast, or for having a conversation with a friend—whatever would be enjoyable and in line with your values. Next to each entry, rate how enjoyable the activity will be, from zero (not enjoyable at all) to one hundred (totally enjoyable). Shoot for the upper end of the spectrum. Enjoyment breeds even greater enjoyment. Even if the numbers on your enjoyment scale are low, this exercise will help you map out the pleasurable activities that are possible for you at this moment in your life, as well as give you hints about activities that could take you further.

The next step is to keep your appointment and do what you planned to do. Don't make it optional.

Finally, go back to your calendar and write down how much you actually enjoyed the activity. You may find (particularly if you're depressed) that you will underestimate your enjoyment up front and have more fun actually doing the activities than you thought you would. But regardless of your accuracy, use the after-activity numbers to guide future planning. If you hit some home runs, put those activities back on your calendar for later.

This self-feedback will help you calibrate your plans as you continue to schedule pleasurable activities in the future. Perhaps a favorite hobby is no longer enjoyable; consider changing it out, or find a way to engage on a deeper level. On the other hand, maybe you had a really nice time talking with your friend and you want to do that again soon. The main thing is to keep scheduling enjoyable activities until it feels more natural and enjoyment becomes a regular part of your life.

Retrain your pleasure receptors by abstaining

If pleasure in some domain is a problem, consider retraining your pleasure receptors. Abstaining from an otherwise good thing can often be a good way to reduce an over-strong pleasure drive for something that is good but not ultimate. Schedule a period where you fast from social media, alcohol, food, or sex. Remember, pleasure is good, but when the best pleasures are replaced by lesser ones, pleasure becomes a problem. Doing without for a period of time can remind your body who's in charge, helping to tame and retrain pleasures to something better. For example, some who choose to fast from food may devote their mealtimes to prayer or meditation instead, seeking a spiritual pleasure rather than a physical one.

Some traditions have fasting or abstaining as part of an annual cycle— for example, New Year's resolutions in the secular Western context or giving up something for Lent in the Christian liturgical year. If an over-strong pleasure has a hold on you, you may want to make fasting from it a regular part of your routine.

Align your lifestyle with what brings you pleasure

If you're ready for something a little more challenging along the pleasure pathway, try adjusting your lifestyle to up the ante on the things that bring you happiness. This may involve asking yourself some questions.

Do I like my job? I hope you do, but if your job brings more grief than enjoyment, maybe it's time to start thinking about making changes in your job or finding a new one.

Do I still enjoy being around my friends? Maybe someone used to be a good friend, but the relationship has become stale. Consider *why* the friendship has become stale. Is there something you could do to rejuvenate it? Finding new friends is an option, but it may be a choice taken too soon in a world of separate individuals drifting ever farther apart.

Other questions might include: *Do I still enjoy going to my book group? Do I enjoy watching sports for as much time as I devote to it? Which voluntary activities drain me, and which ones energize me?*

You need to really think here. You probably can't make *all* the changes you might want to, at least not quickly. This is long-term, large-scale stuff. But by reflecting on your own enjoyment of things, you can begin to make changes in your life so that the way you spend your time aligns more closely with your deeply held desires.

PLEASURE AS A POINTER TO TRANSCENDENCE

Physical pleasure is a pointer to something beyond itself. That's why hedonism—the pursuit of pleasure as an end in itself—is doomed.

One of the most pleasurable moments of my life occurred when my appendix nearly ruptured.

I was scheduled to fly from San Francisco to the Philippines, and I had what I thought was a stomachache when I went to the airport. Then it got worse. Before long, I found myself lying on the floor of the San Francisco airport, trying to gather my strength to sit through what I expected would be the worst flight of my life. Then, still lying on the floor, I asked myself, "When have I ever been in such pain that I lay down on the floor of an airport?" The answer was *never*.

When I attempted a physical exam on myself, I discovered I had Murphy's sign—an even more excruciating pain when I pressed on and released where the appendix was. Clearly, I needed to go to the hospital. I figured an Uber would be about as fast as an ambulance, so I hobbled my way to the curb and went to the hospital.

The emergency department doctor confirmed the diagnosis (apparently I had learned at least one thing while a medical student at Stanford) and pushed one milligram of hydromorphone through my IV. Warmth washed over me. My pain wasn't gone, but now it was okay. Everything was okay. I now understood on an experiential level the potent lure of wanting more of that feeling, but I knew how quickly the naked pursuit of euphoria would lead to ruin.

For many people, the most pleasurable thing they can do is take drugs. Unfortunately, this pathway leads to a destroyed life rather quickly. Even if it were possible to remain in a perpetual drug-induced state of bliss, few would choose that life; fewer still would consider it a life well lived.

When our pleasure system is trained, healthy, and working properly, it teaches us about the structure of the world. In the analogy of the pleasure landscape, the subject of hedonic topography, or pleasure mapping, is one of the most important subjects in life. Food is good, a small incline on the hedonic map, but what is even better than food? Perhaps a good conversation over dinner. If we can chart a path from the pleasure of food to the greater pleasure of a good conversation while enjoying our dinner, we have ascended to quite the elevation. What's better than companionship? Perhaps something that makes it even deeper and more secure, like marriage or best friendship. What's better than a deep relationship? Perhaps being the kind of person your partner can depend on. The "small incline" of fine food is adjacent to the "hill" of good companionship, which is at the foot of the "mountain" of virtue. Pleasure, when not twisted or diseased, is one indicator that we're on the right track—though, like all temporal guides, it's imperfect. Just as we must rely on our eyes as well as our ears, we should not go all-in on any one of these higher senses.

Jesus' famous Sermon on the Mount begins with a series of blessings on unexpected people or groups: the poor in spirit, those who mourn, the meek, and so on.[11] After each example, Jesus gives a reason why that particular group should consider itself blessed. In the middle of the list, Jesus says, "Blessed are those who hunger and thirst for righteousness, for they shall be satisfied."[12] In the end, for this group, there will be something like the pleasurable satisfaction that comes when a hungry person eats food or a thirsty person drinks a cool glass of water. This is a truly good kind of pleasure.

In a later theological expression of a similar truth, the writers of the Westminster Confession chose the following couplet as the first question/ answer pair in their catechism:

Question 1: What is the chief end of man?
Answer: Man's chief end is to glorify God, and to enjoy him for ever.[13]

Acorns grow into oak trees; thus, the oak tree is the "end" of the acorn. A knife's "end" is to cut. The "end" for a human is not "to be authentic to myself," "to have new and interesting experiences," or even "to be a good person." It's certainly not "to make money." According to the Puritans who wrote the catechism, if everything goes perfectly well, the main reason for people to exist is to *experience joy in connection to God.*

There are twists and turns in our stories. There may be phases in which we experience little or no joy. Even though the "end" of a caterpillar is to become a butterfly, there are many days of crawling required to get there. In our lives, there may be years of suffering and seasons without pleasure, happiness, or joy. There may be grueling times when disordered pleasures are bent and retrained into alignment with our values. From that perspective, depression can rightly be seen as an aberration. Depression is not where people are supposed to stay. Even if, heaven forbid, it continues for years and years, I don't believe that depression, discouragement, disillusionment, or dissatisfaction are a person's natural or final state. (We will explore this theme further in chapter 13.)

STEPS TOWARD FLOURISHING

When we are flourishing, we enjoy ourselves. We follow the blips of pleasure throughout the day to enjoy the small things, and we climb up the hills and mountains of great pleasures. When we see that a pleasure is pointing us in the wrong direction, we limit that pleasure and redirect our behavior toward the good, the beautiful, the virtuous. We work hard to develop ourselves into virtuous people who love to be generous and kind. When we struggle to do the right thing, we repeat the lesson again and again until it gives us joy. We build our lives on deep relationships, and enjoy the pleasures inherent and proper to each aspect of our lives.

TRAUMA: BROKEN, MENDED, STRONGER

Choosing hardship, then, the Wise Man
Never meets with hardship all his life.
LAO-TZU, *Tao Tĕ Ching*

One day, in retrospect, the years of struggle
will strike you as the most beautiful.
SIGMUND FREUD, in a personal letter

In 1940, the Nazis seemed unstoppable. After they had conquered France in a mere two months, the fall of Britain seemed inevitable. Hitler offered peace and Churchill soundly rejected it. Then the bombs began to fall on London and around England. The Blitz had begun.

Though more than forty thousand British civilians would be killed by the Germans' bombing of London and the countryside during the war, the physical casualties were not the main worry. Of greater concern was "bomb neurosis," a dangerous combination of hysteria, terror, desperation, and helplessness that might undermine the social fabric and break down Britain's will to fight.

It was understood that, in the trenches of the First World War, the stress and uncertainty of dying by a random explosion caused many soldiers to develop a psychiatric condition they called *shell shock*. This happened all too frequently even among war-hardened soldiers; it was expected to happen at a much greater rate among civilians. When the Blitz began, it was estimated that three to four million civilians would need psychiatric hospitalization. Psychiatric clinics were set up throughout the country.

But no one expected what actually happened.

The psychiatric clinics remained empty. There were only about two cases of bomb neurosis recorded per week, even during the peak of the bombing in September 1940.[1]

The British public responded to the crisis with what came to be known as the "Blitz spirit." The British government printed two million copies of the now famous Keep Calm and Carry On posters. People would discuss the probability of Nazi bombers appearing overhead like they would the chances of rain, speculating that today the weather seemed "very blitzy."

One American observer commented around this time, "By every test and measure I am able to apply, these people are staunch to the bone and won't quit. . . . At the end of a month of this blitzkrieg, the British are stronger and in a better position than they were at its beginning."[2]

The inspiring example of the British people during wartime should make us wonder how we ought to think about psychological stress. How does it interact with depression? What can we do when our life's circumstances are difficult (though probably not as bad as actual Nazis dropping real firebombs on our houses)?

Understanding trauma is critical to understanding depression and being able to picture what its opposite might be. And sometimes we may even be able to use the trauma for our good.

SURVIVING ADVERSE CHILDHOOD EXPERIENCES

The British experience presents a mystery to which we will return later in the chapter. Their mental toughness under bombardment is inspiring but also confusing. We know that psychological trauma can be devastating. To some extent, this has long been known, but it was quantified in startling fashion in the late 1990s.

In a classic study of trauma, Vincent Felitti and his colleagues explored the effects of "adverse childhood experiences," or ACEs.[3] First they asked participants whether events in any of three categories had happened to them in childhood:

1. abuse (physical, sexual, or emotional)
2. neglect
3. household challenges (e.g., parental divorce, parental substance abuse)

Then the researchers dug deeper to find out how these ACEs had affected the study participants.

As you might expect, the effects were enormous. Compared with people who had no ACEs, people with four or more were nearly five times as likely to be depressed, ten times more likely to abuse IV drugs, and twelve times more likely to have attempted suicide.

Observing similar types of psychological consequences in response to trauma, psychiatrist Bessel van der Kolk explains the phenomenon:

Traumatized people chronically feel unsafe inside their bodies:
The past is alive in the form of gnawing interior discomfort.
Their bodies are constantly bombarded by visceral warning
signs, and, in an attempt to control these processes, they often
become expert at ignoring their gut feelings and in numbing
awareness of what is played out inside. They learn to hide
from their selves.[4]

More surprising to some is that the effects from ACEs don't confine themselves to mental health. Women with two or more ACEs showed a doubled rate of developing cancer.[5] Other studies have shown a correlation between higher ACEs and higher rates of cancer, coronary heart disease, and stroke.[6]

The life expectancy of those Americans in the Felitti study with six or more ACEs was worse than the average life expectancy in Haiti or Pakistan.[7]

Certainly there are many people who have lived truly tragic lives. In many cases, they struggle with severe and chronic depression and other lingering effects despite the best treatment and their best efforts. We must not forget about these people, and we should work to improve our understanding, compassion, and treatments. If you are one of them, I hope you will get the help you need. We ought to strive toward a society where these types of trauma don't happen.

Even if your life has been relatively free from major damaging events, however, chances are still good that you may be suffering from elevated levels of stress.

THE STRESS HYPOTHESIS

When I was living in Kenya doing antipoverty work, our tribal neighbors were the famous nomadic hunters, the Maasai. For the sake of my next illustration, imagine yourself as a member of the Maasai tribe living on the savanna in East Africa, searching for acacia bark to treat your wife's fever. You're feeling calm, and your physiology is in a "rest and digest" mode. Your heart is beating slowly, your breathing is even and regular, and your blood supply is shunted to your stomach, helping you digest your most recent meal.

As you approach a shrub that looks promising, you see two eyes within the shadows. *It's a lion!*

Instantly, your body shifts from "rest and digest" mode to "fight or flight." If your spear was at the ready and you weren't alone, you'd fight. But there's no time, so you choose *flight*. Your heart rate accelerates. Blood shunts away from your stomach; you don't need to use any more energy digesting, because if you don't get away, you'll be the one being digested. You start running and you make it to safety.

Whew!

When the harrowing experience is over, you return home and tell the others in your village about how you escaped a lion. Your body goes back to "rest and digest" mode as you enjoy the evening. However, you formed some new emotions around that particular spot in the savanna, and you will behave a lot more carefully the next time you're foraging.

This kind of situation is what our stress system was built for—including everything from how memories are consolidated (e.g., where the lion was hiding) to immediate responses. Our nervous system is designed so that we can respond just like our Maasai friend did.

Robert Sapolsky, in his book *Why Zebras Don't Get Ulcers*, describes the modern conundrum of our fight-or-flight response mode. Though our biology is built for short-term crises, most of us no longer have to run from lions. But what happens when the threat is psychological? What happens when we are constantly worried? We get sick.

Sapolsky says, "Stress-related disease emerges, predominantly, out of the fact that we so often activate a physiological system that has evolved for responding to acute physical emergencies, but we turn it on for months on end, worrying about mortgages, relationships, and promotions."[8]

In our bodies and brains, a cascade of physiological changes occurs in response to a severe stressor as well as to chronic stressors. Sometimes stress can continue affecting us long after the event that inspired it has passed.

WHAT HAPPENS AFTER THE TRAUMA?

In approaching questions about trauma, the most-studied consequence is post-traumatic stress disorder (PTSD), a condition characterized by hyper-arousal (e.g., being easily startled), re-experiencing trauma (e.g., having terrible nightmares), avoidance (e.g., staying away from reminders of the trauma), and mood disruptions. PTSD often includes depression, which only compounds the person's misery.

One group of researchers decided to look at the consequences of one of the darkest moments of the twentieth century: the Holocaust and its psychological fallout.[9] Subjects were examined about forty years after the horrifying events they experienced and were asked about their current symptoms. The participants included both young and old survivors, who were between the ages of three and fifty-one when the Holocaust occurred. They were asked about what had happened to them, and they reported horrors difficult to imagine and unspeakable trauma. Nearly four out of five of the study subjects' closest relatives (sons and daughters, brothers and sisters, mothers and fathers) had been killed during the war. For those who had been in a concentration camp, the average time of detention was more than fourteen months.

Researchers asked the survivors about their symptoms. Nearly everyone still had trouble sleeping, and 83 percent had recurrent nightmares. The study found that an astronomically high proportion of the survivors had symptoms of PTSD, even decades after the events. For point of reference, a study published in 2016 found that 4.7 percent of people in the United States had suffered from PTSD in the previous year.[10] Those who survived the Holocaust but were not in a concentration camp had PTSD rates ten times higher (47 percent). Those who had been in a concentration camp but not at Auschwitz had rates of 51 percent. Those who had been at Auschwitz had rates of 65 percent.

These are the highest rates of chronic PTSD in any population I'm aware of, but there's an important message in the data. If about half the survivors of the Holocaust in general had PTSD, it means that about half *didn't*. And more than one-third of the survivors of Auschwitz—the single worst concentration camp of the Holocaust—*did not* have PTSD. This isn't to make light of the suffering experienced by Holocaust survivors. Their trauma and stress are real and serious. At the same time, however, their experiences show us that PTSD isn't inevitable. As with most of the British public during the Blitz, there seems to be a pathway other than breakdown in response to great stress.

How do we explain this? One source of protection might stem from the kind of influences we get from the people around us.

THE MOOD OF THE GROUP

Though almost all PTSD studies look at individuals and ignore what might be happening at the group level, one study looked at group features of PTSD by studying National Guard soldiers to see what effect the characteristics of the unit had on the development of PTSD.[11] As a way to understand their numerical findings, imagine two different soldiers: Private Smiles and Private Frowns.

- Private Smiles is exceptionally happy. He had a good childhood, and he didn't see much action when deployed with the Guard.
- Private Frowns is exceptionally unhappy and quite pessimistic. He had a terrible childhood, with both physical and sexual abuse. While on deployment, his Humvee struck an IED and his battle buddy died in front of him.

Which of the two would you say had the worse PTSD symptoms? The study confirmed our commonsense intuition that, all else being equal, the previously untraumatized Private Smiles, who had an easy deployment, would exhibit fewer PTSD symptoms than Private Frowns.

Now let's imagine two companies of National Guard soldiers: Cheerful and Caustic.

- Caustic Company soldiers don't smile much, aren't all that happy, and don't think things are going their way.
- Cheerful Company soldiers are always smiling, talking about how happy they are, and believing things will get better even after tragic losses.

Here's where things get interesting. Who would do better: Private Frowns assigned to Cheerful Company, or Private Smiles assigned to Caustic Company?

When I first read the study, I guessed wrong. All my training pointed to trauma as something primarily in the individual's life story, before and during combat. I expected that Private Smiles would be in the better position. But I was wrong. Private Frowns in Cheerful Company had far less PTSD by a large margin. Group dynamics dominated individual experiences, at least in this study. The scientists found that soldiers assigned to units whose other members were happy were protected from PTSD regardless of how they felt personally or their previous experience.

Another interesting finding was that the optimism didn't rub off. Private Frowns was still frowning; he just didn't get PTSD.[12]

The implications of these findings are profound: The happiness or lack of happiness of the people we're connected with is a bigger predictor of PTSD than the trauma itself.

When you think about the trauma in your life that might be keeping you from flourishing, think also about the effect of the people you surround yourself with or perhaps even follow online. Are they generally positive, hopeful, encouraging, and ready to find the humor in a situation? Or are they more likely to be critical, discouraging, and fearful? The attitude of the majority might have more of an effect on you than you realize. Pursuing the good life might, in part, mean reconsidering who you surround yourself with and choose to listen to.

Meanwhile, opening up the potential for moving away from depression and toward flourishing depends on having an accurate perception of the trouble you're facing.

WHEN STRESS BECOMES TRAUMA

The use of the word *trauma* in English-language publications has grown exponentially since 1970.[13] Nowadays, people are far more likely to identify events as traumatic than ever before. This may reflect a growing slipshod use of the term, and it may not be serving us well.

More and more people are showing up at my office with what would otherwise be called PTSD, except their trauma doesn't meet DSM criteria. Criterion A for PTSD requires "exposure to actual or threatened death, serious injury, or sexual violence."[14] I had one patient who had PTSD-like nightmares, avoidance, negative mood, and hyperarousal following a less than stellar performance review at work. In 2016, for the first time in my memory and professional work, some patients started describing nonviolent political events (e.g., Donald Trump's election) as "traumatic."

I'm not suggesting these experiences aren't difficult for these people or that they are unworthy of compassion and treatment. I'm saying that the bar for what constitutes trauma has dropped precipitously. Of course, the DSM allows for other nonspecific diagnoses, such as "adjustment disorder," which only requires a "marked distress that is out of proportion to the severity or intensity of the stressor," or the even more vague "unspecified trauma-and-stressor-related disorder," which has no specific requirements other than my judgment to apply.[15]

Though, without question, words can wound us, it concerns me to see ever more people "bleeding" these days. Worse yet are the increasing numbers who seem willing, and sometimes even eager, to view themselves as permanently broken.

In our day, freedom of speech has become a highly contentious issue. What we should be allowed to say, tweet, or post has been hotly debated.

People seem to have a newfound fragility, and I speculate that it may have something to do with the findings above. Perhaps with a bit less happiness in our lives or by spending time with people online who are unhappy, we are more prone to being damaged by ever more minor traumas. Remember the higher PTSD rates for Private Smiles with his uneventful deployment but unhappy unit.

As traumas seemingly multiply, it is more important than ever to accurately assess the seriousness of the hard stuff we go through, because our culture has also shifted in how we treat those who have experienced trauma.

WHEN WE *WANT* TO BE TRAUMATIZED

In some ways, the increased discussion about trauma is good. Trauma festers in the darkness of secrecy. Remarkable relief can come by confiding in another person. But those conversations can also go too far.

When I was growing up, if there was anything wrong at home, kids would not want to talk about it at school. One of the markers of being respected as a child was to have "respectable" parents. This social norm made things difficult for a lot of my friends who came from what we used to call "broken homes." There was a degree of shame in coming from a dysfunctional household. I'm not saying that feeling of shame was good, but it was the way people generally thought.

Not so anymore.

In 2018, I was working as a psychiatrist in a clinic in San Jose, where a large majority of my patients lived in poverty. I was treating a teenage patient who was generally well taken care of, despite coming from an economically distressed family. She felt frustrated because she was not as well regarded by her peers as her friend, who often talked about having "messed up" parents and a difficult childhood. Her friend received significant sympathy for his troubles and was considered more interesting and textured for what he had suffered. The only problem was it wasn't true!

My patient knew her friend's parents and knew them to be warm and supportive. In private, her friend confessed to her that what he'd said about his victimhood was a lie.

Why would someone lie—even brag—about having experienced

trauma? I think the answer lies in recent shifts in the conversation about people who have suffered.

We have come to see more clearly that there are certain minorities who have experienced particularly difficult roads historically. We rightly have a desire to correct injustice, to show compassion to those we have excluded from our compassion for too long. But in the midst of that conversation, there seems to have risen an idea that is nearly true but ultimately false—namely that people who suffer trauma never get over it. We see them as facing oppression but never overcoming it. We hear about the hardship they've gone through, but rarely about how they have learned to incorporate their suffering into their story—to grow stronger and more resilient.

Willful blindness to the possibility of recovery is unrealistic. Trauma is not a place we have to get stuck. Glorying in victimhood is counterproductive.

This means that not everyone who suffers deserves equal celebration. Yes, I use that word deliberately, though it may seem confusing to think that a person would *celebrate* trauma. But it's happening more and more often. We can feel sad or sympathetic for the person who accidentally smashes his finger with a hammer and has to go to the emergency room; but imagine a lonely person who does it accidentally once and loves all the attention he receives from the nurses and doctors. A month after his fractured thumb heals, he hits his thumb again with the hammer, but this time on purpose. A person who intentionally causes his own injury or illness for the sake of medical attention has what is called a *factitious disorder*. We should still have compassion for this person, but much less so for the pain in his thumb—after all, he caused it himself. The person is indeed suffering from loneliness, but providing extra compassion and attention to the thumb will make the situation worse.

How do we distinguish between true instances of trauma and those that might offer some kind of secondary gain? Some would argue that we should presume the truthfulness and good intentions of anyone claiming a traumatic experience. While that may be a desirable approach, what ultimately matters is the objective truth. If we provide nothing except compassion to those with claims of trauma, without specially celebrating those who bravely face it, we may be *causing* more trauma, as well as hindering people from reaching recovery. Also, if there is no way to identify people who self-traumatize or who are holding on to victim roles because of the compassion they receive, our compassion for these patients worsens their condition. Separating out these people is an incredibly delicate process, but it must have a place in both broader society and private therapy. It's good to provide compassion for an alcoholic, but we mustn't neglect to celebrate the recovery. As a society, I think we inadequately celebrate those who have done, and are doing, the difficult work of trauma recovery.

In a strange way, it's a sign of progress that we've shown such compassion to victims of trauma that there is social incentive to lie about having suffered. We should continue to work to create a society that celebrates the work of *recovery* from trauma, without celebrating the mere fact that someone has *experienced* trauma.

THE DOWNSIDE OF SAFETY

It seems to make good sense that if adverse experiences lead to terrible outcomes, we should strive to avoid them. A recent trend of going to extremes to avoid risk is sometimes called *safetyism*.[16] Seemingly, Gen Z has especially taken this to heart, choosing to, for example, delay driving, drink less, avoid romantic relationships, and avoid going out without their parents.[17]

But research shows there is another edge to this sword.

In a 1972 psychology experiment meant to model an aspect of depression, dogs were given shocks that they could not control.[18] The experiment looked to see how long the animals would try to escape or evade the shocks. Eventually the dogs gave up. They *learned* helplessness.

But when the researchers changed a factor in the experiment—namely, where they got the dogs for the tests—the results changed. Robert Sapolsky explains why: "Dogs born and raised in laboratories, bred only for research purposes, are more likely to succumb to learned helplessness than those who have come to the lab by way of the pound."[19]

Animals that have experienced the stresses of being "on the street," so to speak, don't give up as easily. Their ability to deal with new and unknown situations is greater. They figure there must be a way out of the situation. Animals raised in physically healthy, but ultimately sterile, environments don't have that drive.

Since this early work, other research has found that there is a dose of stress that can "inoculate" an animal from fear. In one study of mice, those that had been subjected to stress when young would freeze for less time in an open field (a stressful place to be for an animal that might be eaten by a bird) and struggle longer to break free when trapped.[20]

Even more recently, other researchers took a closer look at the effect of adverse events. In the classic study of ACEs, the original researchers assumed that the more adverse events a person had experienced, the worse things were for that person. That assumption is true for people with severe trauma histories. The newer researchers wanted to look more carefully at the effects of lower levels of stress.[21]

In a study titled after Friedrich Nietzsche's famous line "Whatever does not kill me makes me stronger," they identified a "sweet spot" of suffering. As expected, the people who expressed the worst PTSD symptoms, depressive symptoms, and overall worst level of satisfaction had lives filled with tragedy. The great surprise, however, was that the next worse-off group was the one that had experienced no difficulties at all. Of course, these are all averages and observations.

FACE THE FEAR

Treatment of PTSD is arguably the most difficult psychotherapy for patients to endure. The dropout rates are high. People hate it. But it works.

The two main evidence-based approaches—prolonged exposure and cognitive-processing therapy—both have as their mainstay the repetition and recapitulation of the traumatic event. Over and over again. This requires patients to demonstrate incredible courage. They must agree to recall the darkest, most terrifying memory they have, and then keep going back to it. Their pulse rises, they sweat, and their breathing quickens.

Some doctors had a great idea to make things easier for the patient: They prescribed an antianxiety medication called a benzodiazepine (e.g., Xanax, Valium, Ativan). Like many great ideas, it completely failed. On the one hand, as expected, patients were better able to tolerate the therapy while under the influence of a benzodiazepine. What was unexpected was that the benzodiazepine eliminated the treatment effect. It seemed that patients could only modify the fear memory if they were *emotionally* back in that difficult place.[22]

This is the key lesson of this chapter: *The worst fears can only be overcome by facing them.* There is no other way. A skillful therapist may help pace the training, gradually increasing the difficulty or detail of the exposure. A friend may create a safe environment and ask you to talk about it. You may have to get it all out in your journal while you work up the courage to tell someone. But it must be faced. As Eleanor Roosevelt said, "You gain strength, courage, and confidence by every experience in which you really stop to look fear in the face."[23]

DROP THE ROCK

Of course, reliving our past traumas so we can move past them may be more difficult when those traumas involve mistreatment from other individuals, possibly including some we still must live with. Here we're not just dealing with a thing that harmed us; the source of our suffering has a face. What do we do about the people who harmed us?

This is a common—and totally legitimate—question when dealing with depression. Often, my patients have been harmed in terrible ways. Unfaithful spouses. Terrible bosses. Rebellious kids. Bitterness is quite common, and it's no wonder. In my work as a psychiatrist, I hear about real tragedies and undeniable malevolence. The difficulty is that bitterness does no one any good. To the person holding on to it, it is destructive and often depressive.

Sometimes the roots of depression are obscure. At other times, ruminating on being a victim or being wronged allows depression to take hold. This pattern of thinking can then morph into greater misery, which justifies more resentment. Resentment can also attach itself to an already spiraling case of depression. Regardless of whether resentment is the root or is grafted in later, there is a way out.

If you've ever been involved with Alcoholics Anonymous, you're probably familiar with this story. A person named Mary is desperately trying to swim to the safety of a boat, but she is holding on to a rock that is weighing her down. People on the boat are shouting, "Just drop the rock!"

Mary has carried the rock for a long time and has grown used to it, so she is reluctant to drop it. Yet now she is drowning. Finally, after more sputtering and more mouthfuls of water, she finally decides to drop the rock. Once freed from the burden, she can swim to safety and get in the boat.[24]

For purposes of illustration here, the rock is resentment.

One of my professors, Fred Luskin, has done a huge amount of experimental testing in this field, and he describes how one way out of resentment is through forgiveness. Approaching the topic from a nonreligious position, he notes that forgiveness changes us, first and foremost, on the inside—not only in mindset, but also physiologically. A key aspect is recognizing that forgiveness is not the same thing as reconciliation; it's not the same thing as excusing the person who harmed us. In fact, Luskin says, it's vitally important to recognize the wrong in what the other person did.

> Forgiveness is the practice of extending your moments of peacefulness. Forgiveness is deciding what plays on your TV screen. Forgiveness is the power that comes from knowing a past injustice does not have to hurt today. When we have good experiences, such as moments of beauty or love, then for those moments we have forgiven those who have hurt us. Forgiveness is the choice to extend those moments to the rest of our life. Forgiveness is available anytime. It is completely under your control. It does not rely on the actions of others; it is a choice you alone can make.[25]

In the most symbolically significant study on the physiology of forgiveness, researchers chose as subjects people who both had heart disease and were holding a grudge.[26] After putting some of the participants through a course on forgiveness, researchers imaged their hearts while the participants thought about the person against whom they'd held a grudge at the start of the study. The hearts of the people who had not worked on forgiveness had blood flow to their already damaged heart tissue drop when they thought about their enemies. Those who had gone through the forgiveness class had significantly more blood flow to their hearts. Quite literally, the people who were unforgiving had cold, dead hearts.

Within this world, there is injustice. There is moral debt. But through forgiveness, we're able to free ourselves from that cycle; we're able to release the debt.

THROUGH THE TRAUMA AND OUT THE OTHER SIDE

I've said that some people today have a tendency to label things as trauma that don't deserve the term. But some people overshoot in the other direction—they *under*estimate the effects of harmful events from the past. Don't make the same mistake. Take the time to assess your history and identify anything that might have been traumatic for you.

Past trauma can easily hold you back from progressing toward the future you desire. If you've suffered severe trauma and have not dealt with it, you may need to seek professional help. It's true, as I've said, that treatment for PTSD can be among the toughest kinds of treatment to undergo—but it *works*. And it's better than remaining stuck for the rest of your life.

In the meantime, let me lay out a process that can help you address less severe traumas. The key is to learn to accept the trauma and also to tolerate the stress connected with it.

Put your trauma on paper

Get by yourself and create a list (either on paper or a device) of the things that have happened to you that were most difficult. These can include tragedies or things that caused an intense emotional reaction at the time. Your list may include loss, mistreatment, abuse, neglect, or exploitation.

Perhaps you'll think of some things that *didn't* create an intense emotional reaction at the time, but as you think back on them now, you feel as if they *should have*. For example, maybe someone in your family died but you didn't do much mourning over the loss at the time. Or maybe you took a bad home environment for granted in childhood, but now you realize it affected you more than you thought.

Write these things down—as many as you can think of—along with how they affected you. Did inappropriate touching cost you your innocence and engender mistrust? Did the onset of a disability cause you to become angry?

Making the list won't be easy, especially if you've had strong responses to trauma. If the exercise seems too overwhelming, you may need to stop until you can confront your trauma with the guidance and direction of a professional. But if you're able to complete the list, this practice alone can go a long way toward helping you understand, integrate, and process the events of your past.

Share your list with someone

This next step will likely be harder than the first. Tell someone else about one or more of the traumatic events on your list. There's something inherently healing about speaking our trauma aloud to another person. This may be a professional—perhaps a primary care provider or a therapist. It may be a trusted friend—but be sure to ask the person's permission before sharing. Not everyone is equipped or prepared to show support in this way. Sharing a secret trauma with someone who is compassionate can go a long way toward defusing the traumatic event.

Practice forgiveness

There are systematic ways to appropriately forgive someone who has harmed you. Many religious communities are well equipped to help with this process. Alternatively, there is a free evidence-based workbook that can be used.[27] As discussed above, forgiveness is more complicated than "just get over it." Either alone or (ideally) with others, walking the path of forgiveness is particularly helpful in cases where the trauma involves being wronged by another person.

Spend time with encouraging people

Remember Private Frowns and the stalwart Brits during World War II? If you've had a tough time but are surrounded by joyful, encouraging people, you're likely to recover faster and may take on the positive outlook of your group. Of course, this is easier said than done, and true loyalties to existing friends and family, happy or not, should be maintained. But as you're able, shift your time toward communities that include the kind of people you want to be like.

Respond to your trauma

After you've identified your trauma and shared it with someone, the next move is to figure out what was upsetting about it. Again, this can be difficult.

For example, let's say that when you were a child, your mother remarried and your stepfather took to beating you for infractions of his arbitrary rules. This was physically painful to you, but it was also shocking. This abuse made you realize that the world is more dangerous and malevolent than you expected. Your stepfather shouldn't have hurt you—but he *did*, and he did it on purpose. You could no longer harbor illusions that such evil is absent from the world.

Or perhaps the blame goes in the other direction. You did something wrong, and you feel regretful and guilty about it. But beyond that, it was traumatizing to you as well. You didn't realize you were capable of such a thing. Now you have to integrate the memory of what you did into your view of yourself. It's going to be a process.

In some cases, it may seem obvious why something was upsetting to you (e.g., sexual trauma, physical or emotional abuse). Other cases may take more exploration. Perhaps your home was destroyed by a fire, but you didn't think it mattered that much to you. Maybe you received a cancer diagnosis, but it came with a good prognosis. Dig into *why* the event was as upsetting as it was, and why it may still be affecting you.

You may wish to share your insights with a friend or trusted loved one.

Review, review, review

Identifying, sharing, and beginning to process your trauma can allow the healing to begin. But it's not a one-time event. In fact, the real benefit comes from revisiting what you've learned from your trauma again and again and again.

As we've seen, one of the key modes of evidence-based treatment for PTSD is reviewing the traumatic event multiple times until it loses its bite. The two main formal approaches to PTSD suggest that either you've "processed it" with rational thinking and integrated the story into your life, or you've allowed the fear to affect you repeatedly until your nervous system doesn't react to it anymore. Particularly for trauma that remains upsetting, you'll likely need to find somebody to help you go through it again and again. Repetitive review takes an enormous amount of courage, but it can really help you overcome the pain of trauma.

Some people might not want to share their trauma with others, to avoid "trauma dumping," a term that implies the traumatized person has psychic "waste" that must be dumped. This concern is based on two misconceptions: that the unfortunate listening friend is merely a dumping ground; and that the exchange is a zero-sum equation—that is, that the dumping party will be relieved while the receiving party becomes burdened. But a stable friend who has agreed to hear your story will rarely feel "dumped on," particularly if your motives are mostly good.

If it feels as if all you've accomplished is transferring your burden, check back in with your friend. Reconsider your motivation to make sure you're not corrupting a path to healing by gossiping, amplifying the wrong done to you, seeking to elevate your status in your friend's eyes, or trying to create an overly strong or intimate attachment to your friend.

If you do these exercises and healing doesn't come, if revisiting the trauma only reopens the wound rather than allowing a scab to develop, you may need to see a psychotherapist who has experience in treating trauma.

BLITZ REDUX

Why were the British able to withstand months of random, indiscriminate bombing and stand strong?

First, they were unified in purpose. They were resolved to stand against Hitler and the Nazis. They had a part to play in an important story. They had close communities (sometimes very close communities, sleeping side by side with one another in subway tunnels and bomb shelters). They were engaged in a collective prolonged-exposure therapy, walking over the bombed-out remains of homes and factories. With each other, and as a culture, they reprocessed the events again and again. They built up the courage to face the next night of bombings.

You, too, can become proactive in relating to your traumatic experiences. You don't have to get stuck in them and see yourself as powerless. You can work through your emotions until you've actually become stronger, not weaker. In a surprising way, trauma can propel you forward in your search to become your best self.

STEPS TOWARD FLOURISHING

When our lives are flourishing, we can face the past with courage. We are part of a joyful community that loves us unconditionally and allows us to share our pain and brokenness. We're able to bravely recall and face the past and speak about it to trustworthy people. We don't use our traumas to manipulate others; we don't nurse bitterness; we don't flaunt our traumas for vanity or power. We work toward forgiving those who have wronged us. We continue to grow spiritually, emotionally, and mentally beyond our traumas, incorporating them into our story but not being defined by them.

5

CONSCIENCE: THE BURDEN OF GUILT

Out, damned spot! Out, I say!
SHAKESPEARE, *Macbeth*

*Blessed is the man against whom the LORD counts no iniquity, and in
whose spirit there is no deceit. For when I kept silent, my bones wasted
away through my groaning all day long. . . . I acknowledged my sin to you,
and I did not cover my iniquity; I said, "I will confess my transgressions
to the LORD," and you forgave the iniquity of my sin.*

PSALM 32:2-3, 5

On September 11, 2001, as eleven-year-old Jessica watched the World
Trade Center tragedy unfold on TV, she was completely panicked. Planes
had hit the Twin Towers. The buildings were on fire. And then one of them
collapsed in a cloud of dust.

"No! No! No!" Jessica screamed. But it was too late. She knew what she
had done. This was all her fault.

To be honest, she wasn't exactly sure *how* she could have accomplished
such an elaborate and terrible plan, but she knew in her heart that she was
the kind of person who *would* do such a thing. Though she lived in rural
America, far from the East Coast, and she didn't even really know where the
Twin Towers were, she was convinced that somehow she had pulled it off.

She would feel intensely guilty about it for years to come.

As I'm sure you realize, Jessica had nothing to do with the events of
9/11. But she had struggled with mental health issues, including depression, from a young age.

Intense and irrational guilt is one of the core symptoms of depression.

Rarely, this guilt can become so extreme that people truly believe themselves guilty of things they could not possibly have done. More often, they have a pervasive sense that they are a bad, evil, or ugly person, with a loquacious inner critic that constantly reminds them of their wrongdoings and shortcomings.

Rightly or wrongly, depressed or otherwise, we all feel guilty at times in our lives. This guilt makes us feel trapped, unworthy, fraudulent. And with the burden of guilt weighing on us, we can never have the kind of life we want. Not with that interior voice constantly telling us we're wrong, bad, or unworthy. We need to find a way to tune it out.

The best response to guilt, it turns out, is *self-acceptance*. If an inner voice is telling people with depression that they are not enough, the appropriate countermeasure is to respond, "I *am* enough." The best meditation techniques emphasize the need to be nonjudgmental. Remember that you are perfect as you are, and there's nothing you need to do to change.

Except . . . *every sentence in the previous paragraph is wrong*. The fact that it *sounds* plausible is partly why, I believe, depression is so common to begin with. We have been told so many times, "You're okay the way you are," and we have tried to believe it. But on a deep level, we know it's not right, and the more we try to suppress the truth, the more it forces itself upon us. The fact is, guilt is an important emotion that can point us to the truth about ourselves. When we ignore or deny it outright, it can fester and lead to depression.

The focus of this chapter is learning how to rightly order this system of guilt.[1]

BANISHING SIN

Everyone knows there's something wrong with humanity—or at least they did up until the tiny sliver of history we call modern times.

In biblical history, the first couple committed the first sin, and the first murder was committed in the next generation. The Jewish religious system—and others—had a sacrificial system that attempted to make some atonement for sin.

Though rituals differed from one culture to the next, there was widespread recognition in the ancient world that human actions had consequences in the spiritual world that one could not ignore. Something *happened* in the world when people failed to do the right thing.

Christians believe that human guilt was done away with by the death of a sinless Messiah. The crucifixion of Jesus was at the very center of cosmic history. Though Jesus didn't establish many religious rituals during his life on earth, he was adamant about this particular one—instructing his followers to remember his death by participating in what is known as the Eucharist or Communion.

"He took bread, and when he had given thanks, he broke it and gave it to them, saying, 'This is my body, which is given for you. Do this in remembrance of me.' And likewise the cup after they had eaten, saying, 'This cup that is poured out for you is the new covenant in my blood.'"[2] By the time the Enlightenment came along seventeen centuries later, followed by Modernism, Freudianism, and Individualism, people had gradually come to believe that all this guilt and atonement was unnecessary.

Today in our society, we put far less emphasis on how *bad* it is when we do something wrong. We have convinced ourselves, despite failing to meet even our own basic moral aspirations, that we are "basically good people." In large part, we have banished guilt. We have no recompense for our minor shortcomings. We have no habits or customs for dealing with our guilt other than denial. We tell people, "You're okay as you are. Just accept yourself."

But when a person doesn't *feel* okay, particularly when he or she has done something truly grievous, such affirmations ring hollow. Less severe failings and harm done to others are simply not part of our daily reflection or discussion.

In some parts of our culture, and largely because of the moral vacuum created by our attempts to completely banish our guilt, we have started talking about guilt as less personal and more collective. Thus, we are meant to feel guilty for racial inequality, colonialism, global warming, and heteronormativity. But it's difficult to individually repent of collective guilt or extinguish it in some lasting way.

We might make some progress if we would consider what our guilty feelings are actually pointing toward.

AUTOIMMUNE GUILT

Guilty feelings are right and proper in helping us identify where we've gone wrong. To use a biological analogy, guilt and shame are a type of pain receptor for the human soul, and the pain we feel comes from the moral harm we've caused. It's like our immune system reacting to a moral contagion that we've invited in. When we're doing something that is damaging to ourselves or to our community, we feel guilty and ashamed.

The problem comes when our sense of blameworthiness begins to attack our normal activities and regular variations in our behavior. A biological analogy may help here as well. If we raise a child in a completely sterile environment, his or her immune system will ramp itself up and food allergies will abound. The immune system assumes there are things for it to attack (which, under normal circumstances, would be true) and that it just isn't looking hard enough. So it begins to attack the body. This is the hygiene theory of autoimmunity.

Some people have "autoimmune guilt." They feel guilty, not about true moral errors or sins, but about other things. That was the situation with Jessica, the eleven-year-old girl who felt terrible about "destroying" the World Trade Center.

Another useful metaphor comes from Jonathan Haidt in *The Righteous Mind*. Building a case for moral reasoning, Haidt writes, "The first principle of moral psychology is [that] *Intuitions come first, strategic reasoning second*."[3] He presents various evidences that minor manipulations to our emotions or bodily states have major effects on our ultimate moral judgments. He says our conscious reasoning can work as a "press secretary" for our emotions—that is, to take whatever we've done and spin a story about why it's justified.[4] One unfamiliar with American politics might mistake the person doing all the talking and justifying (the press secretary) for the one making the decisions (the president). In depression, this is often the case: The rational thinking part of the brain is hijacked and conscripted to spin convincing stories about why guilt *would be* justified. What would have to be true of me for these feelings of guilt to be appropriate? The rational brain sets to work constructing narratives that would otherwise be considered absurd: "I'm actually a terrible person." "I must have done something really, really bad." Sometimes, it goes *meta*, with the depression itself being drawn into a narrative: "I feel depressed as a punishment for having been such a bad person."

Whether our feelings of guilt are rational or irrational, they are not something we can simply dismiss or ignore. Sensitivity to right and wrong is deeply tied in with our being human. In fact, it develops extremely early.

BORN TO FEEL GUILTY

Psychologist Paul Bloom devised an ingenious set of experiments to determine whether a moral sense comes before or after language development. It was already known that babies would stare longer at scenes that didn't make physical sense. For example, babies shown optical illusions would look curious, as such an image seemed to violate an expectation. Bloom took this to the next level and showed babies as young as nine months a series of scenes depicting moral or immoral behavior in a puppet show. In one version, a puppet was trying to climb a mountain while another puppet was pushing him down. In another version, while one puppet was playing with a ball, another puppet would come up and steal it. When the babies were then given an opportunity to pick one puppet to play with, they showed that they did not want to play with the "bad" puppet. In other experiments, they showed surprise when a "bad" puppet was rewarded.[5]

There are important questions to be answered about when and how this sense of morality develops, but it's certainly very early. Either it is taught wordlessly at a very young age or it is innate. It may be that we are all born with a "first draft" morality that encodes things such as reciprocal fairness, and that society fills in the details of when exceptions to the rule can occur (e.g., harming others is bad, *except* in self-defense).

Moral awareness—and thus the capacity to know right from wrong—is something that develops incredibly early and is more foundational than even language. Though some would argue that rules of fairness are "nothing but a social construct," it looks much more like a developing physical sense than a set of arbitrary, learned social rules. Moral awareness develops in the same way and around the same time as a rudimentary understanding of physics. In the construction of the later brain, one of the early foundational levels includes the capacity to "see" *right* and *wrong*. In other words, babies have this sense—with no conscience-dulling concept of "being okay as you are." Even infants are refining their sense of right and wrong and learning how to better discern the difference.

GUILT AS A GUIDE TO THE HIGHEST SELF

"He'd still be alive if not for me." That's what Daniel—a man in his thirties who came to the clinic reporting terrible depression—said to me. He believed he was guilty of his father's death.

When I administered a standardized interview for determining the severity of Daniel's depression, his number was in the stratosphere. On top of that, his anxiety was as bad as I had ever seen. He carried himself throughout the interview in a state of terror, like a character from a horror movie stuck in that moment when the monster is revealed.

His brother was in jail and his father was dead, and both situations were his fault, as far as he was concerned. He had some tenuous explanation for how these family tragedies should be laid to his account: "If I hadn't moved out here for work . . ." Beyond that, he was unable to explain how he had single-handedly affected the justice system and his father's fate. But by the time I met him, he had carried this guilt for years.

As we discussed the merits of accelerated TMS, I told him that one possible risk of the procedure was that he might no longer feel guilty. We talked about how his feelings of guilt were good in some ways, in that they proved he cared about his father and brother. That if he truly was responsible for what had happened to them, and he was a decent person, he *should* feel guilty. But he had enough awareness to acknowledge that his guilt might not be reality-based.

We completed the treatment, and he responded remarkably well. His depression and anxiety scores dropped to zeros, and he was completely well after the full week of treatment. He now realized that he wasn't really to blame for his brother or his father. The emotional root of the guilt was cut, and the rational branches shriveled immediately. When the foundation of his guilty feelings was undermined, his feelings of being to blame collapsed in a moment of epiphany—though he still felt a bit of guilt for having moved away. When potent biological treatments shut down the out-of-control emotions and epiphanies occur, it helps show that their foundation was an irrational emotion.

Every time in my career—except once—when I've delivered TMS to a patient who was feeling guilty, it restored him or her to a proper sense of moral proportions. That one time, a patient came to me feeling guilty about something he had done that was legitimately wrong in his own estimation. He had no intention of confessing it or making it right, but I assumed the exaggerated weight of guilt was too much to bear and was part of his depression. With relief from the depression, I assumed he would be free to make right what was wrong. And indeed he was. But he did not use his freedom to make things right. While the TMS relieved his depression, it also completely removed any conscious concern for his wrongdoing. TMS can relieve depression, but it doesn't make people good.

GUILT RESPONSES

There are three main pathways for dealing with guilt. The first is to *deny that there is any reality to moral duties, so there is no wrong and no guilt*. In other words, we try to suppress our guilt feelings or convince ourselves they mean nothing.

Though denial of moral duty is a popular refrain among college freshmen and people wanting to experiment sexually, it's a hard position to defend. I can't recall ever meeting a patient or another person who arrived at this viewpoint rationally. The closest I have seen are sociopaths—though they also have a code that they fail to live up to, albeit one that is bizarre to most outside observers.

Denial is helpful only when the wrongdoing in question isn't actually wrong but only *feels* wrong (in which case, it is irrational guilt). However, healthy humans simply aren't able to live in denial as a global approach to life. The guilt will find a way to manifest itself.

The second pathway is to *accept that guilt is a real and useful capacity for seeing the moral universe*. It ought not be ignored or suppressed, but must be dealt with.

Wrongdoing leaves a permanent stain on the conscience—as with Lady Macbeth, who is complicit in the murder of the king of Scotland in Shakespeare's famous play. While sleepwalking, she "sees" her hands still bloody from the murder and cries, "Out, damned spot! Out, I say!"[6] But she can't wash herself clean.

In Shakespearean justice, Lady Macbeth descends into madness and suicide. That is not the outcome we would want for ourselves, but we all have guilt, so what are we going to do with it? If we take the second pathway, we accept that everyone has their "damned spots," and we try to make matters better.

This is the pathway of most moral systems. In Islam, one's good deeds and bad deeds weigh against one another to determine one's place in the afterlife. In Hinduism and Buddhism, one's *karma* cannot be "reset" and will determine the conditions of a person's next reincarnation. The best one can hope for is to try to "do better" with the time that remains.

There is much to be said for this approach. In therapy, by accepting the reality of guilt, we can begin to understand ourselves and the influences that may have led to a wrong decision. We can come to see the universal nature of human failing.

One well-known approach to true guilt comes from Alcoholics Anonymous. Its Twelve Steps include the following actions:

- Made a searching and fearless moral inventory of ourselves (Step Four).
- Admitted to God, to ourselves, and to another human being the exact nature of our wrongs (Step Five).
- Humbly asked [God] to remove our shortcomings (Step Seven).
- Made a list of all the persons we had harmed, and . . . made direct amends . . . wherever possible, except when to do so would injure them or others (Steps Eight and Nine).
- Continued to take personal inventory and when we were wrong promptly admitted it (Step Ten).[7]

The process of making the best of it after truly doing something wrong is well described in these steps.

The third pathway for responding to true wrongdoing is to *find a way to be forgiven*. Guilt is real, and we don't have to try to manage it or minimize it; we can acknowledge it and leave it behind permanently. An excellent resource for exploring this from a Christian perspective is Timothy Keller's book *Forgive: Why Should I and How Can I?*

One of the foundational beliefs of Christianity is that our guilt can be wiped away through the death and resurrection of Jesus. Fully embracing the availability of forgiveness is transformational. Of course, we may still have to make amends, as AA encourages, and there may be lifelong consequences to our actions. But the burden of guilt is gone.

LAZY JACK

Jack was a recovering alcoholic. Though he hadn't had a drink in fifteen years, he continued to attend AA meetings, where he always introduced himself in AA fashion: "My name is Jack, and I'm an alcoholic."

Even without alcohol, Jack was in trouble. He was the sole breadwinner for his stay-at-home wife and three school-age children. College was in their future, and that was going to be expensive. The mortgage on their home was also expensive. The problem was that Jack was so lazy that he was afraid he was going to lose his job. He came into my office for treatment.

Wanting to get a sense of what exactly he meant by "lazy," I asked about his daily routine. He woke up at 5:00 a.m. and went for a run with the family dog. He'd cook a healthy breakfast for himself and his wife. Then he'd have "personal growth time," which included going to an AA meeting, meeting with his sponsor, and journaling. He'd arrive at work at 8:00 a.m., work all day, and get home around 6:00. After dinner and spending some time with the family, he'd usually try to put in a little more work before going to sleep at 11:00 p.m.

This did not sound lazy to me. Having not gone for a run, cooked breakfast, or spent time on my personal growth that morning, I might have been especially concerned to prove that Jack was not lazy. I explored further.

It turned out, he felt lazy because his productivity at work was down. He was having a hard time concentrating, and he couldn't push himself to do the unpleasant but necessary parts of his job. Ten years ago, he was at the top of his game, getting promotions and advancing in his career. Now he felt that he was on the verge of losing his job.

He also felt sad all the time. He had always been a doting father who loved to spend time with his kids. He remained dutiful, but now the joy was gone. Life, which had been so full, now felt like a burden. Food had lost its appeal, and he had lost weight.

He was clearly depressed, and I agreed to take him on as a patient. We started with psychotherapy, but it wasn't enough. I added a medication. His "laziness" improved to some degree, but he was still stuck on the idea that he wasn't measuring up.

In the process of therapy, I discovered that guilt was a recurrent theme in his life. He felt guilty for being lazy (though he wasn't). He felt guilty for being an alcoholic (though he hadn't had a drink in fifteen years), a bad son (he wasn't), bad husband (he wasn't), and bad father (he wasn't). Over the weeks, and then months, we explored these feelings. When he was young and poor, guilt had driven him to get good grades and build a materially successful life. Guilt had gotten him sober. Guilt kept him in line at work. But like many a thing that works until it doesn't, guilt was no longer enough to goad him into action. What he was describing as "laziness" was the failure of guilt to get him to do even more.

He identified as a Christian, and we explored the meaning of forgiveness. He told me he "didn't really connect to that part of Christianity." He didn't understand it. He knew he had to suffer the consequences of his actions, and he was prepared for that. We had been making marginal gains for about a year. The medications had helped somewhat to bring down the temperature of his guilt and push him a bit further in his productivity. But the deep feelings of guilt remained.

Then, in one of our therapy sessions, it finally clicked: *He didn't have to hold on to the guilt.*

Like a flood breaking through the levee and overwhelming smaller dams and riverbanks downstream, the epiphany flowed. For the next few sessions, he shared what he had discovered and unlocked by accepting forgiveness. What I witnessed was a complete transformation. He no longer had to *continue* feeling guilty about being an alcoholic; he could confess it as a sin and release it. The same with his problems at work and how he treated his wife and kids. The same with his childhood experiences. He saw that his motivation didn't have to come from lashing himself with guilt; it could come from his love for his family. He could be free. His Christian faith began to make more sense, and he got more involved at his church.

His performance at work improved. His relationship with his family improved. His mood improved. We started to have trouble finding issues to work on in therapy, because his life was now so full of love and peace. So we took the win and concluded the therapy.

GET IT OUT, LET IT GO

The applications for this chapter involve varying degrees of confession. Holding on to the burden of guilt and self-recrimination can become unbearable. Confession allows us to separate real guilt and shame from what is not real, so that we can dispense with the part that isn't real, while acknowledging, owning, and seeking forgiveness for the part that is.

Acknowledge your guilt

Step Four of the Twelve Steps of Alcoholics Anonymous involves taking "a searching and fearless moral inventory." You don't have to follow the AA method entirely, but dare to accept the searching and fearless part. In seeking to move past guilt, it is helpful to write down the things you feel guilty about. Simply make a list on a piece of paper or in a journal of whatever you've done wrong.

Don't include things that you feel guilty about irrationally or that others are mad at you about but aren't really wrong. Do include things that you have never confessed or that continue to come back to you with guilty feelings.

Sometimes guilt isn't black-and-white. As you write down things you feel guilty about, try to separate what you may have done in ignorance from what you did with full knowledge that it was wrong. Writing things down has a way of making our opinions clear and concrete. Is this something you ought to feel guilty about or not? It's also an important springboard for later application steps.

Confess and make amends

As you consider a more intensive intervention or application, try talking about your wrongdoing with a friend or confidant—someone unrelated to the act for which you feel guilty.

If you're a person of faith and are open to it, confess your sin to God while in your friend's presence. Ask forgiveness, trusting in God's willingness to give mercy. Having someone with you to witness your prayer and pray with you will help you remember this moment as a turning point.

After you've confessed, make amends with the people you've harmed—unless doing so would cause further injury. Sometimes "making it right" will be costly. This can be a complex topic, particularly for big offenses. If you're estranged from the person with whom you need to make amends, it's still a good idea, but you should game-plan with another person what you're going to say before giving it a go.

Turn confession into a way of life

A third and more systematic approach is to make confession a regular part of your life, particularly confessing to another person. An example of this would be a sponsor in AA—someone you talk to weekly (in person or on the phone) and with whom you must be perfectly honest. It's a very effective strategy in recovery, and there's no reason why it wouldn't also be helpful elsewhere. Regularly seeking forgiveness is a great way to clear out a backlog of guilt and keep your accounts short going forward. It will also reveal areas where you still need to grow.

THE SHORT-TERM PAIN THAT LEADS TO HEALING

A flourishing life is one with robust and potent emotions of guilt that are rarely active. As your errors become less grievous, your conscience will become appropriately more sensitive. This process is reflected in the writings of ancient prophets and saints, like Isaiah, one of the heroes of Jewish tradition, who saw a vision of God seated on a throne and cried out, "Woe is me! . . . I am a man of unclean lips."[8] The apostle Paul referred to himself as the foremost of sinners.[9]

We're not all prophets and saints, but when our conscience is functioning properly, we may find ourselves increasingly able to detect even small shortcomings in ourselves. Fortunately, this allows for quicker confession and prevents guilt and shame from taking root.

Rumination on past sins, problems, or symptoms that lead nowhere is not a part of a flourishing life. *Rumination*—a word that refers to chewing the cud—is great for bovines but terrible for people. Mental rumination refers to "going over the same matter in one's thoughts again and again,"[10] but it doesn't lead to action and thus serves no useful purpose. Reflection on a past situation—trying to understand it and how to act differently—is good and useful; but continuing to chew on it is when it goes too far. It's like the difference between washing your hands after using the restroom and compulsively washing your hands hundreds of times per day.

Rumination is a bad mental habit that is typical of depression, and also a cause of it. People without depression who ruminate are more likely to develop depression. According to one review article, "rumination exacerbates depression, enhances negative thinking, impairs problem solving, interferes with instrumental behavior [i.e., actions performed to reach a goal], and erodes social support. . . . Further, evidence now suggests that rumination is associated with psychopathologies in addition to depression, including anxiety, binge eating, binge drinking, and self-harm."[11]

Physical pain can alert us when our bodies are at risk of being damaged; it gives us incentive to change and can help us remember not to do something again—like putting your hand on a hot stove, for example. Physical pain is good and protective. Insensitivity to pain can be quite dangerous, leading to serious injury for those who lack pain perception. At the other extreme are numerous conditions where the perception of pain is always present without there being any actual physical injury.

Like pain, guilt can be useful when it prompts us to take action. But like pain, if it's always present, it provides no useful or actionable information. Guiltlessness can be a symptom of sociopathy. Flourishing involves listening to our guilt when it is accurate and in line with the truth, and learning to dismiss it or explore it further when the guilt is false or excessive.

Accept guilt as a "pricking of the heart," something that moves you to confess your misdeeds, seek forgiveness, and change your ways. But don't listen to the voice of evil that accuses you "day and night,"[12] hoping to keep you trapped. If guilt is an impelling force that moves you toward a better future, it's something to be thankful for.

STEPS TOWARD FLOURISHING

The opposite of depression is clean, sharp guilt. When we are flourishing, we feel bad when we do something wrong. We confess our wrongdoing quickly and are swift to make amends. We do not dwell on past wrongs for which we have confessed and made amends, and we do not accuse ourselves of things we haven't done.

6

ATTENTION: CHOOSING WHERE TO FOCUS

Can you purify your mystic vision and wash it until it is spotless?
LAO-TZU, *Tao Tĕ Ching*

The eye is the lamp of the body. So, if your eye is healthy, your whole body
will be full of light, but if your eye is bad, your whole body will be full of
darkness. If then the light in you is darkness, how great is the darkness!
MATTHEW 6:22-23

As humans, we have a truly remarkable ability: *concentration*.

There is a Niagara Falls of data flowing down through our eyes and ears and into our brains. There is an ocean of past memories, future plans, and present calculations. Our minds could be reflecting on a timeless truth about nature, calculating the relationship between the sides of a triangle, or deciding what we're going to have for dinner tonight. But in order to figure out anything, we have the ability to focus our attention on one small part of what's possible to think about in any given moment.

What do we focus on? Do we rehearse the memory of having been wronged from earlier in the week? Think about what we'll have to do at work tomorrow? Meditate on what we have to be grateful for? I can turn my attention toward brooding, or I can turn my attention toward loving my neighbor. In a very real sense, we always have a choice, and the choices we make about what we pay attention to today will shape what we become tomorrow. In fact, where to focus our attention may be the only real choice we have about anything.

The eye is both a specialized sense organ and a symbol for concentration. Let's explore the realm of physical sight to see if we can gain some understanding of spiritual sight.

TO SEE IS TO CHANGE

Most matter in the universe can't "see" anything. Stars emit photons that travel endlessly through the sightless void of space. Along the way, some might strike gassy planets or rocky ones, where they are either absorbed forever or bounce off to continue their journey into the blind darkness of space.

On at least one planet, though, there are creatures that are able to capture that stream of photons and put it to use. Trees and turtles, bushes and bacteria, people and plankton all have this ability. Most, like plants, use it merely for energy through photosynthesis. Fewer organisms can extract some basic information, such as directionality or color. But an animal with eyes can do something even more remarkable: It can piece together an array of photons into a depiction of a three-dimensional world. This world is modeled using the light coming through two quarter-inch openings in the front of the brain.

Plato conceived of the eye as a spotlight, shooting out "vision" from the eye, bouncing off things in the world, and coming back to the eye, almost like a sonar system. Though wrong in a literal sense, his view is useful conceptually. Wherever we turn our gaze, our consciousness lights up the world (at least from our perspective).

The philosophical implications of conscious attention in the physical world are also mind-blowing. Everything in the material world has objective properties. A paper clip is shiny and curved, and weighs about one gram. You and I can look at the same paper clip and ascertain the same properties. Objective properties are the very basis of science itself. But some things have subjective properties as well. What it's like being *me* is not something *you* can ever really know. Reading a description of what it's like being me can't capture it: it's ever only you in your subjective experience trying to empathize with me. This concept is hard to explain within the confines of the belief that the world is nothing but physical matter.

Observation itself also seems to have powers far beyond what we once thought possible. Some of these concepts were discovered in the field of quantum mechanics about a century ago but have been simply too weird to incorporate into our workaday world. Take the phrase "a watched pot never boils." In reality, water boils at the same rate no matter how often we check it. Yet the same is not true in the quantum world.

In one particularly creative experiment, scientists checked on a "pot" of beryllium ions as they were "boiling" (increasing from a low initial energy state to a higher energy state) on a "stove" (a beam of radio waves). Normally, this process takes about a quarter of a second (250 milliseconds). But when the scientists "checked the pot" sixty-three times in that quarter-second by shining a brief pulse of light at 4 millisecond intervals, the beryllium ions never reached the "boiling point," the higher energy state.[1] It seems that "watching the pot" literally changed the speed of boiling. In other words, the scientists' *observations* changed the physical world.[2]

Though this research had "no immediate practical applications,"[3] the implications are profound: If observations can literally change the physical world, it may be that our *attention* can be the mechanism by which our physical brain changes. It may be that our attention is like the laser in the experiment: Wherever it shines, things change. Whether this happens is the subject of delightful debates at the intersection of philosophy and neuroscience.

Though the science and philosophy remain unsettled, I am persuaded that every single change we could ever make to ourselves is made via attention. Attention is the rudder of the ship. Mastering our own attention is the only way to achieve a flourishing life amid the Good, the True, and the Beautiful, having left the Bad, the False, and the Ugly of depression behind.

ATTENTION FOR SALE

In depression, it can be incredibly difficult to pay attention to anything. Sometimes it's because the negative voices are so loud that they crowd out time for any other thinking. Sometimes it's just that any attempt to focus slips away, like trying to hold water in a sieve.

As if things weren't already hard enough because of feeling down and lacking interest or joy, the inability to concentrate makes life doubly difficult. Particularly in an age when bureaucracy reigns and everything from renewing a vehicle registration to doing our daily work has outsized consequences for minor lapses in attention. While doing those annoying tasks is hard for all of us, they create an amplified burden on depressed individuals.

When looking for a sense of how bad a person's depression is, I will sometimes ask how long he or she can focus. By the time people come to see me, they are often unable to work and instead fill their time with passive entertainment. So I'll ask, "Is your depression so bad that you can't watch a TV show?" Sometimes it is. Their attention is so scattered that even trying to follow the plot of a twenty-four-minute TV show is too much.

But it's not only depression that can lead to this kind of outcome. Attention, it turns out, is an incredibly valuable thing. Much of the inconceivable wealth created in the past twenty years was in the commoditization of your and my attention. The tech sector does a lot of things, but one of the biggest is its ability to capture human attention by making engaging content (e.g., Facebook), or by organizing and displaying relevant information (e.g., Google), and then showing ads that you'd be especially interested in. Some tech companies are largely buyers of attention (e.g., Amazon, Apple, Microsoft); some are mostly sellers (e.g., Google, Facebook, Netflix). As I'm writing this paragraph at 1:30 p.m. on a Tuesday, my phone informs me that it has tried to alert me to things requiring my attention 286 times. No human can give serious attention to 286 things in half a day.

As finite beings, we have only so many moments of attention every day. If we are languishing, it is difficult to resist the lures placed out for us. If we are depressed, it can be harder still. In the most extreme states, there isn't much attention left; some of my patients will simply sit and do nothing while their thoughts assail them. To flourish, we must do our best to use whatever attention we have in ways that align with our ideals. Those tech platforms vying for our attention don't care one whit about us; we must do what we can not to become "wares."

Attention is the only currency we have that can buy a different future. But it can also be sold—and for not that much money. Facebook, for example, sells your attention at a rate of about a dollar an hour.[4] Is that a good deal for you? Do you deserve better?

For people who are depressed, their inability to concentrate is a big part of the reason they are not living the good life. And for those of us who are not depressed, and who have the ability to sustain our attention on something, we may be too often focusing on the wrong things, and thus not making progress toward the good life.

THE COST OF DISTRACTION

In one study I was involved in, called SoulPulse, we were interested in how best to deploy limited attention.[5] Using an innovative survey method, we interrupted people via their smartphones (the irony of interrupting people to investigate focused attention is not lost on me) at random times during the day to ask questions while they were out living their lives. This allowed us to study people outside of a laboratory in their "natural habitat." Included among other questions were these three:

1. Are you rushing through activities without being really attentive to them?
2. Are you doing jobs or tasks automatically, without being aware of what you're doing?
3. Are you thinking about something other than what you're currently doing?

We wanted to know whether failing to focus attention depleted a person's willpower. Or to put it another way, does living life rushed, mindless, and distracted lead to such things as difficulty in making decisions, feeling irritable, and being fatigued?

In the course of our study, we followed people for two weeks. Some consistently had divided attention; others were consistently focused. Those who were consistently divided in their attention more often had depleted willpower: They were more irritable, had low energy, and struggled to make decisions. The effect was quite pronounced. For a point of reference, we also asked people whether they were in physical pain. We found that physical pain also affected a person's ability to make decisions, and contributed to their feeling irritable and out of energy. But rushing (by itself) affected people 46 percent more than physical pain.

Also notable were the differences seen in people who answered consistently higher on these measures. Among those who were consistently distracted (either because of habit or disposition), the impact was nearly doubled. In SoulPulse, some effects were ameliorated when they became habitual; but for inattention, they were substantially exacerbated.

Clearly, our attention is best used in a focused manner. Being distracted or scattered, doing multiple things at once, or rushing from one thing to the next all lead to our feeling more depleted.

TRAIN YOUR BRAIN

A fascinating experiment, conducted over a period of twelve weeks, set out to test the effects of directed attention.[6]

The researchers asked the control group to exercise a particular muscle—the *abductor digiti minimi*, located on the outside of the hand at the base of the pinky—for fifteen minutes a day over the course of twelve weeks, and then measured the change in strength. The people who did the exercises developed abductor muscles that were 53 percent stronger than before.

Meanwhile, the researchers told the experimental group to simply *think* about moving the *abductor digiti minimi* for fifteen minutes a day over the twelve weeks. This group, which literally *did not move a muscle*, had a 35 percent increase in muscle strength!

This finding is incredible, but other groups have replicated the results, so it seems to be a real effect.[7] What it suggests is that some percentage of our muscle strength is related to changes of neurons assigned to control those muscles. In other words, it's possible we could reprogram and rewire our bodies with the power of thought alone.[8]

This finding isn't nearly as important as the broader implication: You can reprogram your own brain. How? Through repetition. As in the experiment, repeatedly thinking a particular way strengthens the pathways in the brain.

What is true of the physical body is even more true of mental pathways.

In a classic experiment, researchers compared the brains of London cabbies with those of London bus drivers and found (with comparative controls) that the part of the brain that retains spatial memory was larger in the cabbies, who might take a fare anywhere in the city, than in the bus drivers, who followed established routes on the job.[9] In violinists, the part of the brain controlling the left hand—the hand that makes all the delicate movements along the fingerboard—was substantially larger than the corresponding area in the other hemisphere.[10] Purely mental practice has been shown to be effective at improving performance in things as varied as playing the piano to surgery.[11] This process is called *neuroplasticity*.

The term comes from material science. Imagine a paper clip. It can bend a certain distance and return to exactly the same shape afterward; this is *elastic change*. Bend it too far, and it will stay in the new shape; this is called *plastic change*. A small paper clip holding three pages will exhibit only elastic change; a small paper clip holding fifty pages will experience plastic deformation and will not return to its original shape. Our brains are the same way, except what "bends" the brain is *repetition* and *significance*.

Do you remember what you ate for lunch three Tuesdays ago? Your brain changed to be able to remember that for a short time, but without another process of repetition or significance, the memory disappears from conscious thought. More people would likely remember what they ate at their wedding. But if, at some unpredictable time in the next year, a quirky billionaire offered to pay you $1 million if you accurately remembered what you ate for lunch three Tuesdays before, you'd figure out a way to remember your Tuesday lunch choices.

To sum it up, beyond accumulating knowledge, your brain can also learn new skills. Although some organs or body parts can certainly be changed by physical training (e.g., stronger muscles through exercise), it's likely that most learning happens in the brain. Some would argue that there is an objective reality to our "gut feelings," and others believe that an immaterial soul holds information that it shares with the brain. Regardless, it's very likely that most everything you learn is stored in your brain and encoded as physical changes, some of which can be grasped with our current crude understanding of neuroscience.

This goes for learning in psychotherapy as well. Neuroplasticity is facilitated by the therapist—either by creating a safe environment or by guiding the patient to healthy, true, and helpful patterns of thought. This process starts to train the brain to think regularly in a better way.

CRYSTALLIZED THOUGHT

The other thing that seems abundantly clear to me, though it's controversial, is that highly focused attention is quite depleting. When I do something that requires me to be continuously *on* and focused, I get a special kind of tired by the end of the day. After an all-day licensing exam or after lecturing for six hours in a seven-hour period, I'm exhausted. There is an interesting technical debate about the neural mechanisms that underlie these common experiences, but it's nonetheless clear to me that we cannot simply direct more and more attention at things.

God, in his infinite wisdom, has given us a way out. Our brains have a way to automate tasks. We can delegate parts of tasks or sometimes entire tasks. This near-miraculous ability is called creating a *habit*.

My sixteen-month-old daughter is currently learning to brush her teeth. It requires every bit of her concentration to achieve a brushing motion that is as faithful to effective toothbrushing as most movie adaptations are to their source material. In other words, full attention and it's still not right. For me, I tell my brain to initiate the "brush my teeth" routine and no additional concentration is required until the task is done. My brain has been brushing my teeth quite well for decades.

How? By doing what my daughter does: I applied concentration again and again, and my brain changed. I wanted clean teeth, so I "programmed" my brain to do it for me. Habits are tools for helping us get what we want. They are crystallizations of our repeated choices.

I believe this lines up precisely with Aristotle's position from many centuries ago. Will Durant's synopsis of Aristotle's philosophy highlights one of the key lessons of this chapter: "We are what we repeatedly do. Excellence, then, is not an act but a habit."[12]

While this is true of brushing our teeth or going to the gym, the most important habits are habits of thought. Where do we focus our attention?

What do we think about hour after hour? If we redirect that stream of thought again and again, we can train our brains to live a better life.

There are certainly limits to this, and those with severe depression sometimes bump up against those limits. Though we should be sympathetic, we should also keep looking for a mental way of escape. No one should ever assume they have reached the limits and thus give up hope. I could tell you countless stories of full remission from severe depression with therapy alone. I have even heard of people having their own breakthroughs, without therapy.

Whether you're depressed or just weary, you can learn to direct, or redirect, your attention so that it helps you in your journey toward a flourishing future. Let's look at some practical ways to start.

ATTENTIONAL PUSH-UPS

The applications in this chapter are subtle, but they are potentially life transforming. Learning to control and direct our attention is a dimension of life that some philosophies put at the very heart of the good life.

As usual, I'll start with small exercises that are not only good in themselves, but that also contribute to something bigger.

Breathing mindfully

Mindfulness is central to several spiritual traditions. It involves a simple activity that teaches experientially how our attention works.

Pick a quiet location and sit in a comfortable position—straight but not rigid—with your feet flat on the floor. Close your eyes and focus your attention on the *feeling* of the air as it enters and exits your nostrils.

You may want to count as you breathe in (1-2-3-1) and again as you breathe out (1-2-3-2), but the essential activity is to focus your attention on the sensation of the movement of air.

Naturally, as you do this, your attention will wander to other things—perhaps a worry, a source of stress, or a plan for tomorrow. That's okay. It's part of the process. Whenever you notice your mind wandering, redirect your attention back to your breathing and start again—1-2-3-1 (in), 1-2-3-2 (out), 1-2-3-3 (in), 1-2-3-4 (out), and repeat.[13]

An important thing to learn about the human condition is that we really can't keep our focus on anything. Our minds wander. But that's kind of the point. The point of the exercise is to keep bringing our attention back. It's an exercise that demonstrates that we all have a lot to learn. As you practice this exercise, you will find yourself in one of three modes: (1) paying attention to the sensation of your breath; (2) mind-wandering; (3) noticing that your mind is wandering and directing it back to your breath.

Though the exercise described above originated in Buddhism, it isn't necessarily a religious practice. It is an exercise that very quickly reveals our failure to do the things we want to do. It proves in short order that we are not of one mind; that we fail to live up to our own standards, even with something as seemingly simple as focusing our attention. The selection of the nostrils, though it has mystical significance in the East, also happens to be where God breathed the "the breath of life" into humanity.[14]

I learned how to meditate from my mentor Jeffrey Schwartz, who has spent an hour a day for decades practicing mindful meditation. When he first taught me the practice, I grew curious about the deeper mysteries that might be unlocked if I were as diligent with the exercise as he was. So I asked him, "I know these instructions are where I'm supposed to begin. But what are *you* doing when you meditate after all these years?" He looked puzzled for a moment and then answered me patiently: "I'm focusing my attention on my breath, and when my mind wanders, I redirect it to my breath."

In one of the more clever studies on mindfulness I've seen in recent years, Wendy Hasenkamp and her team asked participants to practice mindful meditation while undergoing fMRI scanning, and to press a button as soon as they realized they were mind-wandering.[15] Using the button-press timing, they were able to identify three distinct brain states—the default-mode network, the salience network, and the executive network—corresponding to the three basic aspects of mindfulness meditation.[16] In other words, the research team found that mindfulness meditation worked like an attentional push-up. Like a push-up, you start in one position (focusing on your breath), move through another position (mind-wandering), and end up back where you started (focusing on your breath). But in so doing, you've exercised the different parts of your brain.

The other fascinating thing was the involvement of the salience network. It's mainly famous for being the "snake detector," the brain state that gets us to pay attention to a threat. Even novice meditators can repurpose the salience network to identify mind-wandering as the "snake" and alert the conscious self of the intruder.

As you practice mindful meditation, you will learn to control your attention. If you're having a conversation with a loved one, you won't be distracted by past fights or emotions that aren't relevant. You'll be present in the moment. If you're at work, you won't be thinking about recreation; you'll be focused on the job at hand. If you're in church and you realize that you're thinking about something else, you'll be able to bring your mind back to worshiping God.

Wouldn't you like to have that kind of power of attention? If you were able to better attend to the people in your life and the situations you encounter, you would be a better friend, spouse, and worker. Mindfulness meditation can help you get there.

Spending even five minutes a day (for starters) in this kind of meditative practice is a great way to explore the possibility of harnessing your attention. As you become accustomed to the practice, you may wish to increase the time you spend meditating.

Learning metacognition

With or without formal meditative practice, you can learn *metacognition*— the process of paying attention to paying attention. This is not an activity in itself, per se. It's something you can learn to do throughout the day, in the midst of all your other activities.

Sometimes it helps to find an anchor to remind yourself to ask, *Am I paying attention?* Sometimes it's a trigger word or a particular action. Then you direct your attention to where you want it to be. A hospital chaplain once told me that he says a prayer for the patient he is about to visit as he's

THE OPPOSITE OF DEPRESSION

washing his hands to enter the room. He sees dozens of patients a day, and every time he washes his hands to go in to see another patient, he focuses his attention by saying a brief prayer for that patient.

This exercise is as deep and as hard as you like. If you're depressed, you might be able to manage it a few minutes a day. Or maybe you're focused most of the time on what you want but struggle with distractions at the end of the day. Or maybe when speaking to others, your focus is good but you're not adequately expressing compassion. Metacognition is the process of intentionally improving the pattern of your thoughts—and thus your actions.

Practicing the presence of God

From a Christian perspective, metacognition leads into what some spiritual writers have called *practicing the presence of God*; that is, learning to be aware of God's presence at every moment of the day.[17] How often are we aware of God's goodness? Or God's love? It may be precious few minutes per day. What if we could have at least some level of awareness of God at all times? We can learn how to move in that direction.

Learning to control your attention and direct it toward God is a lifelong task. If we could do it all the time, it would lead to perfection. While perfection isn't attainable in this life, with God's help, growth in this direction is possible.

WIPE YOUR GLASSES

I opened the chapter with quotes from Lao-tzu and Jesus. In both cases, they were talking about a spiritual kind of vision—one that allows us to truly see light and dark, good and bad.

The centrality of our internal vision and where we direct it is, in a very real sense, the only choice we ever have. When tempted to cheat on a test, our attention may be directed to the rewards of cheating or to the knowledge that it's wrong. When we see someone who is suffering and we can help, our focus might go to our smartphone or to the great commandment written on our hearts to love our neighbor as ourselves. If our internal vision were perfect, we too would be perfect. But as Lao-tzu asks rhetorically, "Can you purify your mystic vision and wash it until it is spotless?"[18]

Attention and redirection make up one of the core tasks of the human experience. Where does your mind go? Where do you look with your physical eyes? Where do your thoughts go when you're alone? If you were perfect, you could direct your mind perfectly to those things that are good.

Eastern Orthodox Christians have a practice of praying what is sometimes called the Jesus Prayer: "Lord Jesus Christ, Son of God, have mercy on me, a sinner." They will pray this countless times per day with the intention that it would become "a prayer of the heart." That is, they would like to pray these words at all times, literally without ceasing as the apostle Paul instructs.[19] They hope for this mindful attention to God to become the background hum of their lives.

Whatever approach we take, in every moment we have the opportunity to nudge our attention toward something wholesome and good. In every moment, we have the opportunity to rub the fog from our internal lenses and maybe see things as we ought to see them. If we do that often enough, we might gain a moment of true clarity.

With a moment of truly clear attention, what would be impossible for us?

STEPS TOWARD FLOURISHING

The opposite of depression is paying attention. When we're flourishing, we will resist the ever-present distractions in life, both internal and external. Through long years of practice, we will develop habits that help us attend to what is most important. We will pray and meditate regularly, strengthening and ever purifying our inner vision.

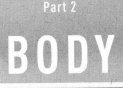

Part 2

BODY

FOOD: WHAT'S ON YOUR PLATE?

Behold, I have given you every plant yielding seed
that is on the face of all the earth, and every tree
with seed in its fruit. You shall have them for food.

GENESIS 1:29

To eat is a necessity, but to eat intelligently is an art.

FRANÇOIS DE LA ROCHEFOUCAULD

Linda was a woman in her sixties who had been depressed for some time. As she sat on a gurney in the emergency room, she was quite anxious, folding and unfolding her arms and looking down at the floor. Her eyes darted around as if certain of impending danger. As the psychiatrist on duty in the emergency room, it was my job to determine whether a patient should be admitted to the hospital. This was the first time I had met Linda. She and I discussed her options.

Linda's primary psychiatrist had sent her to Stanford Hospital—one of the few remaining voluntary psychiatric units in existence—hoping she would meet the criteria for admission. Linda said she was doing "just fine" at home with her husband, and she made it clear to me that she'd prefer to keep trying to get by at home.

A choice had to be made. Did she really need one of our psychiatric beds, which were always in high demand? Or could we arrange more support for her so she *could* get by at home?

Unable to reach a decision based solely on what Linda was telling me,

I contacted her regular psychiatrist and found out more of the story. One detail tipped the balance in favor of admission: She had lost twenty pounds over the previous few weeks.

Weight loss isn't easy. In fact, Linda had previously struggled with being overweight in the midst of moderate depression. So a drop in weight of this degree, in such a short amount of time, indicated something was now seriously wrong. There were no medical reasons for it other than depression, and a profound depression at that. I recommended admission.

DEPRESSION BELOW THE NECK

As it did in the diagnostic drama that played out in the emergency room with Linda, depression is often identified by changes in appetite, sleep, and movement. Interestingly, the effect for all three of these indicators can go in either direction. Depression can cause either *overeating* or *undereating*. It might lead to sleeping *too much* or *too little*. It can produce *agitation* or *lethargy*. In severe cases, these changes can be profound.

Depression is a medical condition that affects the entire person, including the body. In other words, more than just the neurons in the brain are involved. Though many of the clinically significant changes occur inside the head, depression also changes things below the neck in profound ways. For example, depression increases the risk of developing heart disease. Depression also makes a person more likely to get cancer. Depressed people have changes in stress hormones and changes in their immune system. They even show differences in blood clotting.[1]

One way to tell that depression is a physical illness is that it can cause profound changes in our microbiome—the writhing mass of microorganisms living inside us that outnumber our human cells ten to one.[2] If you transfer microorganisms from depressed people into nondepressed mice, the mice act depressed.[3] (Nobody knows if the mice are actually depressed, because we haven't figured out how to ask.)

Another piece of physical evidence is that depression is encoded in the genes. By studying identical twins raised separately, scientists concluded that major depressive disorder is 37 percent heritable.[4] So as much as some psychoanalysts want to lay all the blame on parenting, a large part of the explanation is in the genes passed down from our parents rather than their parenting style. While depression may be mostly due to *nurture*, nature also plays an important part—albeit a minority role.

How does the physical component of depression manifest itself?

Though the course of depression isn't consistent from one person to the next, a common progression begins with self-critical thoughts followed by depressed mood. Physical symptoms develop later. It's likely that some cases of depression start in the brain and then anchor in the body—but sometimes it's the other way around. Many patients have no self-critical thoughts initially, but find themselves inexplicably sleeping longer than usual, or eating more than they normally do. As these symptoms intensify, the person starts thinking self-critical thoughts. For some people, physical symptoms are the seed that grows into full-blown depression.

I had a patient with a particularly difficult case of depression. I prescribed an aggressive treatment plan: psychotherapy with me, medication management, and TMS. She did so well that I successfully weaned her off all medications and she "graduated" from needing to see me for therapy. Years later, she called to tell me that the depression had come back full force immediately after she started taking prednisone, a steroid, to treat inflammation. This prescribed medication was the trigger for another depressive episode. Even after the prednisone course was done, the depression persisted. Her circumstances hadn't changed, but her physiology had. It took more therapy, medication, TMS, and a lot of hard work on her part to bring her out of it again.

However depression develops, the physical aspects of the disease are important to understand because they affect how responsible the person may be for their depression. The naive belief that someone just needs to "be happy" or "stop being lazy" is counterproductive if the person has physiological reasons for why that's not possible. There may be genetic reasons why the person is depressed in the first place, or why he or she became depressed after a tragedy that others seemed to bounce back from.

But here's the good news: Though the body may be a cause of depression and a place where it resides, it is also the door through which healing can enter. Indeed, we can flourish *only* if we pay attention to our physical composition and nature.

Overeating, undereating, and eating poorly can be symptoms of depression or contributors to depression. Either way, they are signs of problems in our lives. If we want to flourish, the most basic place to start is with *what* and *how* we eat. That's where we're going in this chapter. Then the following two chapters will address the related issues of *sleep* and *exercise*. Happily, the evidence shows that there are specific, positive steps we can take in all three areas to promote greater health, vitality, and productivity.

THE FOOD/DEPRESSION CONNECTION

Humans have the ability to consume an incredible variety of food. Some foods are better for us than others, but can bad eating make you depressed?

One ambitious group of researchers embarked on a meta-analysis—a study compiling other studies—to summarize the results of the reams of science already done on the food/depression connection.[5] They wanted only the best studies and ones that spoke directly to the question of whether eating well protects against depression. Starting with 3,400 studies, they culled them down to 21 that best met their criteria.

Each study represented an enormous amount of work. Scientists asked people from all over the world detailed questions about their diets and also about how they felt. In the end, researchers looked at the eating patterns of 127,773 people—more people than would fit in the Rose Bowl. What did they find? Healthy eating was associated with a 16 percent reduction in the odds of developing depression.

Though 16 percent might not be a *huge* reduction in depression, it is a *big* reduction. If every American suddenly started eating healthy tomorrow, there would be three million fewer cases of depression than there would have been otherwise.[6] I think it's enormously significant that healthy eating reduces depression *at all*. It is evidence against the simplistic idea that depression is "just a brain disease," or worse, "just in your head." Many people who develop depression would not do so if they ate a healthier diet.[7] Depression is partly biological, but not purely neurochemical.

In some cancers, there are two versions of a gene and you need just one that's functional to prevent the cancer. Some people inherit a broken gene and thus are especially prone to cancer if the other gene has a problem.

This is called a "two-hit hypothesis." Depression may work the same way: A person who is eating well and suffers a major catastrophe may not develop depression, but someone who is eating poorly would be more likely to develop depression given the same circumstances.

Now let's look at it the other way around—that is, from the "opposite of depression" standpoint. Eating well—though far from being the only factor for a flourishing life—is an important component. A foundational component. Better eating can improve both the length and quality of our lives.

Though we might be tempted to overlook this most basic of factors—after all, "it's just food"—we shouldn't downplay our food choices. Instead, we should begin our quest for the flourishing life at the kitchen table.

EAT LIKE A GREEK

Most diets have some positive value, and few are likely to be any worse than thoughtlessly eating takeout and packaged foods, as so many of us do. Nonetheless, in the research literature there's one diet that stands out above all the rest: the Mediterranean diet.

Long established in Italy, Greece, and the Middle East, and now popular around the world, the Mediterranean diet looks roughly like this:

1. Lots of olive oil
2. Nuts, seeds, and beans
3. Whole grains
4. Fresh fruits and vegetables
5. Fish
6. Small amounts of non-fish meats
7. Moderate amounts of dairy products, mostly cheese or yogurt
8. Moderate wine consumption.[8]

From a scientific standpoint, the Mediterranean diet is arguably the most-tested diet in the history of diets. In an era when the Food Pyramid reigned, and mainstream recommendations included sparse fats, no alcohol, and a hefty base of grains, it was observed that those eating more traditionally Mediterranean foods, heavy in olive oils, and regularly drinking red wine, lived a remarkably long time. Researchers began to examine what these people were eating, in contrast to a typical Western diet.

The story really got interesting in 2018 when a team did a randomized controlled trial—the gold-standard type of experiment.[9] Researchers randomly assigned people to get counseling in the Mediterranean diet and then assigned a key supplemental food to be consumed over the course of the study (either two pounds of nuts or a gallon of olive oil per month). The researchers then picked a high bar to clear: Does this diet actually *prevent* heart attacks? Remarkably, those assigned to the Mediterranean diet did have fewer heart attacks!

The Mediterranean diet helps reduce risks of such major killers as heart disease, stroke, cancer, and diabetes.[10] It also helps improve cognition, attention, and mental processing speed.[11] It makes it more likely that a person will age healthfully.[12]

LET FOOD BE YOUR MEDICINE

But what about depression? Can a Mediterranean diet help there? Another group of researchers set out to answer that question.[13] They also chose a randomized trial to test their hypothesis. They provided a social support group to one set of depressed patients, and a diet support group to a second set of patients, encouraging them to eat a Mediterranean-style diet. When they followed up after twelve weeks, they found that the diet support group had truly changed their eating patterns and were eating more healthily, whereas the group with the general social support had not.

The population these researchers were trying to treat was quite depressed. Most had tried at least one psychiatric medication that wasn't working. Patients with profiles like this can be hard to treat.

Did it work?

It worked incredibly well. One way to quantify and compare effects is to ask how much it moves the average of a particular score. With depression, we're usually more than satisfied if we can move the average by 0.3 or 0.5 standard deviations; this is common for psychiatric medication studies. The effect size they found in the Mediterranean diet study was an enormous 1.16! In this hard-to-treat population, the average patient who participated in the diet support group moved from moderately depressed to mildly depressed; and for nearly a third, their depression went into remission entirely.

Food is good medicine indeed. Let's enjoy a bowl of whole-grain pasta with fresh vegetables and olive oil as we contemplate those results. But not too big of a bowl. It's not only *what* we eat that matters; it's also *how much*.

PORTION CONTROL

Temperance has long been considered one of the four cardinal virtues. But temperance, in this sense, is far different from the 1920s-era prohibition against drinking alcohol. Aristotle talked about a "golden mean"—the idea that the virtuous path leads to having neither too much nor too little of something. On this basis, he would probably have called teetotalers *intemperate*.

Though we might be more likely to use the term *moderation* or *balance*, the idea of navigating to the good life by avoiding extremes is still compelling. Food gives us a chance, three times a day, to be mindful of this. What size portion are we going to put on our plates? How much is too much, and how much is too little? When will we decide we've had enough and stop eating?

Depression disrupts the body's cues for hunger and satiety, so using these to guide meal portions might not be easy in the throes of serious depression. But as you emerge from your depression, it becomes possible again to learn how to pay attention to your body and the social cues about eating.

Though some people, like Linda in our example, undereat because of depression or because of an eating disorder, overeating is far more prevalent in our society. In 2018, more than 73 percent of Americans over the age of twenty were overweight (BMI 25+).[14] Americans spent almost $71 billion on weight management in 2020.[15]

Context also matters. Though eating past fullness on Thanksgiving is an American tradition, feasting and carousing at a funeral would be frowned upon. Eating heavily when training for a marathon is appropriate, as is eating less when sedentary. When we pick food from the menu or plan our meals for the week, we have an opportunity to think ahead about how much to eat.

I find it interesting that Jesus went to a lot of dinner parties—where he probably ate some version of the Mediterranean diet. He ate at others' homes so often, in fact, that he was slandered by some who called him a glutton and a drunkard.[16] But he also said and demonstrated that there were appropriate times for fasting.[17] Knowing the difference between times for feasting and times for fasting (or eating less) is a key skill to learn as we begin to pursue a life of greater flourishing.

SLOW FOOD

Two of the hardest months of my life were when I was a medical student on the dreaded surgery rotation. There were stretches of days when I didn't see the sun much. Rising in the early morning darkness, I had no time for a proper breakfast, but I knew I needed fuel. So I plunged a spoon into a jar of peanut butter and stuck it to the roof of my mouth, like I was some poor dog whose master needed a laugh. Then I ran out the door. En route to the hospital, I worked my way through the calories plastered to my hard palate.

Even back then, I realized this was not a good way to eat. But if I'm being honest, I have to admit that it would be years before I developed a better routine. Here's a case where you'd be better off following my words and not my example. Unfortunately, too many people are stuck in the habit of grabbing food on the go, and we may not even think there's a problem with this.

In years past, more people would gather around the table to eat a home-cooked meal as a family. Mealtimes were social times—opportunities to converse and connect.

Nowadays, fast food has displaced some home dining. And even when we do eat at home, we're more likely to dine on processed and ultra-processed foods.[18] Processing foods does many things, but perhaps the most dangerous is that it concentrates calories, sugars, and fats, so that we feel full too late, and thus we eat more food than we need.[19]

Cooking, by nature, is a transient artform. Once the food has been prepared, it may last for less than an hour before it is consumed and gone forever. Yet while it lasts, it is a primary way to bring pleasure to others, and a way to bring people together in a relaxed and social way.

Depression flourishes in isolation and loneliness. It can accelerate in the context of depression-induced poor nutrition. People who are depressed may not have normal hunger cues, but if dinner is always at 7:00 p.m., at least there's a chance that they'll eat.

For those who are not depressed, having at least one meal per day—on a plate, sitting down at the table—can go a long way toward elevating their mood and sense of well-being. Mealtime can be an anchor in a day that may otherwise be a continuous blur.

Eat healthily and enjoy what you eat; but don't overeat. Take your time, whether you're at a restaurant or at home. Eat with friends or family. Savor the relationships as much as the food.

A FRESH APPROACH

In the early 1920s, two doctors at Harvard Medical School offered a radical plan for treating epilepsy: starving their patients.[20] It had been shown that fasting seemed to help hyperexcitable brains, but for obvious reasons, the treatment could be applied for only so long.

Around the same time, Dr. Russell Wilder at the Mayo Clinic proposed a high-fat, moderate-protein diet that would convince the body that it was starving without actually starving the patient. Unlike starvation, or even fasting, it could be sustained over a longer period of time. It worked. What came to be known as the *ketogenic diet* soon became a mainstay for treating a debilitating brain disorder.

For about a hundred years, this is where the treatment remained, coming in and out of fashion as a therapy of choice. Very recently, researchers have begun trying this diet with patients suffering from mental illness. In one study, extremely treatment-resistant patients suffering from depression, bipolar disorder, and schizoaffective disorder were put on a ketogenic diet. For the patients who were able to stay on the diet for at least two weeks, the results were "significant and substantial."[21] Every single patient got better—and these were people for whom nothing else had worked.

More research needs to be done to confirm these initial very exciting findings. As with all early studies, we expect astonishing results to be tempered at least a little, and sometimes entirely. Until more research can be done, I urge caution when considering a ketogenic diet. There are reports that it can cause mood elevation/hypomania, significant shifts in cholesterol, and difficulty in maintaining weight. Enlisting the help of a dietician—and discussion with your psychiatrist (if you see one)—is certainly warranted. Nonetheless, a ketogenic diet is certainly something to consider, especially in more severe cases.

An ongoing lively debate continues about whether dietary changes work—and if so, *why*. What's curious, for example, is that on some questions, the diets give opposite advice—e.g., the Mediterranean diet encourages whole grains; keto strictly prohibits them. But one thing they have in common is that both prohibit quick-to-digest or processed foods (Mediterranean partially, keto entirely). If unprocessed foods prove to be a factor, then both diets may work to reverse recent cultural dietary trends.

THE BANQUET OF LIFE

If the goal is to change your eating from an unhealthy pattern to a healthier pattern, I have some advice to share. It's pretty straightforward, but there's a lot of psychology behind it that should be taken into account. With food in particular, small changes can really go a long way. So let's start there.

Take something away, add something in

What are you eating that isn't good for you? If you're like many people, you know exactly what you're eating that's unhealthy in your diet.

Select one bad dietary habit to change. For example, maybe you drink a soft drink every day. You know sugary drinks can lead to weight gain and raise your risk for diabetes and other health concerns. Decide to go from drinking one soda every day to drinking only one per week. That's a small change that you can handle, and it will make you feel better about yourself.

Cutting something out is only half the exercise though. The other half is to *add* something healthy into your diet.

As we saw above, the Mediterranean diet has been proven to offer substantial improvements in health. In one study, researchers asked some participants to add a serving of mixed nuts (containing healthy fats) to their diet every day. They asked other participants to use olive oil (also a healthy fat) as a salad dressing and in other ways in their food. Both strategies led to substantial improvements in overall health.

You can try the same thing. Add nuts, olive oil, or some other staple of the Mediterranean diet to your regular eating. This is a tasty way to improve your diet, and it may help you replace unhealthy calories with healthy calories.

There are a hundred small but bold food changes you could make to start improving your eating. Eliminate something or add something to your diet today to improve your well-being.

Claim one meal as your own

Once you're ready for a bigger change to your eating habits, here's what I suggest as an intermediate step: Don't completely revolutionize your diet in one big step; instead, change *one meal of the day*.

I had a patient who knew she wasn't eating well and that her bad habits were contributing to her depression. She decided to start cooking a healthy dinner with her partner every evening. For the time being, breakfast might still be something grabbed on the go; lunch might contain more processed foods than were good for her; but at least in the evening she would enjoy a healthy home-cooked meal, eating leisurely in the company of her loved one.

You might set a similar goal. Pick one meal of the day and try to transform it into a healthier eating experience—if not every day of the week, at least as often as you can manage. You should notice a substantial change in how you feel, and it may motivate you to make even bigger changes.

Head to the Mediterranean—diet, that is

A bigger dietary change you could make would be to strictly adhere to a Mediterranean-style diet. Sound daunting? It might take some work and a lot of habit changes, but it's an excellent—and proven—way to upgrade your physical well-being. There are plenty of websites, videos, and cookbooks that can help you eat like a (traditional) Greek for three meals a day. If you need some external support, consider contacting a dietician, nutritionist, or health-and-wellness coach to help you to get on (and stay on) track with your eating.

If you live with a partner or family, try to get them involved in the change. Making changes in your diet will be much easier with the support of other people. In particular, having moral support when you're tempted to slip back into old habits can be useful and helpful. Besides, switching to a healthier eating plan is good for your family as well!

Kill the carbs

If you want to embark on one of the most difficult diets to adhere to (but one that might also be highly effective), consider a ketogenic diet, or keto. In this case, I strongly recommend that you find a dietician and/or doctor to work with who is experienced in the diet. If you can't find a local dietician, there are a variety of dietetic counseling services available online. Depending on your situation, saying goodbye to carbs may be worth trying.

GOOD FOOD PAIRED WITH GOOD LIVING

Just as wine connoisseurs think about how to pair their food with just the right bottle of wine, you can enhance your opposite-of-depression approach to eating by pairing dietary changes with other helpful practices. Here are two good ones.

First, eat *mindfully*.

Do you tend to rush through your meals without paying much attention to what you're eating? Maybe you've been eating such bad foods that your palate has become accustomed to mostly sugar, salt, and fat. As you transition to a diet filled with fresh fruits and vegetables, whole grains, and lean meats, focus your attention on really *tasting* and *appreciating* what's there. Subtle flavors take more attention to appreciate.

As you eat, become more thoughtful about what you're consuming. Focus on every sensation while you're eating—the appearance of the food, the aromas before the first bite, the flavors as you start to chew. Such mindful eating can help to increase your appreciation for the food, as well as slow down your eating—something that many of us are not very mindful of.

Second, eat *socially*.

If you tend to eat alone, or at your desk, or in front of the TV, think about sharing more of your meals with other people. If your family has fallen into the habit of everybody eating on their own schedule, have a conversation with them about reinstating a beautiful tradition: the family dinner. If you live alone, make a date with a friend to eat together. Or invite a coworker to join you for lunch. It doesn't have to be a big deal, just a *together* deal.

You may not be able to, or want to, eat every single meal with other people. But if you can make more of your meals a social experience, you may come to love it! In a later chapter, we'll be looking at the importance of good relationships in living the good life, and dining together is one of the best ways to build relationships.

We're all busy, and we all have a lot on our plates—figuratively, and perhaps literally. But among your other time commitments, I encourage you to take the time to become more intentional about what actually goes on your plate when you eat. Moving away from depression, and toward a life of flourishing, begins here.

STEPS TOWARD FLOURISHING

When it comes to food, the opposite of depression means being so active and engaged that we are hungry when it's time to eat. The flourishing lifestyle means eating and enjoying a healthy amount of food—not too much and not too little. It means eating mostly healthy foods—perhaps a Mediterranean-style diet. It means not being rushed at mealtimes, enjoying good company, and using mealtimes to build relationships with those who are important to us.

SLEEP: MIND AND BODY AT REST

Gonna live while I'm alive;
I'll sleep when I'm dead.

JON BON JOVI

What is sleep? Believe it or not, this is one of the deepest mysteries of animal and human biology. We spend one-third of our lives asleep; it's an experience common to all. Scientists have done lots of research on sleep, which has revealed that all manner of things in our physiology are different while we're sleeping. And we still don't really know *why* we sleep.

William Dement, the father of sleep medicine, founder of Stanford's Sleep Research Center, and codiscoverer of REM sleep, has said, "As far as I know, the only reason we need to sleep that is really, really solid is because we get sleepy."[1] This is profound wisdom that comes from a place of deep humility.

Though the rationale for sleep remains elusive, it's clear that several important things happen while we slumber, including consolidating memories and draining toxic waste from our cells. If we don't sleep adequately, these processes are disrupted.

Even if we had no clue what was going on in our brain and the rest of our body while we sleep, no one would doubt that good sleep is important.

Many *wish* they could sleep better but don't know how. Is there anything that can be done?

Yes. Just as there are habits and practices in the realm of eating that contribute to a flourishing life, so too there are things we can do to improve our sleep at night and order our waking time during the day, to live more restful and productive and satisfying lives. These changes may not be easy. People in depression are typically starting from a baseline of terrible sleep and few resources. People who are weary, burned out, or dissatisfied with life often have years of bad sleep habits. As with every other aspect of flourishing, the benefits become obvious over time. The longer we practice good habits, the easier they become.

I've addressed sleep and rest with many of my patients, and the insights that have come out of treating their depression can help all of us who are pursuing a life of flourishing.

I LITERALLY CAN'T EVEN

Too much or too little sleep in an otherwise healthy person is strongly connected to the odds that the person will develop depression. In one aggregate study analyzing nearly fifty thousand people, researchers found that those who slept too little became depressed at a 31 percent higher rate than those who got adequate sleep. Those who slept too much did even worse, becoming depressed at a 42 percent higher rate.[2]

It also appears that lack of sleep is a reliable way to increase suicidal tendencies, regardless of the presence or absence of depression. There is a fairly strong correlation between "voluntary sleep curtailment" and suicidal ideation.[3] In one of my all-time-favorite examples of researchers inventing a formal name for a common phenomenon, teenagers staying up too late was called "behaviorally induced insufficient sleep."[4] Even this kind of sleeplessness can temporarily make life appear not worth living.

Anyone who has ever had insomnia or stayed up late working on a project or had a baby cry through the night knows how this feels. Everything becomes too much. It seems that irritation with life itself emerges with insomnia. "I literally can't even" becomes the person's deepest reality. In research I conducted, we found that poor sleep was one of the top two contributors to feelings of depletion, irritability, and the inability to make decisions.[5] For those who are already near the edge emotionally, a lack of sleep can push them closer to it.

This experience is hardly just a modern phenomenon. A famous prophet in the Bible experienced the same type of feelings.

YOUR JOURNEY IS TOO MUCH

The crisis followed one of the most epic showdowns in the Bible.

The Hebrew prophet Elijah had challenged the prophets of the Canaanite deity Baal to a death match. Both sides erected altars and prepared sacrifices for burning. Elijah said he would appeal to the God of Abraham, Isaac, and Israel while the other prophets cried out to Baal. Whichever side's sacrifice was consumed by fire from heaven would prove their God was most powerful.

After the prophets of Baal prayed to their god and he did not respond, Elijah upped the ante by soaking his altar and sacrifice with water. When Elijah prayed, God consumed not only the sacrifice with heavenly flame, but also the stones of the altar itself.

Queen Jezebel, who had been rooting for Baal, was displeased with this result, and she swore that she would kill Elijah within the day. Even on the heels of his great victory, he was afraid, and he ran for his life into the wilderness.

When Elijah finally stopped in the middle of nowhere, his fatigue was overwhelming. The same hero who had been so publicly bold just hours before now confessed to God that he was feeling suicidal despair: "He asked that he might die, saying, 'It is enough; now, O LORD, take away my life, for I am no better than my fathers.' And he lay down and slept under a broom tree."[6]

Throughout the Hebrew Scriptures, God responds to despair among his people in various ways. Sometimes he responds with a rebuke. Sometimes with punishment. Sometimes with words of encouragement. In Elijah's case, God sent an angel to feed him. But the prophet was so overwhelmed and exhausted that the angel had to rouse him twice.

"Arise and eat," the angel said to him, "for the journey is too great for you."[7] And so it feels to many of us. Depressed or not, we all have journeys that feel like they're too much.

But regular rest can restore us like nothing else. This is the most important thing to know and remember about sleep: When you get enough, you feel better. The restorative power of sleep is easy to forget in a culture that overvalues productivity, but the benefits are clearly understood by anyone who has ever had a good nap or a good night's sleep.

Let me give you a few reasons, from a mental health standpoint, why sleep is so important.

MEMORY'S INSCRIBER

I have been around many doctors in my training who have tried to convince their patients that sleep is important. As I've said, the most common reason for sleep is simple and obvious: so you don't feel terrible. An even better reason is that sleep helps us consolidate our memories. There are good studies showing that we don't really learn some things until we sleep.

In one study, the participants were taught a motor task and tested after a similar amount of time (twelve hours), but some slept between the tests and others didn't.[8] The ability to learn the task was improved in people who were able to sleep during the twelve hours compared to those who didn't. This makes good sense.

When I was first learning to snowboard, I went for a weekend excursion. In case you've never had the experience, let me say that learning to snowboard is a lot like life: it involves falling on your butt again and again and again. After taking a lesson on Saturday and repeatedly falling, I got a normal night's sleep and my brain did its thing. When I woke up on Sunday, my brain had figured out how to snowboard in a way that hours of additional practice on Saturday without sleep never would have accomplished. I wasn't going to win a gold medal, but when I hit the slopes on Sunday, I was definitely better at snowboarding. Simply going unconscious for a few hours and *not practicing* was the most effective way to learn.

What is true of snowboarding has been tested in a wide variety of other memory domains as well, including declarative memory (learning facts that can be consciously recalled and overtly declared).[9] This medical fact can easily be confirmed by personal experiment. In most areas of life, not sleeping causes a person to be less mentally sharp.

BRAIN DRAIN

Most of the energy we use comes from burning something, whether it's gasoline in our cars or glucose in our muscles. As big molecules are broken down into smaller molecules and energy is released, waste products are also created. Out of our tailpipes come such things as carbon dioxide, nitrogen oxides, and particulate matter. Our muscles, when adequately supplied with oxygen, burn glucose and produce carbon dioxide and water.

Neural metabolism also produces waste. In fact, as 20 percent of the body's energy goes to powering our incredibly hungry brains, it creates quite a mess during the day. Scientists were pretty sure that the waste products of metabolism were expelled from the brain somehow, but they knew it didn't happen in the same way as with our muscles. Until quite recently, however, we didn't have a good understanding of how these waste products left the brain.

Then, scientists using special new techniques identified the fact that microchannels open up in our brains, draining the poisonous waste products that build up during the day.[10] The cell bodies themselves shrink during sleep, allowing for drainage. During the day, the brain is like a fantastical medieval city with buildings stacked on top of one another, so crammed together that there's no space for sewers. But when we sleep, the buildings shrink and sewers appear, and the "buildings" can flush their waste. We wake up in the morning with a clean brain, ready to go for the day.

The cumulative effects of the buildup of waste products in the brain are not fully understood. We don't know how much sleep deprivation affects us by inhibiting the drainage. But the general principle is quite straightforward: Let the literal poison drain out of your brain. Sleep!

CINEMA OF THE UNCONSCIOUS

Sleep is a mystery. Dreaming is a mystery within a mystery.

Dreams can be wonderful or terrifying experiences. Also absurd, elusive, or inscrutable. With dreams, there is the sense of floating in a deep ocean of significance that may or may not be explorable. Humans have pondered the interpretation and significance of dreams throughout our history, yet we still don't know exactly how or why they occur.

My profession has a long history of certain members speculating about what dreams actually are or what they reveal. Sigmund Freud's 1900 classic, *The Interpretation of Dreams*, helped bring the idea of the unconscious to the world and suggested that dreams are the pathway to understanding it. "The interpretation of dreams," said Freud, "is the royal road to a knowledge of the unconscious activities of the mind."[11]

This process of interpretation is central to certain types of psychotherapy (for example, psychoanalysis and psychodynamic therapy). According to psychiatrists in these areas, the visions in dreams are stand-ins or symbols for other things, and it is up to the therapist and patient to unravel what they mean. *Everything* matters. According to Freud, "Dreams are never concerned with trivialities."[12]

Although some claims about the meaning of dreams seem to me to stretch the data, I have seen cases where dreams really did, to all appearances, reveal a deep, curative insight into a patient's problem. For instance, I recall one patient who, in the midst of accelerated TMS treatment, took a nap between stimulation sessions. Afterward, she said she had dreamed that she was jumping over hurdles. When she woke up, her depression was gone.

Some argue that the specific content of the dreams isn't all that relevant or may be truly random. Some of my colleagues treat dreams merely as symptoms. Many biological psychiatrists end up discounting the details of the dreams, writing "vibrant dreams" in the side effects section of their notes. Proper dream analysis doesn't fit into the fifteen-minute doctor visits that have become typical even for psychiatrists.

The fact that there is a human phenomenon about which smart people can disagree so much is humbling. The fact that humans have incredible experiences every night is remarkable. It's like being the captain of a ship who understands how much of it works but then has large sections of the ship with machinery he doesn't understand, manned by people speaking a foreign language.

The reasons for sleep are many, including consolidation of memory, opening up drainage for the brain's waste products, and facilitating dreaming. But it goes even deeper. In order to better understand this, we need to take a detour into biology.

THE BODY'S RHYTHM

According to the book of Genesis, when God created the universe, he said, "Let there be lights in the expanse of the heavens to separate the day from the night. And let them be for signs and for seasons, and for days and years."[13] As far back as human memory or myth goes, the movement of the earth and heavenly bodies have marked the rhythm of time.

Throughout human history, we have lived in a world where the sun "rises" and "sets" every day. Up until the creation of artificial light, we have mostly risen with the dawn and gone to bed after dusk. But ever since the invention of the electric light bulb and the discovery of affordable energy, we have less and less compunction about staying up late at night. Disconnection from the diurnal rhythm of the sun is almost a defining part of what it means to be a modern person. Now, with access to infinite information and unlimited entertainment 24/7, we have plenty of things to do after the sun goes down. We wake up with alarms, stay up and work or play as late as we please, and may go months or even years without seeing a sunrise.

Unfortunately for our well-being, we can't escape the natural cycles of life. As much as we can untether our lives from the rising and setting sun, our bodies and brains were not designed to be out of rhythm, and it shows.

Along with all the other multicellular organisms on earth, human beings have a control mechanism known as *circadian rhythm*. The term derives from the Latin roots *circa* (around) and *dies* (day). American scientists Jeffrey C. Hall, Michael Rosbash, and Michael W. Young won a Nobel Prize "for their discoveries of molecular mechanisms controlling the circadian rhythm."[14]

Working with a previously discovered self-regulating gene called *period* (they actually named it that), they found that it encodes a protein that builds up in the cell nucleus at night and degrades during the day.

The harmonious interplay between *period* and two other "clock genes," named *timeless* and *doubletime*, creates an oscillating circadian clock, which, in much-simplified terms, functions like sand in an hourglass. This clock then "anticipates and adapts our physiology to the different phases of the day," regulating the rest of the body—including our "sleep patterns, feeding behavior, hormone release, blood pressure, and body temperature."[15]

It is truly astonishing how many organs and systems in our bodies "know" what time of day it is. Nearly half of all proteins in our bodies cycle with the time of day.[16] Our esophagus "knows" what time of day it is. So does our heart. They have cycles, too, and it takes each organ a different amount of time to adjust if the light changes. This is probably why jet lag hurts so much—our organs are each adjusting as fast as they can to get their "workers" (proteins) to show up at the new times they're needed.

Light drives this entire process. The internal clock is good, but it drifts if not led by the sun.

For people with seasonal affective disorder, depression often comes on in the winter and is better in the summer. It can be effectively treated with an obnoxiously bright light-therapy lamp, especially in places that don't see much sun.[17]

The inability to see light is also a big part of why blind people have a higher rate of sleep problems, including a common "free running" sleep pattern that doesn't follow day/night cycles.[18] In fact, there are cells in the retina that plug directly into the hypothalamus. They don't help us *see* anything, but they contain cells that contribute something so fascinating that scientists had to coin a new term: "non-image forming vision."[19]

We are creatures whose biology is inextricably tied to the sun; we should not forget it. A regular rhythm of sleep tied to nighttime is part of maintaining good health and well-being.

That said, I know that sleep can be an incredibly frustrating domain for many people, whether they're depressed or not. Many folks are doing everything they can think of to sleep better, yet good sleep remains elusive. If that includes you, maybe I can suggest some things you haven't thought of yet. The goal is not just to get a good night's sleep, but also to have a restful day and week.

AN EVIDENCE-BASED WAY TO SLEEP BETTER

Poor sleep is a common complaint, and any number of sleep products, fancy beds, and nutritional supplements are designed to help with this problem. As far as I'm aware, however, the most effective action is to take the advice of Harvard researcher Gregg Jacobs in his book titled *Say Good Night to Insomnia*.[20] Jacobs and his team accomplished something rare in the history of science: They showed not only that psychotherapy works, but that it works *better* than a medication. Their treatment, cognitive behavioral therapy for insomnia, worked better than zolpidem (Ambien), a really potent sleeping medication.[21]

In his book, Jacobs explores ways to think differently about sleep, stress-reducing techniques, and habits. It's cognitive behavioral therapy for sleep.

One of Jacobs's key recommendations is counterintuitive: *Sleep less.*

Every insomniac is trying to get more sleep—because when they don't sleep, they feel terrible. Often they will lie in bed wide awake, frustrated and anxious about the passing night and the coming day. Jacobs's advice, interestingly enough, is to limit your time in bed so that you fall asleep quickly.

If you find yourself unable to sleep after fifteen or twenty minutes, get up and go do something that isn't activating. Then try going back to sleep when you feel sleepy again. If it so happens that you only get a few hours of sleep as you're starting to implement this, almost certainly after another night—or two or three—of this, you'll start to fall asleep quickly. When this happens, your brain will relearn that the bed is a place for sleep.

I tell my patients that I'd rather have four good hours of sleep than eight bad hours of sleep. I'd rather have four hours without striving than eight with stress and anxiety.[22] The best thing about this particular piece of advice is that many people end up getting both length and quality of sleep because they stop working so hard at it.

While this practical tip can be helpful for people with insomnia, it holds within itself a secret wisdom. Some things can only be gained by giving them up. "Trying harder" at some things only makes matters worse. Some victories are won by *resting*, not by striving.

YOUR NEW SLEEPY-TIME PRACTICES

One of the worst things about having poor sleep patterns is the helplessness you feel. By now I hope you're encouraged by the potential to take charge in this area of your life. You should also know that several aspects of a healthy sleep life can contribute to a flourishing waking life. I'm going to take you through some escalating steps, with the goal of systematically changing your sleep habits.

In seeking to improve your sleep, start small. Even incremental changes to your sleeping and waking routines can have a big positive impact. You can set yourself up for a better night's sleep by removing obvious barriers and obstacles that are *getting in the way of your getting a good night's sleep.*

Take it easy on your nervous system

Are you consuming caffeine in the afternoon or evening? If so, set a rule for yourself: no coffee, tea, or caffeinated energy drinks after 1:00 p.m. Even if you are already restricting your caffeine intake to the mornings, cutting back on the *amount* of caffeine you consume might help with sleep.

Have a standard bedtime, and stick with it

Going to bed at ten o'clock some nights, midnight other nights, even later on other nights, is disruptive to your circadian rhythm. Special events (such as a late-night concert or ballgame) might force you to stay up occasionally. But if you're regularly staying up past your bedtime to work, watch TV, or fiddle around on your phone, then let's be honest: You don't have a sleep disorder; you're simply choosing other activities that are more tempting. As much as possible, go to bed at a regular time and wake up at a regular time. It will help you feel more consistently rested.

Put your devices to bed before you put yourself to bed

You know that scrolling social media on your phone, sending emails, or using a computer close to bedtime can be too stimulating for sleep. You've probably also heard that screens emit a blue light that can keep you awake. It's true.

If you *must* use a device close to bedtime, it may be helpful to limit the blue light or electronic light given off by your screens. Unfortunately, "night mode," which reduces the blue-spectrum light, doesn't help.[23] Wearing glasses at night that block blue light actually does help.[24] It really is *blue* light that matters, not ultraviolet or other invisible parts of the spectrum. This means your naked eye is a great judge of whether a blue-light-limiting product will work. If your glasses don't *look* yellow, or if you can clearly see blue through them, they're not blocking blue light.

In any case, it's *much* better not to engage with your devices before bed. Power them down. Spend the last hour of the day in a peaceful activity like reading, talking, or listening to music.

If you really struggle with "scrolling fever," I recommend that you leave your phone outside your bedroom so you won't be tempted to pick it up. If you use your phone to wake up in the morning, and putting it outside your room sounds crazy, let me introduce you to a little contraption called an *alarm clock* that you can keep on your nightstand for waking you up, and that won't tempt you to go online. If your phone is still too much of a temptation, there are more extreme measures you can take, such as software to shut your phone down at night and mechanical boxes that will lock your phone away for a certain amount of time.

Reset your internal clock

Another small change you could make *after you wake up* is to get light exposure.

One of the major drivers of poor nighttime sleep is an internal clock that doesn't know what time it is. The circadian rhythm is largely driven by blue-spectrum photons that hit the retina, especially those that come in during the morning. If you live in a sunny area, make sure that you go outside and see full sunlight for at least half an hour—particularly during the morning. Maybe you could convert a meeting from a typical sit-down-inside meeting to a walk-around-outside meeting. Or take a phone call outside, where you can sit on a sunny bench and get the photons your body needs to realize that it's daytime. By calibrating your circadian rhythm during the day, you will help your body know when it's time to start shutting down for sleep at night.

If you don't live in a sunny area, or you can't easily go outside, another option is to purchase a phototherapy or light box and use it in the morning. This has been shown to be an effective treatment for major depressive disorder as well.[25] But even if you're just a bit down, or having trouble sleeping, some manner of "light therapy" is a reasonable way to help your body remember what time it should be sleeping.

Become your own sleep coach

If practical changes such as restricting caffeine use, maintaining a regular bedtime, and powering down your devices aren't enough to fix your sleepy-time troubles, consider going through a self-help version of cognitive behavioral therapy for insomnia (CBTi). This involves a number of steps that are centered on sleep restriction. For the background on this technique, reread the section above titled "An Evidence-Based Way to Sleep Better."

It's usually best to do CBTi as part of a program. Again I recommend Gregg Jacobs's book *Say Good Night to Insomnia* as the definitive template on how to do this. The underlying principle is straightforward: By systematically restricting sleep and focusing on *quality* of sleep over *quantity* of sleep, you can reset your internal clock and get *both*—a sufficient quantity of good quality sleep.

For the tech savvy, the Veterans Administration has developed an app that teaches the basics of CBTi and comes with some incredible clinical evidence that it's as effective as taking a sleep medication.[26] Best of all, it's "free"—that is, your tax dollars already paid for its development, so you might as well get your money's worth.

See a medical expert

If self-help steps don't work, or if your sleep is really problematic, then it's reasonable to consider seeing a doctor, either a sleep doctor or perhaps a therapist—but make sure your provider is formally trained in cognitive behavioral therapy for insomnia. In an era when you can see any therapist licensed in your state remotely, it may even be feasible to find someone trained directly by Dr. Jacobs.[27]

You also may need to see a doctor for a physiological cause of sleeplessness or poor quality sleep. If you're not sleeping well, or not feeling restored when you wake up, it could be that you're not getting enough oxygen while you sleep. If you snore heavily at night, particularly if you sound like you're choking, you should be evaluated for obstructive sleep apnea, and you may need to start with a CPAP machine. This could be a game changer for both improving your sleep quality and possibly alleviating depression and other health problems.

A MIND AT REST

Once you're sleeping better, you may begin to see more clearly that sleep is just one component of a peaceful and restful lifestyle that you can enjoy every day. A passage in the *Tao*, attributed to the ancient Chinese philosopher Lao-tzu, is useful for our immediate purposes—and, whether by happenstance or revelation, sounds not unlike the apostle John's *Logos*:

> The Way is always still, at rest,
>   And yet does everything that's done.[28]

The typical person's mind in our contemporary culture is buzzing with ten thousand things all at once. The same is true of people who are depressed, but for them the buzz consists largely of negative things about themselves or their future.

But another way is possible. We can aspire to have minds that learn from our bodies. There are times to be active, and times to rest. Even within our activities, we can be buzzing and rushing about or we can be still and focused. Even when we're busy, our minds can be at peace, not striving for the next thing but able to be present in the moment.

A busy pastor with many people under his pastoral care recalled a conversation he'd had with a friend back when "long distance" phone calls were an expensive proposition.

> What did I need to do, I asked him, to be spiritually healthy?
>   Long pause.
>   "You must ruthlessly eliminate hurry from your life," he said
> at last.

Another long pause.

"Okay, I've written that one down," I told him, a little impatiently. "That's a good one. Now what else is there?" I had many things to do, and this was a long-distance call, so I was anxious to cram as many units of spiritual wisdom into the least amount of time possible.

Another long pause.

"There is nothing else," he said. "You must ruthlessly eliminate hurry from your life."[29]

"Ruthlessly eliminating hurry" and being "always still, at rest," doesn't mean not doing things. It doesn't mean sitting in quiet contemplation all day long (though a good day will most likely include *some* time of solitude). It refers more to a state of mind that is unhurried in its approach to life.

A DAY TO ELIMINATE HURRY

One day when I was a junior in college, I came across something in the Bible that stunned me. I had grown up in the church and had a good grasp of the key concepts of Christianity, so I wasn't often surprised by what I read. But this time, as I was reading the Ten Commandments, it was as if I'd never seen this part before:

> Remember the Sabbath day, to keep it holy. Six days you shall labor, and do all your work, but the seventh day is a Sabbath to the LORD your God. On it you shall not do any work, you, or your son, or your daughter, your male servant, or your female servant, or your livestock, or the sojourner who is within your gates. For in six days the LORD made heaven and earth, the sea, and all that is in them, and rested on the seventh day. Therefore the LORD blessed the Sabbath day and made it holy.
>
> EXODUS 20:8-11

How had I failed to see this? Everyone knows it's wrong to murder people. Everyone knows it's wrong to commit adultery. But why had keeping the Sabbath not ever risen to my awareness as something that God expects us to do?

I was in a demanding engineering program at UCLA, running a nonprofit organization, and preparing to apply to medical school. I had limited time to accomplish all these things, and so like everyone else I knew, I worked seven days a week. I was faithfully involved at church, but otherwise I worked hard and without any days off.

I sat for a few minutes, my mind spinning, trying to justify my lifestyle. Surely I had read this commandment before. Maybe it wasn't meant to be taken literally? Maybe it was written for a different time, a different culture? None of these lines of reasoning took me very far. I felt personally convicted and believed that God was calling me to take this commandment at face value.

I counted the cost. What if taking off one day a week affected my grades and I didn't get into medical school?

I decided that had to be God's problem, not mine. If he was telling me to stop working on Sundays and he still wanted me to go to medical school, then he would have to help me get everything done. That's the beauty of obedience. If God's commandment is clear, the results that come from obedience are no longer my responsibility.

The following Sunday, I didn't work . . . and I had a day I would never forget. I felt free. It felt like the first day of summer. All the underlying guilt I often felt—about not working, or not working *harder*, or not prioritizing things "optimally"—and all the stress I had accepted as normal, fell away. I woke up unburdened. The creeping rebuke that had robbed the joy from every other break was gone. The internal voice that often whispered, *But David, you could be getting something done*, was silent for once.

I kept up my commitment through all the ups and downs of medical school. One professor, to maximize our study time on weekends, set all our exams on Mondays. I shut my books late on Saturday night and did as well as I could on the tests. When it came time to apply for my residency, I hoped that recent reforms in work hours would make it easier to keep my personal commitment. I noted my religious commitments on the applications and was told explicitly (and illegally) by one program that I would not be accepted as a resident if I wasn't willing to bend on this.

Despite the challenges, this rhythm of respite has become an anchor of my own stability. No matter how hard the week is, I know I will get a day of rest. It is an axis around which the rest of the week revolves.

I'm not saying that everyone should be as literal as I was, but I think it was necessary for me. When something is sacred, there's no question about whether something else is "more important." Having a rule without exceptions banished the accusing voice more effectively than half measures ever could.

Sabbath is a day to remind ourselves that we are not God. The world can go on for a day without us. In fact, the world may be better off without our trying to do one more thing for one more day. Even if we sell ourselves as slaves to the cruel god of productivity during the week, a day of rest ensures that we never become the tyrant's permanent possession.

Observing Sabbath was my own path to solving the problem of overwork and not enough rest. There are many other ways to work some rest into the busyness of our lives. Most full-time jobs allow for some vacation time. Some jobs allow and encourage periods of rest—called sabbaticals—between "productive" years. Other people have found ways to carve out some time for rest in the middle of their days.

Getting a good night's sleep and building rest into your daily and weekly rhythms will give you the energy to move toward the opposite of depression.

STEPS TOWARD FLOURISHING

A life of flourishing includes times of rest and replenishment. We make it a point to see the sun regularly—especially early in the day. We don't stay up too late on a regular basis, striving to finish "just one more thing." If we dream, we reflect on the deep mysteries of the unconscious mind. If we struggle to get to sleep at times, or to stay asleep, we don't let it bother us; we just try again the next night. Our minds are unhurried and unharried, and we incorporate cycles of rest into days, weeks, months, and years.

EXERCISE: GET MOVING

A dead thing can go with the stream,
but only a living thing can go against it.
G. K. CHESTERTON, *The Everlasting Man*

If a man achieves victory over this body,
who in the world can exercise power over him?
He who rules himself rules over the whole world.
VINOBA BHAVE

When my family first got our German shepherd, Mister Samwise, he was an energetic puppy. My wife and I took turns walking him regularly, and he bounced along merrily whenever we went out. One of those days when I was walking Sam, I suddenly realized, *I haven't been walking* myself *as much as I now walk this dog.*

I knew Sam would be healthier if I walked him. I also knew *I* would be healthier if I walked *me.* Yet I didn't exercise much. I thought I was too busy to work out regularly—but really it was a choice. And what was I saying by choosing not to exercise? Did I not believe that my own health was at least as important as Sam's?

Which brings me to a gentle exhortation (which I need to hear as much as anyone): Please, treat yourself at least as well as you would treat a dog. If you would make sure your dog gets exercise, why not help yourself get some exercise?

Like eating well and sleeping well and getting regular rest, exercise is a big part of living a flourishing life—that is, the opposite of depression. I'm not necessarily talking about running a marathon or climbing a mountain. I'm talking about getting up, getting out, and getting moving.

We are designed to move—and when we do, we see improved energy, decreased health problems (such as heart disease and diabetes), and extended life spans. Not only that, but there's a certain type of enjoyment that comes from being active, and it holds a prominent place in making life worthwhile.

LASSITUDE

Of all the words I've learned over the past few years, *lassitude* is on the short list of favorites. I hadn't heard it before I started working in mental health, and yet it succinctly captures a world of suffering. There's even a bit of onomatopoeia in the word: *lassitude* . . . one almost sighs when saying it. It refers to "a condition of weariness or debility . . . characterized by lack of interest, energy, or spirit."[1] As a symptom, lassitude reveals how much depression changes people.

Generally, when we're healthy, we have sufficient energy to go about our daily lives. We go to sleep, and we wake up refreshed. We have some pep. In depression, on the other hand, the energy to do even simple tasks can be limited. Some people with depression call it "low energy," but that doesn't begin to capture how difficult it feels, or the Herculean effort required, to perform basic self-care. Showering and personal hygiene can be so burdensome that people struggling with depression can't manage to do them regularly. One of my very depressed teenage patients spent so much time lying down that her mother had to cut off tufts of the girl's formerly beautiful hair because they'd become so knotted and tangled.

In depression, lassitude often prevents people from working on productive tasks, doing chores at home, enjoying hobbies, and even maintaining relationships. A person might not be able to reply to a text from a friend, because the effort required feels so enormous. Mail goes unopened. Phone calls go to voice mail (which is soon full). The guilt of disengagement often drives further disengagement.

What does this say about the nature of the good life? It tells us there's an aspect to flourishing that involves engagement with work and relationships.

Like a power plant, our energy is meant to be used. And it's damaging when our energy is *not* used.

ACTIVE VIRTUE

The good life is *active*—in the sense that it is self-directed and not passive. It may also involve moving our bodies, but not necessarily. We might be diligent in prayer, for example, moving our soul rather than our muscles.

That said, there is little room, even in the monastic or contemplative traditions, for someone who is only passive; in fact, physical labor often accompanies spiritual practice. This is perhaps most evident in the rule of St. Benedict: "Idleness is the enemy of the soul. Therefore, the brothers should have specified periods for manual labor as well as for prayerful reading."[2]

The chief virtue of love is also active in Christian tradition. I will expand on this idea in a later chapter on relationships, but here I would like to note that love itself is *active*—it is not primarily intellectual or emotional. Jesus said, "There is no greater love than to lay down one's life for one's friends."[3] It's not that those who express the greatest love have certain feelings for their friends, though they most certainly do. It's not that they have a particular disposition toward or belief about their friends. Love is like the string of a drawn bow: The action of shooting the arrow is *in* the tension of the bowstring as the action of sacrifice is in the loving friend.

Depression largely robs a person of the ability to take action; it removes all motivating force. In thermodynamics and chemistry, there must be a difference in energy for work to be done. Hoover Dam has water piled up behind it that is higher than the water below it. The US Bureau of Reclamation uses turbines to capture the "difference" in the falling water as it travels down the canyon. There is more heat and pressure in one part of a steam engine than another, so blades spin and work can be done. In depression, everything is at the same level; with all "pressure" the same, there is no way to do work.

The opposite of depression is being active—mentally, physically, and volitionally. The most direct application here is exercise—in every aspect—which equates to all sorts of movement and activity. In fact, life is almost synonymous with movement.

THE MIRACLE OF MOVEMENT

James, who was in his seventies, couldn't move. He just lay in his hospital bed as if paralyzed, his face frozen into a frown, with a permanently furrowed brow. He was experiencing psychomotor retardation, a slowing of movement and speech that can become quite profound in severe cases. This condition sometimes goes along with major depressive disorder.

Because of his psychomotor limitations, James had stopped eating on his own. His wife helped out as much as she could, spoon-feeding James as if he were a child. But this had not been enough to sustain him and he'd lost a lot of weight. His doctors had tried medication after medication to no avail, and finally recommended him for admission to Stanford's voluntary psychiatric ward, with me as one of his inpatient psychiatrists.

After discussing options with James and his family, I ultimately recommended electroconvulsive therapy, sometimes called shock therapy. We'd exhausted all other options, and he was rapidly getting worse. We asked for second opinions from other colleagues, and everyone agreed: If we didn't do the ECT, James wouldn't last much longer. He was taken early the next day to start treatment.

Later in the day, after James was taken to ECT, I was walking down the main hallway of the ward, and I noticed a new patient walking toward me. I was supposed to be informed of any new patients being admitted, but I had not been paged. Perhaps my colleague had admitted this man?

Then I looked again. It was James. His appearance had been transformed.

After being incapable of even raising a spoon to his lips the night before, he was now up and walking after only a single session of ECT. His face was no longer frozen into a frown. He definitely still had depression; he wasn't exactly beaming like Santa Claus. But at a glance he looked . . . normal.

The change seemed almost miraculous. Simply being able to move made him look like a new person. And his ability to get out of bed was a huge part of his ultimate full recovery.

A FINITE LIFE-FORM IN THREE-DIMENSIONAL SPACE

Movement is a capacity uniting humans with other life-forms, down to the microscopic. Certain bacteria can move by spinning their whiplike flagella. Other tiny organisms move toward food or away from threats by using leglike cilia. In more complex organisms, muscles serve to move animals in ways that help them meet their needs. Even some plants have the ability to optimize photosynthesis by moving their leaves to capture more sunlight. As human beings, before we're even born, we announce our vitality by kicking our mothers (sorry, Mom).

Our cognition is framed around the reality of movement. Even our abstract expressions draw upon our imagination in the world of motion. Your boss "moved the goalposts." Your child is "throwing" a fit.

Even as our lives move increasingly online, we cannot escape the fact that we are fundamentally physical creatures who operate in the dimension of space. In the 1990s, we met in cyber*space*, and now we interact in a realm of many "threads" woven together: the "inter*net*." We conceive of our stored data as existing in a "cloud." Tech giants are betting big that we'll set up our lives and businesses in "virtual reality," a reimagination of space.

C. S. Lewis, creator of the Narnia tales, once called his fellow humans "amphibians—half spirit and half animal."[4] The metaphor is apt, and this chapter is about the physical "water" where we spend most of our lives. The spiritual "air" is where we are from time to time, perhaps in prayer or while working out mathematical theorems. But eventually we must eat. And communicate. And move.

With movement so basic to our nature, we would do well to consider *how* we are moving and whether we are moving enough. In particular, if we're seeking the good life, we need regular exercise. Just like my dog, Mister Samwise.

Exercise is one of the most straightforward and fascinating treatments in medicine. On the one hand, doctors since the dawn of the profession have been telling patients to exercise. Very early studies suggested that we need exercise in order to flourish. We need exercise to prevent heart disease. We need exercise to prevent obesity. It's how we're made.

The apostle Paul said, "Physical training is of some value, but godliness has value for all things, holding promise for both the present life and the life to come" (1 Timothy 4:8, NIV). Paul builds his argument on what he and his first-century readers would have taken for granted: that exercise has "some value." Like Jesus, Paul was a man who walked long distances. And judging by his references to foot racing, boxing, and the wreaths placed on the brows of victorious athletes, we know he paid at least some attention to sports.[5]

We can never achieve a flourishing life without paying attention to our souls, and we'll get to that topic at the end of the book. But as long as we are in our mortal bodies, we must take care of them through exercise.

THE MULTIPURPOSE ANTIDEPRESSANT

In medicine, we've learned some things . . .

- *Some things may offer prevention but not a cure.* For example, eating oatmeal can help prevent a heart attack, but it doesn't treat heart attacks.
- *Some things may offer treatment but not prevention.* Inserting a stent into a blocked blood vessel is a treatment for a heart attack, but it doesn't prevent heart attacks.
- *Some things neither prevent nor treat a condition, but they may prevent a recurrence.* Daily aspirin use is not usually recommended to prevent heart attacks in the general population, but it is often used to prevent *another* heart attack from happening.

Which of these three things—prevention, treatment, or prevention of recurrence—would you say best describes what exercise does for depression?

You might be surprised to learn that it does *all three*. It can prevent the onset of depression, treat existing depression, and reduce the risk that depression will come back after improvement.

One group of researchers looked at people who didn't already have depression. They followed them over time to see who got depressed. Those who were sedentary got depressed at a higher rate than those who exercised.

In people who were previously depressed, those who exercised felt better than those who didn't.[6]

More importantly, those who engaged in exercise programs showed substantial benefits to their mood. For reference, the standard "effect size" of an antidepressant medication is usually between small to medium (0.2 is small; 0.5 is medium; 0.8 is large). Those who were assigned to an exercise program showed an effect size of 1.24.[7] That's gigantic!

If all that weren't enough, exercise also works to prevent a person from relapsing into depression. All it takes is a cumulative hour of exercise *per week* to ward off depression; those who were completely sedentary had a 44 percent higher chance of developing depression compared to the 1+ hour exercisers. Remarkably, even a tiny amount of exercise, one to thirty minutes *per week*, was quite protective. (Minimal exercisers had only a 19 percent increased chance of developing depression compared to the 1+ hour exercisers).[8]

Other studies that explored the optimal amount of exercise for overall health set the bar at more than sixty minutes per week. The CDC recommends 150 minutes.[9] There are important and interesting debates on the optimal type of exercise in addressing depression, but there are no firm conclusions at this point. Any type of exercise will get the job done.

Depression loves lethargy.

The opposite of depression is powered by exercise.

COGNITIVE CONDITIONING

What happens in the brain when we physically exercise?

It has long been established that the motor cortex—an area within the cerebral cortex at the top of the brain—is the likely center for controlling muscle movements. But scientists wanted to know if there was more to it than that.[10] They placed study participants into an MRI scanner and asked them to squeeze a hand gripper at various intensities. What they found was that muscle contractions require coordination and communication (functional connectivity) between the motor cortex and the prefrontal cortex, the part of the brain related to rational thought.

What's going on here? It might be that the prefrontal cortex tells the motor cortex what to do. The prefrontal cortex might be like a captain, with the motor cortex as a lieutenant, obeying orders. The motor cortex then delivers the commands to more specific neurons, the enlisted soldiers that need to fire to get the job done.

Another interesting finding in the study was that, when the muscular strength required to make the contraction was higher, more of the prefrontal cortex connected with itself, and in particular the number of hyperconnected spots increased. During these contractions, the connections between the prefrontal cortex and the motor cortex seemed especially tight.

This means that exercise requiring greater muscle contractions compels your brain to practice coordinated firing. When you push against physical resistance, your prefrontal cortex's ability to command and control other parts of the brain is recruited. In exercise, it does this "for no reason," almost like a military training drill. Yes, your muscles get stronger, but it's also a way for your brain to practice coordination. Later, when your prefrontal cortex needs to act in concert to respond to a negative thought originating in an emotional center of the brain, push harder to finish something at work, or resist bickering with your spouse, it has an officer corps that is well drilled.

Exercise not only strengthens your body below the neck for the needs you'll encounter in the future; it also trains your brain to work better.

USING ENERGY TO MAKE ENERGY

Now that we have confirmed the benefits of physical exercise and physical movement, the application is to find ways to move your body more. I'm not trying to turn you into a world-class athlete, but I *am* hoping to overcome any resistance to exercise you might have and help you become a person who gets some good exercise—*any* kind of exercise—regularly.

Whatever exercise you choose will be good for your mental health *and* your physical health. Not only will the exercise itself be enriching, but your mind and body will be better equipped for the life goals you have in mind.

Start tiny if you must

Some people with severe depression or other health problems, or who have had a negative experience with exercise, may hear a deceptive brain message telling them they *can't* exercise, that it's beyond their ability.

The bad news about this lie is that if you believe it, it's crushing.

The good news is that the lie is easy to disprove if you set a reasonably small goal.

True, you might not be capable of vigorous or sustained exercise at this point. But that doesn't mean you aren't able to do *some* exercise. Here's how to get out of that trap: Simply set a goal that's undeniably achievable, doing something you wouldn't have done otherwise. For example, decide to walk out to the mailbox—not to get the mail, but just to get the exercise. Put on a sweater, sweatpants, and slippers, open the front door, walk down the driveway, touch the mailbox, and walk back. If you live in an apartment complex, go out of your apartment, walk down the hall, open the door to the complex, see the sun, and go back to your apartment. If you do this twice a day, you will prove to yourself twice a day that you can do something to get some exercise.

If you're already getting up and out every day, you can find ways to get a little more exercise in your day by making small changes in your routine. For example, take the stairs instead of the elevator, or park your car on the opposite side of the parking lot. These simple strategies can increase the number of steps you take during the day.

Okay, let's be completely honest. How much difference does this kind of exercise make physiologically? Not much. But the difference it makes psychologically or emotionally can be huge, because it helps to convince you that depression is a liar when it says you *can't*. And if once or twice a day you do something to get some basic exercise, you're taking control of your circumstances for at least a few minutes every day, which is something you can build on. Remember, in the study I mentioned above, even those people who exercised for *one minute per week* were better off than those who didn't exercise at all.

Do whatever you have no excuse not to do

Maybe for you, my walk-to-the-mailbox or take-the-stairs options seem way too easy. You want more aggressive goals. Good for you. Go ahead and set them.

You can do whatever kind of exercise you want, because just about anything you can do is bound to be good for you. Pick whatever is most appealing, because there doesn't seem to be a big difference between the health benefits of different types of exercise. If an important goal for you is to improve your mood, it may be that high-intensity exercise is better than moderate-intensity exercise.[11] Team sports also correlate with better moods, possibly because of the social component.[12] But whatever exercise you choose, make sure to have a fallback position—something that is so easy you have no excuse not to do it.

Let's say you've set a goal to go to the gym for an hour three days a week. You keep it up for a while, but one morning you just don't feel like going. What then? Well, don't do *nothing*. Skip the gym if you must, but do your predetermined fallback exercise—say, thirty push-ups—instead. Now you've kept the exercise momentum going and you can get back into your gym routine without feeling as if you've let yourself down.

If you make sure to have at least *something* you can do when things don't go according to plan or when your gumption fails you, you'll always be on track. The best exercise is always the one you actually do.

Do whatever you can do consistently

Doing anything repetitively will eventually make it easier. Something that initially takes energy and attention will become more automatic the longer you maintain the habit. Exercise is a particularly good habit to cultivate.

Maybe you're getting thirty minutes of exercise, three times a week. That's a great start, but maybe your next-level goal is to hit the CDC target of 150 minutes per week. If so, choose the kind of exercise that you can do consistently for that amount of time, an exercise that appeals to you as a long-term habit.

Creating a habit doesn't necessarily mean you're going to *like* the exercise—at least not at first. Our initial impressions of an exercise or a sport don't always match with a long-term perspective. Some runners, for example, will tell you that the first few weeks of running were misery; but over time, they came to love running.

If you need a boost to get yourself over the difficult period of starting to exercise, you might find that a workout buddy can help. Having an exercise companion may make all the difference. In any case, pick something that you can do relatively consistently, and keep going until the benefits provide their own motivation.

Think beyond exercise

There is a ceiling to the mental health benefits of exercise. It's not easy to say where that ceiling is, but people who go all-in on exercise aren't necessarily better off. In fact, they might even be worse off than someone who exercises a reasonable amount—say, a few times a week for a few hours.

To increase the benefit of exercise, you might want to pair it with something else that you know will contribute to living a better life. For example, if you have shyness and social fears, switch from going to the gym alone and join an athletic team. As you participate in the team sport, you'll not only be continuing the workout that's good for your body but you will also be learning how to coordinate with other people.

Be mindful of the ways that regular physical movement can become movement *away* from depression.

IF SHAWNDA CAN . . .

One day, in a video session, a patient named Shawnda told me she'd been buying a lot of clothes lately. I immediately became worried. Shawnda had bipolar disorder and was at risk for mania. One of the symptoms of mania is a lack of inhibition that could lead to wildly inappropriate purchases.

"Why so many new clothes?" I asked.

"My old clothes didn't fit me anymore."

Because our session was by video and Shawnda had been out of state for the past year under the care of another doctor, I hadn't noticed that she had lost weight since the last time I'd seen her. At that time, she had been morbidly obese and had a very painful back condition that took multiple surgeries to partially preserve her ability to walk with a walker.

"I lost a hundred pounds, Dr. Carreon."

A pang of fear gripped me. Was she now depressed and losing weight?

But she wasn't depressed. She was happy and smiling. There was a note of justifiable pride in her voice when she said she'd lost weight. She had *intentionally* lost that weight.

I was stunned. An aggressive weight reduction like that meant she had lost about two pounds per week over a fifty-week period.

Shawnda explained that she had bought a small under-desk pedal machine (like a tiny exercise bike) and was always on it when working or using her computer. "In fact, Doctor, I'm on it right now."

Despite being on medications that contribute to weight gain, Shawnda had been able to lose substantial weight. And exercise was an important component in her success.

I give this example because she had plenty of good reasons not to exercise. I have far fewer reasons to keep me from exercising like I should, and I think that's probably true of most people.

Let's get out there and move more, like we were meant to.

Exercise can help you become a new person.

STEPS TOWARD FLOURISHING

The flourishing life includes being active—in body, mind, and spirit. We learn to take active, volitional control over our bodies. We practice the limits of our embodiment through exercise, learning to bring ever more of ourselves more completely under our own control.

Part 3

SOUL

10

MEANING: A *WHY* TO LIVE FOR

Love and work are the cornerstones of our humanness.
SIGMUND FREUD

He who has a why to live can bear almost any how.
FRIEDRICH NIETZSCHE

It was only 3:00 p.m., and I was done. I couldn't do any more work. I had always thought of myself as a hard worker, but I couldn't put in a full day anymore. The motivation just wasn't there.

In many ways, it seemed like I should have been energetic and enthusiastic. I was nine months into a twelve-month project in rural Kenya with a great nonprofit, Nuru International. Our work—trying to end extreme poverty—was about as important as it gets. My own job for my year-long commitment—helping to set the foundation for training community health workers—was important too. But there was also a lot to be cynical about.

On the one hand, the leaders of the villages were incredibly enthusiastic about our work. We had broad support among the farmers who were banding together, dramatically increasing farm yields and seeing improvements in health and education. My colleagues were motivated and hardworking, passionate about helping the people in the villages. The government officials, on the other hand, were not as excited. Though I had originally anticipated that the resources and ideas we brought would be welcomed, now I felt that the local officials were more interested in milking our start-up nonprofit for cash than in helping to make changes to benefit their people. The project stalled.

As ennui set in, I decided that I had to do something to give myself a visible, tangible sense of doing worthwhile work.

I bought a *jembe* (basically a heavy-duty hoe, wielded like a pickax) and went to work digging on a goat path. With a lot of labor, this path could become a road that would enable more convenient travel for my neighbors.

At first, however, the neighbors were confused. A *mzungu* (the slightly derogatory Swahili word for "white man") swinging a *jembe* was a strange sight to see. In their culture, manual labor was something to avoid, and surely a mzungu could afford to hire someone to do whatever digging was necessary. I was accosted more than once—even interrogated—by women passing by who were utterly baffled by what I was doing.

In broken Swahili, I did my best to explain, and I kept going. I dug and dug and dug.

My other work, as a medical adviser, was important, but it wasn't challenging for me. My brain sat idle for most of the day as I participated in meetings that seemed unnecessary.

The digging, however, required a certain amount of skill. As I was widening the path into a road, it needed a certain grade to drain the massive amounts of Kenyan rainfall without washing away. I wanted the incline to be as smooth as possible.

Every day, I spent about an hour on the road, and every day I went home from work feeling like I had actually accomplished something. The physical exercise felt good as well. I liked being tired at the end of the day.

When I started, I didn't think I would be able to finish. It was a long path and I was a knowledge worker, not an expert at wielding the *jembe*. But it was important that finishing the project—whether the work was done by myself or by others—was at least theoretically possible. This endeavor had what classical philosophers and theologians would call a *telos*—an end or purpose. I was working *toward* something. And it was a *good* something. That's why it felt more inspiring and fulfilling than my medical assignment at the time.

As it turned out, I was wrong about not being able to finish. By the time my tour was done, cars had started driving up and down the now-widened path.

The former Stanford psychiatrist Irvin Yalom said, "To live without meaning, goals, values, or ideals seems to provoke . . . considerable distress. . . . We apparently need absolutes—firm ideals to which we can aspire and guidelines by which to steer our lives."[1]

That's what I found to be true in Kenya and still believe today: The good life requires doing good things. A worthwhile destination brings motivation. Meaning gives momentum. Our paid work is one obvious place where we might find meaning (or else miss it keenly), but we can also find purpose in many domains of life, including faith, family, volunteerism, and creative output.

If you haven't taken stock lately—not only of how you're living, but of what you're living *for*—then consider this chapter as your invitation. Take aim and shoot your life like an arrow.

DGOOB

Why get out of bed? Depression puts this question front and center. Depressed people have a profound experience of not mattering. Their actions seem to have all the meaning sucked out. Sometimes they can be completely blind to their own significance. I have had patients with all varieties of jobs that others would consider significant and desirable, and some with home lives that others might envy; yet, to the patient, everything is meaningless.

Twenty-year-old Matt had ambitions of becoming a fantasy writer, but he began to not see the point. He loved the idea of exploring humanity's biggest questions, and he had been a great student, but now he was struggling in school for the first time. The heavy blanket of depression that had descended on him made movement itself difficult, let alone taking upper-division courses. Worse, he had begun to question the point of everything. He had no grand, unifying purpose in his life, but before depression hit, he had found glimmers of meaning when he practiced his writing. Since depression came, everything he did, from schoolwork to writing, seemed pointless. With death as the eventual common outcome, the void of meaninglessness seemed inescapable. The resulting inaction only worsened the depression, perpetuating a vicious cycle.

In my sessions with depressed patients, I see a specific symptom so often that I use an acronym to jot it in my notes: *DGOOB*. It stands for "difficulty getting out of bed" and captures the untold human anguish afflicting those who are depressed. In short, *What's the point?*

Normally, we have intrinsic motivators that get us up and out the door in the morning. We like our job, or the money it provides, or we enjoy our colleagues. Maybe we're afraid of getting fired, don't want to be seen as lazy, or simply don't want to miss a commute window. But what if all those motivational cues were flatlined? It would be difficult to get out of bed, to even move.

Meaning ought to be something perceptible, but depressed people may have distorted vision here, as in other domains. Sometimes we think we have a clear purpose . . . and then we lose it. Big time. It's called burnout.

THE EX-WHY

To those in the medical field, burnout is considered something separate from, but related to, major depression. We see it often enough, even among our own numbers. Burnout occurs when, for example, a doctor continues showing up to work but doesn't feel the passion she once did. She feels fatigued and frustrated. She feels a lack of significance in her work and a lack of connection to her patients. This phenomenon is becoming much more common. One study found that the number of doctors with at least one symptom of burnout increased dramatically during the COVID crisis, up from 38 percent in 2020 to 63 percent in 2021.[2]

What, exactly, happens when a person burns out?

One of my mentors, Mickey Trockel, was part of a team who set out to understand burnout in medicine.[3] A particular area of concern was performance. Nobody wants to commit a medical error. It's one of a doctor's greatest fears. After all, "do no harm" has been at the heart of the Hippocratic approach to medicine since 400 BCE.[4]

Trockel found that burned-out doctors at every level of training—both residents and supervising physicians—admitted to making more medical errors. Anyone who has burned the candle down to nothing isn't able to perform at the same level as someone who hasn't gotten to that point.

Incidentally, Trockel's study determined that sleep deprivation was the other major factor leading to medical error. It makes sense that people who feel sleepy will make mistakes. Further—in the category of findings that surprised no one—people who feel sleepy *and* are burned out make more mistakes than doctors who are only sleepy or doctors who are only burned out.

I've been talking about medical burnout, but the problem of absence of meaning goes much, much further. It can even run rampant among populations where you might least expect it.

THE VALLEY OF DISAPPOINTMENT

Those who make it to Silicon Valley as tech geniuses come with stars in their eyes. They know that the San Francisco Peninsula is the epicenter for making things to solve humanity's problems. Corporate vision statements are never more grandiose than they are in the tech industry. While other fields of endeavor seem not to be making the fundamental breakthroughs they once did, technology's advances continue to be amazing. However, for some, when they see how the technology "sausage" is actually made, they lose their appetite. The stars begin to fade.

I readily concede that my frame of reference is the mother of all sampling biases, because I mainly see depressed people and very many of my patients live in Silicon Valley, but I can attest to a level of cynicism in many technophiles who have been here for a while. They see the futility of their work. Obsolescence is practically baked into the products that come and go, and the latest features are constantly changing.

One patient told me of visiting a phone recycling facility in China. The workers were smashing phones by hand with hammers to extract the precious metals. He recognized the model of the phone—it was the top-of-the-line model from five years ago.

He saw it as a parable.

Such is the fate of all technology—and not even in the distant future. In just a few years, stuff being designed now will be deemed not worth fixing. So why invest your heart in it? Why care at all?

Other tech workers know their projects are doomed before the product even comes into existence. The goal is impossible, or the application is too soon for the market. Still others lapse into despair once they realize that the main purpose for developing search engines and social media is to sell ads. Jeff Hammerbacher, a millennial employee at Facebook, summed it up well: "The best minds of my generation are thinking about how to make people click ads. That sucks."[5]

Although your work may be totally different, does that disillusioned attitude seem familiar? It's not enough just to say, "Oh well," or to wait for retirement and hope that isn't empty too. Feeling a sense of meaning is crucial to our well-being, even our very lives.

WHAT'S AT STAKE

Viktor Frankl, one of the most influential psychiatrists of the twentieth century, survived the Holocaust and wrote a book called *Man's Search for Meaning* about his experiences in Nazi concentration camps. He concluded, "Striving to find a meaning in one's life is the primary motivational force in man."[6]

This turns out to be literally true. In a 2016 study of 136,265 people, researchers found a connection between "having a higher purpose in life and reduced all-cause mortality."[7] It seems reasonable to expect that if I don't have a meaningful life, or if I don't feel purposeful, I would feel sad or depressed. But I wouldn't expect a heart attack; I wouldn't expect cancer; I wouldn't expect to literally *die* from this. But a comparison of outcomes for the top 10 percent and the bottom 10 percent showed that those with the highest levels of purposefulness had a much lower chance of dying. Specifically, the study found a 17 percent reduction per year in the odds of dying.

The stakes are high. If we're feeling aimless, not able to articulate a reason to get up in the morning, we would do well to work toward finding meaning.

WHEN FEELING FOLLOWS DOING

One straightforward but profound approach to therapy is called *behavioral therapy* or *behavioral activation*. The primary focus is to have people who are depressed engage in activities that may not feel meaningful to them now, but would feel meaningful if they weren't depressed. In other words, this therapy doesn't delve into the *source* of depression, current thoughts, or the past. It's based on the idea that focusing entirely on changing behaviors (even in small ways) can break the cycle of depression. This approach might not work for people who are severely depressed, but for those who are still capable of some activity, experience has shown that they can sometimes be nursed back to mental health by behavioral activation.

It should be noted that behavioral therapy is still a specialized psychotherapy that requires special training; it's not simply telling depressed people to try harder. Nonetheless, the approach of structuring a series of small steps in a special way to help people exercise whatever small amount of meaning-making or meaning-engagement they can muster will gradually help to fill the person's life with meaning.

With Matt—the would-be fantasy writer—I employed existential psychotherapy with a cognitive bent, exploring his beliefs about meaninglessness. We spent many hours discussing the justifications for his *certainty* of the meaninglessness of life. Even when we found inconsistencies or self-contradictions in his philosophy, his conviction that everything was meaningless remained unshaken.

So I switched my approach. I assigned him the task of trying to write short fantasy stories for ten minutes every day, even if he knew it would be ultimately meaningless. I also told him to go for a daily walk. In combination with medication, exercising his mind and his body did the trick. He began to feel little glimmers of significance when he wrote, and the walks themselves felt significant, though he couldn't explain why. Months after Matt was in full recovery, he and I reviewed the arguments he had used to justify his view of universal meaninglessness. But now he could find nothing convincing in them at all.

For some people, if they can be coaxed into small activities, even if it's something as basic as cooking a small meal or going for a short walk, they experience little bits of significance and start to see that there is still meaning in those activities. I say *see* that there is meaning because I believe it is more like seeing something tangible than other mental experiences. For analogy, we can believe that the atmosphere contains oxygen, and we can see that the sky is blue; experiencing meaning is closer to the latter.

What is true in small ways in the depths of depression is true at all levels of human experience. When we have a sense that what we're doing matters, we're able to do it more. When we don't have a sense that what we're doing matters, we don't do it as well. When we lack a subjective sense of meaning, it's as if we lack the fuel to engage.

MEANING, MOMENT BY MOMENT

Many people who have studied the role of meaning have approached it as a global state. So they may ask questions about a person's life in general. In our SoulPulse research, we looked at whether a person's sense of meaning varied from hour to hour and in various situations.

The first thing we found was that the results were *highly* variable. Certainly there were people who consistently answered on the high end, and others who consistently answered on the low end, but when we looked at everyone together, some trends emerged. Perhaps the most unexpected factor was time of day. It turns out that 6 a.m. is the time when people feel least meaningful, and noon is when they feel the most meaningful. People's sense of meaning builds to a peak from the time they wake up and then recedes until the time they fall asleep.

We also took note of the activities most associated with feelings of meaningfulness. Far and away the activity most associated with a sense of meaning was *prayer*. No other activity could hold a candle to it.

People whose lives were characterized by prayer, reading or watching news, and food prep were the ones with the greatest sense of meaning; those whose lives were characterized by video games, resting, and work breaks had the least sense of meaning. The activities that correlated with higher meaning in the moment were prayer, music, and play; those that correlated with momentary low meaning were resting, watching TV, and playing video games.

In SoulPulse, we found that one of the major drivers of what a person finds meaningful has to do with simply having other people around.[8] Being with one's partner, children, friends, coworkers, customers, acquaintances—and even one's boss—correlated to a deeper sense of meaning. Interestingly, however, the study found that being around one's parents did *not* improve the person's sense of meaning. Neither did being around strangers (which might be expected).

These results seem to align with what we experience in life. It may be that the healthiest way to experience meaning is through the rising and falling patterns of daily life. It may be like cortisol, a hormone whose daily rise and fall is normal and healthy. A consistently high, low, or erratic level is unhealthy. My interpretation of the data is that it's good to have times of rest and times of meaningful work.

FINDING AND CREATING MEANING

The applications for this chapter focus on becoming aware of and engaging with sources of meaning in the world. Once we do this, we can move toward doing more meaningful things.

Name three good things (and three reasons why)

One of the best-tested interventions in positive psychology is the practice of gratitude. Of course, expressing gratitude isn't the same thing as finding meaning, but I think it is closely related to seeing and appreciating how the things in our lives connect and have significance.

There are many ways to consider what we have to be thankful for, but my favorite, from psychologist Martin Seligman, is called the "three good things" exercise.[9] This exercise seems to build more happiness the longer it is practiced, including six months *after* the experiment ended (probably because the people kept doing the exercise).

Here's how it works:

At the end of the day, write down three good things that happened that day. These can be good things that others have done, good things you have done, or good things you find in the natural world or from God. Examples:

- "My husband brought me flowers."
- "I was productive at work."
- "The weather was beautiful."

Next, write down how each of these three things came about. This step reveals the web of connections that make up a meaningful story. Examples:

- "My husband brought me flowers because he loves me."
- "I was productive at work because I care about the people I work with."
- "The weather was beautiful because God likes to create beautiful things."

Try making this exercise a regular part of your daily routine.

Become a helper

Another effective way to find meaning in our day-to-day lives is by helping other people. Find something that needs to be done—and do it. This might be a task around the house, at work, or in the community. Tidy up a common area at your office, even though it's not in your job description. Return someone else's shopping cart. Pick up trash you didn't leave behind. Maybe fix the fence between your yard and the neighbors'. I find it often feels particularly meaningful to fix something that will be physically different after you're done—like the road I started in Kenya.

Consider volunteering, preferably with a group. Do something charitable, something that helps other people. Some people who don't feel their jobs are meaningful find deep significance in volunteering on the weekends or during a vacation. Find a cause you care about, a cause that speaks to you or that expresses your values. You're likely to find more satisfaction and meaning if you choose something that aligns well with what you believe in.

If you can't think of a cause that's meaningful to you, *just pick something*. Really. It's that simple. I have known people, including some of my depressed patients, who started volunteering without any prior experience. Through a process of exploration, they were able to find out where they fit in a volunteering environment. After trying different things, they were able to say, "I liked this aspect of it, but not that. This felt meaningful, but that didn't." Eventually they found their niche.

Bend your career toward the meaningful

In one sense, nearly every job is meaningful in that it provides an income and produces useful goods or services, though the value to humanity of what your company produces might seem abstract and philosophical. But you can make money doing just about anything. (Have you ever seen the show on the Discovery Channel called *Dirty Jobs*?) For some, their career is not where they find meaning. Maybe it's with their family, their faith, or their friends. But if you can choose to do work that is meaningful, it can be an excellent way to pursue a life that is satisfying and flourishing.

Sometimes it's possible to find deeper meaning in your job by reflecting on the impact it has (or at least your company has) on others. In one famous study of workers in a university's call center trying to raise money for a scholarship fund, a single, brief interaction with a scholarship recipient increased productivity 171 percent—a result that persisted even a month later.[10]

I am grateful for the opportunity I have to do a job I find very meaningful. Before psychiatry, I pursued the most meaningful jobs or pathways I could find; but when I eventually discovered that what I thought was most important or most significant wasn't as compelling as a new opportunity, I decided to do something else instead. But I wouldn't have known about the new opportunity without undertaking the old one.

Is there some way you can turn your job or career into a greater source of meaning?

MEANING SHADOWS

Meaning involves connection to a larger story. By volunteering to help build a home for a poor family, for example, we become part of that family's story, their history. Indeed, anything we do that transcends our tiny circle of self-absorption is a move toward finding a deeper purpose and more profound meaning in life. But to expand on the question from the beginning of the chapter, what difference does it make if everything just ends at death? What transcendent meaning can be found if we're simply part of a random assortment of highly evolved primates? Existentialist philosophers have been grappling with these questions for the past two centuries.

As a psychiatrist, I've found that any glimmer of meaning is enough to work with. Even the faintest flicker of hope can become a rung on the ladder that leads out of the pit of depression and toward a life of greater meaning. Even if a person is never drawn to the question of ultimate purpose, it is pragmatically helpful to be part of something bigger than ourselves. That part I find to be indisputable.

As a Christian, I believe that our common human desire for meaning points to something ultimate. And I believe that our sense of meaning and purpose derives, at least in part, from our having been created in the image of God. The story that unfolds in the Bible—the culmination of which we still look forward to with anticipation—is the epitome of a bigger story. Some of the stories in the Bible are inestimably ancient, far older than the written versions we have. The text of the Bible is at the foundation of the Western Canon, with its influence extending onward into the future. The Bible is multivocal, including perspectives of women and men, enslaved people and kings, priests with unbroken lineage and prophets who come out of nowhere. All these stories are in a beautiful and unresolved tension that invites our participation. It is the greatest story ever told, not merely because it's a good story; it's the greatest because it is best able to draw people from across time and space together into the same shared narrative.

STEPS TOWARD FLOURISHING

Moving toward the opposite of depression involves finding something meaningful and purposeful to do in our lives. To flourish, we will seek out activities that contribute to the world and to others. As we are able, while still providing for those who depend on us, we gravitate toward actions that will make the world a better place. We try to align our good intentions with good actions to achieve good outcomes. We keep the end in mind from the beginning so that we don't lose our motivation.

TRUTH: IT WILL SET YOU FREE

You will know the truth, and the truth will set you free.
JOHN 8:32

We suffer not from the events in our lives but
from our judgment about them.
EPICTETUS, *The Enchiridion*

The object of the superior man is truth.
CONFUCIUS, *Analects*

Joe had a job in an auto shop, but he was having trouble working because he thought he was dying. Normally that would send him to a different kind of doctor, but Joe had already seen the others and they had assured him he wasn't dying. Several times. At great expense. He had been diagnosed with panic disorder, and his panic attacks certainly made him think and feel that he was having a heart attack. He was starting to develop depression as a result.

One of the things that can keep panic attacks going is the belief that we're about to die. Joe genuinely believed he was having a heart attack. His heart raced, sweat poured out, his chest constricted, and he had a sense of impending doom. Chemically and psychologically, it wouldn't have been much different if he really had been dying.

But he *wasn't* dying, and somehow I had to convince him of that. When you *feel* like you're dying, however, it's hard for a rational explanation—"It's 'just' a panic attack"—or external expertise coming from your doctor to overcome your lived experience. In most cases, our assurances convince a part of the brain that is irrelevant to the panic attack. Patients *say* they believe it, and they *say* they trust their doctor, but really they don't.

In Joe's case, I decided to use an approach called the *experimental technique*, which I learned from my mentor David Burns. The technique uses a variety of approaches to help people overcome their self-defeating beliefs and negative thoughts by exposing them to the very thing they fear most.

With Joe's permission, I induced a panic attack in my office. He closed his eyes and focused on my words as I led him through the opposite of a relaxation meditation. I had him imagine his worst fears happening— having severe chest pain, calling 9-1-1, going by ambulance to the hospital. It took only a few minutes for him to go into a full-blown panic attack.

His heart rate increased.

He was consumed with dread.

He began sweating.

He was sure he was dying of a heart attack.

I asked him, "If you were actually having a heart attack, do you think you'd be able to do exercise?"

"No, I wouldn't be able to."

I said, "All right, then, let's test that. I'm a medical doctor. We are in a medical clinic. If you do, in fact, have a heart attack, we're very well equipped to treat you. So let's test this out. Start doing jumping jacks."

"What?!"

"Jumping jacks. I'll do them with you."

So I started doing jumping jacks in the small office.

Joe joined me. No heart attack occurred, and his performance was unimpaired.

"Maybe we can try a different exercise. Let's run in place."

I started high-stepping in the office (to the probable confusion of the clinicians in the room below us). Again, Joe joined me. Then the most remarkable thing happened: The same young man who was convinced he was dying started laughing instead.

"Why are you laughing?" I asked.

"Well, because clearly I'm not dying."

The second he believed with his whole self that he wasn't dying, he was cured. Years of crippling panic attacks resolved in a moment of laughter.

The experimental technique isn't magic. I've had plenty of other cases where it didn't work at all. But Joe's success serves to illustrate a few important points:

- Belief is not necessarily constant.
- Belief is deeper than "conscious" or explicit assent.
- When belief is misplaced, it can be changed by a voluntary choice.

Joe's belief that he would die if things continued as they were sustained his misery. Similarly, what you and I believe about ourselves and about the world is critical to how we live our lives. Whether what we believe is *true* or *false* will either bring enormous relief or enormous suffering to our lives.

It's always extremely satisfying in therapy, or in life, to find the key quickly. Dramatic cases like Joe's help us realize it's possible. But sometimes it isn't all that obvious what's wrong with our current beliefs. The process of uncovering the truth may take moments, or it might take years; either way, rejecting false beliefs about yourself or the world can help you achieve a better life.

WHEN THOUGHTS ARE SYMPTOMS

Sometimes our beliefs—or even just a single belief—can be the root of much of our suffering. This is the foundational assumption (usually unstated) of cognitive therapy, one of the major types of psychotherapy.[1] According to the cognitive model, particular thoughts can perpetuate depression; and as soon as the person changes those thoughts, the depression begins to lift. In other words, the root of depression is one or more "cognitive distortions" or "distorted brain messages."

People with depression (and many people without it) can get lost in a maze of their thoughts—ever circling, never able to get to where they want to go.

They need to know that escape is possible.

What if the solution to a problem were as "simple" as connecting one specific neuron to another specific neuron in the brain?[2] With 86 billion neurons to choose from, finding the right connection would take a very long time. Nevertheless, the hope of the cognitive approach is that once we find a pathway to navigate through the maze, we don't need to do it again.

"A BAD PERSON"

When I was a third-year medical student, I had a hard time during my internal medicine rotation at the Palo Alto Veterans Administration hospital, taking care of patients with everything from heart failure to bad ulcers. It was one of my first rotations, and I was still pretty green. It didn't help that my team included a couple of bright young doctors fresh out of med school, a particularly brilliant fellow med student, and an attending who had been practicing for many years.

Despite years of study in basic physiology, I wasn't able to translate what I knew to my patients (that's what I was supposed to learn by being thrown into the deep end on this rotation), and I didn't know how to present a case to my superiors. Before long, I started to panic.

The attending physician was smart, but she wasn't patient. My voice began to tremble, and my ability to think on my feet seemed to disappear as she asked us increasingly more difficult questions. My feeling ignorant and stupid intensified at every turn.

I started thinking I must be too stupid to graduate. Sure, I was at Stanford, but maybe the admissions committee had made a mistake. Maybe I didn't have the intelligence needed to pass this rotation and become a doctor. As you can imagine, this line of thinking did not help my anxiety.

The downward spiral of my confidence continued as my anxiety went through the roof during our daily rounds. I was so tied up in knots that whatever knowledge I actually possessed could barely make itself heard through the wavering staccato of my shaky voice.

Finally one day, I realized I had been listening to—and believing—three false messages in my mind:

1. "If my attending thinks I'm stupid, then I must be."
2. "I'm not going to graduate."
3. "I'm a bad person."

When I stopped long enough to think about it, I realized that every one of these conclusions was false. First and foremost, I had forgotten that my worth as a person did not depend on my work. I am loved and valued by God regardless of my accomplishments. Even if it happened that I didn't graduate from Stanford, my value as a person would be unchanged. So it didn't matter what the attending physician thought of me—and to be honest, I didn't actually *know* what she thought of me; I just knew how I *felt*. While it remained to be seen whether I actually had the chops to graduate, I could probably figure out a way to make it through. In any case, lacking certain skills was nothing to feel guilty about. It didn't make me a bad person. My job was to do my best. If my best wasn't good enough, so be it. I just needed to stay the course.

With the pressure of these false messages removed, my shaking hands and trembling voice improved. I learned how to give a better presentation and how to think like a doctor of internal medicine. With renewed confidence and some generous help and tutoring from others on the team, I passed the rotation. The key to a successful outcome was a change in my thinking.

INSIGHTS FROM THE SUBCONSCIOUS

Another aspect of depression that isn't necessarily tied to conscious thoughts or beliefs is sometimes called the *psychodynamic perspective*. Sigmund Freud and Carl Jung, among others, developed a psychodynamic approach to patients that centers on the process of storytelling and listening to get at the subconscious.

Our deep emotions match the entrenched stories we believe about ourselves. For some people, those stories are instrumental in keeping them depressed. Depression is rarely "for no reason." Very often, people are depressed because how their life has turned out doesn't line up with their deep yearnings, values, character, or hopes. Depression is often the result of a person's frustrated noble aspirations, even if it appears to be undesired and unattractive failure.

I realize this might sound counterintuitive. Depression is a debilitating condition. Why would anybody want to stay depressed?

My mentor David Burns loves to explore this question with what he calls a "magic button" question.[3] He'll say to the patient, "Imagine there's a magic button right here. If you push this button, your life circumstances won't change at all, but your depression will vanish. Do you want to push the button?"

Almost every patient immediately says, "Of course I'll push the button. That's why I'm here."

But then Dr. Burns will say something like, "I can think of a lot of good reasons why you might want to be depressed, and I wouldn't want to take that away from you, even if I could." Then he'll explore good reasons for holding on to depression.

For example, imagine that a mother comes in for treatment. She is estranged from her adult son because she feels she's been repeatedly wronged by him. Using Burns's technique, I might ask something like "Do you really want to feel happy in a situation where your son continues to be terrible to you? Remember, if you push the magic button, you'll be happy, but your son won't change how he acts toward you. There will be no consequences for him. He will basically get away with how he's treated you. Would you want that? Would that be acceptable to your sense of justice and fairness?"

Or consider a young man who failed to complete college because of his severe depression. As a result, he feels guilty and worthless. I might say, "If you push the magic button, your depression will be gone and you'll feel happy. You still won't have a college degree, and your crippling student loan debt will remain. Would you want to feel happy about failing? In other words, it seems that your sadness is connected to your having high personal standards and great ambition. Is that something you want to give up?"

This technique helps patients recognize that there are good reasons why they have the emotions they have. Their depression helps to demonstrate the value of these things. So in order to overcome their depression, they must be able to identify these subconscious blocks. They must become consciously aware of what is causing the resistance. When they become motivated, they are more likely to engage with therapy in a way that relieves their depression.

Even if you're not depressed, you may need, and benefit from, a similar clarification of your motivations.

There's a story in the New Testament about a time when Jesus approached a man who had been unable to walk for thirty-eight years. The man had been trying to heal himself, but without success. Jesus asked him a question that seems obvious, but isn't: "Do you want to get well?"[4]

Instead of answering the question, the man explained how hard he had tried and what he had done that hadn't worked. But the question still stood: "Do you want to get well?" Jesus knew that healing the man would change his life completely. He would have new responsibilities along with new opportunities—and even a new identity, as he would no longer define himself by his disability.

Moving toward the opposite of depression may begin by truly desiring the change we think we want. We need to ask ourselves whether complete healing—with all its results—is really what we want. If it is, we need to remove the barriers to healing.

COGNITION AS VISION

A devout friend once asked me whether it was possible to help people with depression by using verses from the Bible to assure them they are known and loved by God, and that God has a plan for their lives.

I appreciated my friend's intentions, but the trouble with depression is that it dims our ability to see the truth. So it might not matter how many hopeful and affirming Bible verses we share with others. Knowledge by itself is ineffective if the person is unwilling or unable to see the truth in it. In other words, the chief problem is not with *understanding* but with *vision*.

A related phenomenon occurs with anorexia. People with this eating disorder often think of themselves as fat even when their weight is dangerously low. It was long believed that this was a problem with their thinking—that is, the patients *see* themselves as thin in a mirror or photo but *think* they're fat. But in a clever and classic experiment, women with eating disorders were given an apparatus that worked like a carnival fun house mirror and were asked to adjust it to be "accurate." They consistently set it to where it would be if they were actually overweight. They didn't *think* they were fat; they "*saw*" they were fat.[5]

People with depression seem to have distorted emotional "vision." In the same way that an anorexic person cannot see that she is dangerously underweight, depressed patients sometimes cannot *see* the good things in their lives.

Depression not only affects one's perspective about the present, but like a weed planted in the present with roots stretching into the past and future, it strangles old happy memories and kills hopes and dreams for the future.

A depressed person has a hard time believing that any time in the past was happy. They either can't recall happy memories or they recolor them in the melancholy light of depression. Hopelessness, one of the key symptoms of depression, is partly created by this experience. Trying to encourage a depressed person by describing things getting better or being different can often lead to frustration. He or she may rigidly insist that any proposed good is actually not good or is not possible. To people in this state of mind, the most real reality is the depression, which eclipses all other possible realities.

Treatment for these symptoms may involve challenging the irrationality. In mild to moderate cases, this distorted vision can be challenged in therapy or even informal conversation.

I have also seen a person's vision of the truth suddenly return. I remember a patient I once treated using TMS. She had bravely struggled through cognitive therapy, challenging one cognitive distortion after another. She had worked hard in therapy, both in session and at home; it just never made a difference. The logic used in cognitive behavioral theory (CBT) seemed thin in comparison to the "visible" fact of her worthlessness. Then, halfway through a course of TMS, she told me, "It just clicked. I *saw* what my therapist has been saying all this time!"

Our team at Stanford found that one of the ways TMS works is by increasing the connection between the prefrontal cortex and the rest of the brain.[6] It may be that the patient for whom it finally clicked had been performing the cognitive exercise in the island of her rational thought, but it just wasn't connected, literally, to the rest of her brain.

How can we determine whether we're believing lies? How do we know if our perception is distorted? There are two main strategies.

The first is to assess whether a belief holds up to scrutiny by multiple senses or capacities. For example, the familiar pencil-in-water visual illusion is impossible to *see* differently. But if we take the pencil out of the water and look at it, or feel it with our hands, that will dispel our false impression that the pencil is bent.

The same thing works with false beliefs. Except with more severe cases of depression, patients are still able to logically analyze their own beliefs. "Is what I believe *true*?" "What evidence do I have that it's true?" "Is this consistent with my other beliefs?" Questions like these may help to sort things out.

Another strategy is to look at the situation from another person's perspective. Even if our own sensors are broken, it's highly unlikely that another person's sensors would also be broken in the same way. Friends can often tell us whether we're thinking rightly, or if a belief has no foundation. Sometimes even *imagining* what another person would say can help us come up with a good, rational response.

We'll soon put these strategies to work, but first we need to take a step back and look at some larger social and philosophical reasons why we may resist the idea of pursuing truth.

POISONS FATAL TO TRUTH

Two false *isms* that are pervasive in our culture are *determinism* and *subjectivism*. They aren't commonly talked about because they have become such a part of the social fabric, but they affect our beliefs about what is possible, and we must address them if we're at all interested in truth and how it relates to flourishing in life. To adapt a phrase from G. K. Chesterton, "There are thoughts that stop thought. Those are the only thoughts that ought to be stopped."[7]

Determinism is "the belief that we are not free to choose what we are like or how we behave, because these things are decided by our surroundings and other things over which we have no control."[8]

Subjectivism is "the theory that all knowledge and moral values are subjective [i.e., based on our own ideas or opinions] rather than based on truth that actually exists in the real world."[9]

I believe we have the capacity to look outside ourselves and see a world of truths, illumined by beams of reality that originate from God.

We can see that 2 + 2 = 4, or that A = A, or that the sky is blue, because God gives us the ability to see reflections of himself in his creation—in math, science, logic, and the physical world. I also believe we have at least some ability to choose truth over falsehood. But we can also choose to deceive ourselves and others through lies and deception. Determinism and subjectivism are the first falsehoods we must overcome if we want to eliminate other falsehoods in our lives. We have to believe it's objectively possible.

EMBRACING HELPLESSNESS

The extent to which we've been influenced by subjectivism and determinism may help to explain why we don't believe in truths that will help us move toward a better life for ourselves.[10]

Three main types of determinism work to undermine the concepts of free will and personal responsibility. The first is *psychological determinism*, which can be summed up in a statement by Sigmund Freud, who suggested that individual and personal influences shape an unconscious self that drives our decisions: "There is within you a deeply rooted belief in psychic freedom and choice, [and] this belief is quite unscientific, and . . . it must give ground before the claims of a determinism which governs even mental life."[11]

Another challenge is *social determinism*, the theory that it's not so much our *personal* psychology, but *collective* psychology, that matters—that is, we only act out what we have been conditioned to act out according to social interactions, and constructs, such as race, class, or gender, follow a socially determined script. A key advocate for social determinism was Karl Marx, with his focus on class struggle. Contemporary discussions focus more on race, but the message is similar: "You're only saying X because you're a Y." Alternatively, "You're not a Y, so you could never understand or speak to something that affects us." Marx said, "It is not the consciousness of men which determines their being, but on the contrary, their social being which determines their consciousness."[12]

A third variety is *biological determinism*, the theory that we lack free will because of something in our biology—sometimes said to be our genes, neurons, or neurotransmitters. From this perspective, a man is an alcoholic entirely because his father was an alcoholic; it's in his genes.

The error in these three models is not in their saying that we are influenced, or even highly influenced, by one or another of these factors. The error is when they become the sum total of what drives us. Each one subtly pulls us to believe we are not ultimately responsible for who we are or what we do. Consequently, there are things for which we are truly responsible that we instead blame on our parents or on society. After all, "that's just how I am."

Few people hold fully to any of these theories, but they're tempting excuses to avoid responsibility in tiny—and sometimes not-so-tiny—ways. Those tiny ways can add up year by year into a large bundle of denial.

Another opponent to truth is an extreme view of *authenticity* that has become surprisingly common. "This is the way I am, and I must express my true self."

On a certain level, it sounds admirable. But on closer inspection, it's just another excuse not to act responsibly.

THE LONE WOLF

I once had a patient who intended to be as *free* as possible. Though he'd had major depressive disorder for years and said he wanted to be rid of it, he declined medications and therapy because "that would be cheating."

I suggested an evidence-based self-help book to help him respond systematically to negative thoughts that might be contributing to his depression. He refused to consider it because "that would not be authentic." Such was his position on any ideas that might come from someone outside of himself. That included all learning, training, and coaching. He felt it was more "authentic," and thus more admirable, to teach himself a skill than to bend his neck to a coach or teacher. "I've always admired the lone wolf," he told me more than once.

Because this lone wolf wanted only his "own" ideas, and limited himself to his instincts and what he himself could learn, he remained trapped in his depression. "Authenticity" was a deep pit where the light of the wisdom of others was completely obscured.

This commitment first and foremost to one's supposed authenticity makes major depression harder to treat. Though few examples are as extreme as the "lone wolf," an increasing number of my patients are convinced that the dark or suicidal thoughts that correlate with their moods are their *true* desires and must be satisfied, come what may. All my talk of curing a disease or addressing cognitive distortions is an affront to their "true selves." Those who choose to serve their "authentic self" become beholden to an inner tyrant who convinces them that they are captain of their own ship and master of their own fate. It chills my soul to think of how many people have never even sought treatment and instead followed these dark whispers into death.

CORRECTIVE LENSES

If we're telling ourselves things that will determine our direction in life, it is important to evaluate those messages on the basis of truth.

Challenge your distorted thoughts

The first step is to write down thoughts you have about yourself—both positive and negative—and do your best to measure them against the truth. The tool we use in TEAM-CBT—the kind of therapy I most commonly practice—is the Daily Mood Log (DML). An example and description of the DML can be found in *The Feeling Good Handbook* by David Burns. The form (without the instructions) is also available online.[13]

But you don't need a special tool to get the benefit of this activity. With a sheet of paper in front of you, think about a moment recently when you had a difficult interaction. Write down the emotions you had at the time. Then write down the *thoughts* underlying those emotions.

Don't think only about *negative* emotions.[14] It's possible that *positive* emotions can also be a problem. For example, pride is often considered a good thing, but is it possible you have been thinking too highly of yourself?

Once you have written down things you believe about yourself or things you believe about a particularly difficult situation, evaluate those statements for truth. Sometimes, in simple cases, merely writing down your feelings and thoughts enables you to see where your line of thinking is wrong—and why—and what the truth is. But if the exercise isn't that easy (which is more than likely), there are a number of ways you can challenge your thoughts. My favorite comes from Jeffrey Schwartz, who advises people to consult their "Wise Advocate," which is his way of describing how to "take a third-person perspective on your first-person experience—to see yourself, and the way you interact with the world, as a trusted, caring, and dispassionate observer would see it."[15]

Imagine there is someone who knows you perfectly, loves you completely, and wants only what's best for you. What would that person say about the things you wrote down? Record the response you imagine that person would give. This is a safe way to get a loving and truthful perspective on your negative thoughts.[16]

Consider the following interaction: John has just been laid off by his company. After years of working hard and doing a good job, he just wasn't needed anymore.

If John were to do the Wise Advocate exercise, he would start by identifying his feelings: sadness, anger, anxiety, fear. Then he would write down the thoughts or self-talk that accompany those feelings—perhaps something like this: "I'm a worthless failure who will never be able to find success." The goal then is to identify what is false about that thought. To broaden your perspective, ask yourself what a loving person or a good friend would say about that negative thought. Consult your Wise Advocate.

Here's one possible response: "I'm a good worker who's experiencing hard times. Though I haven't been able to get where I wanted to yet, there's a good chance I will in the future."

As you complete the steps, identifying your feelings and their accompanying thoughts, reflect on whether your emotions have changed. If not, or if they've changed but incompletely, try the exercise again but with different arguments.

Enlist a friend's help

A step up from imagining what someone else might say about your thoughts is to work through the same exercise with a friend or loved one—someone with whom you're comfortable discussing your thoughts (or at least are able to). Other people are often better able to see into our blind spots. Even if they may not have a perfect perspective, a good friend may be able to tell you where you're deceiving yourself.

This may start as a single conversation; but if it goes well, consider making this type of conversation a regular part of your friendship.

Reflect on your speech

Telling the truth is hard. Lying is easy. Even "little white lies" are destructive—whether they're lies you tell others or lies you tell yourself. Start by trying to *identify* and *eliminate* conscious lies. Next, think about ways you've been subtly dishonest in your speech, and stop doing it. Once you've stopped actively deceiving yourself and others, or obscuring the truth through your words, it will become much easier to speak the positive truth about yourself, others, and the world.

Each evening, reflect on the words you've spoken that day and write down what comes to mind. Was your speech truthful and honest? If not, why not? In what ways have you engaged in deception? Why did you want the other person to believe something that was untrue, or not entirely true? What does that say about you and your beliefs?

This is a deep exercise. But if we are truthful in our thoughts and our words, even when we feel intense pressure to compromise the truth, we are on our way to living lives of honesty and integrity. That's all part of the good life. And even when we stumble with the truth, forgiveness is available to get us back on track.

HERO OF THE TRUTH

Refusing to seek after the truth—or sometimes, to even *want* to—is a sure-fire way to get stuck in depression or languishing. But you've come too far on the journey to the *opposite* of depression to turn back now. You're ready to make a habit of interrogating your own beliefs to determine whether they conform with what is true. And though this habit may not always flatter you or make you happy, it *will* lead to flourishing.

"Your feelings result from the messages you give yourself," says David Burns. "In fact, your thoughts often have much more to do with how you feel than what is actually happening in your life. . . . In contrast, you can learn to change the way you think about things, and you can also change your basic values and beliefs. And when you do, you will often experience profound and lasting changes in your mood, outlook, and productivity."[17]

Challenging your own thinking by putting away distorted thoughts and clinging to true ones will lead you to a better life. And who knows? Maybe you'll also persuade a few other people to set out on the journey to a life of flourishing.

STEPS TOWARD FLOURISHING

A flourishing life is one that celebrates the truth. To that end, we critically examine ourselves and our beliefs to find out what the truth actually is. We search our motivations for reasons we might be holding on to lies. We do what we can to clear our vision so that we can see clearly. We reject ideas—such as determinism—that undermine us and our community. We value truth over so-called authenticity.

12

RELATIONSHIPS: THE POWER OF TOGETHER

It is not good that the man should be alone.

GENESIS 2:18

Among all worldly things there is nothing which seems worthy to be preferred
to friendship. . . . It is what brings with it the greatest delight, to such an
extent that all that pleases is changed to weariness when friends are absent,
and all difficult things are made easy and as nothing by love.

THOMAS AQUINAS, *On Kingship*

Without friends, no one would choose to live,
even if he had all other goods.

ARISTOTLE, *Nicomachean Ethics*

Much of our understanding of the human brain and its response to drugs is based on rodent research. Rodents are relatively easy to keep in captivity, and their brains and physiology are similar to ours in many ways. They also behave in similar ways to humans, which can make them useful for modeling a disease. We can reliably get them to exhibit what we call "depressive-like behaviors," but we haven't yet figured out a way to ask a rat how it's actually feeling. Also, it isn't addiction per se when a rat seems unable to stop pressing a lever that delivers cocaine to its brain, but the rat's behavior reflects something that looks very familiar. These types of similarities have been used to legitimize the application of conclusions from rodent research to the human population.

But what if, despite all appearances, animal experiments don't approximate human behavior at all? What if the depressive-like and addictive-like behaviors are simply responses to the rodents' living conditions?

In the late 1970s, Canadian psychologist Bruce Alexander set out to test these questions in a series of studies that came to be known as Rat

Park. Alexander and his team kept one set of rats in standard laboratory conditions. These rats were caged, kept in isolation, and given little stimulation apart from their food and water. The experimental group, by contrast, had a wonderful assortment of open space, toys, and—perhaps most importantly—other rats with whom to socialize. After about two months, half the rats from each group were swapped into the opposite situation. Then the research team gave all the rats free access to morphine and measured how much they took.[1]

The results?

The rats who spent the entire experiment under standard laboratory conditions were the largest imbibers of the morphine and were quickly "addicted." They were followed by the rats that transferred into the lab from Rat Park, and then the rats that had started in the lab before moving out to Rat Park—though these rats tended toward the lowest concentration of morphine.

Meanwhile, the rats in Rat Park who had been engaged full-time in exploration, play, and breeding weren't really interested in morphine. Their use was dramatically lower.

In the world of neuroscience, a study from the 1970s is ancient history. But apart from that, it seemed to me there had been a strange lack of interest in this study for several decades.[2] Why? Was the relative silence in the face of these findings because so many scientists didn't want to face the implications? After all, the medications we prescribe every day assume the validity of experiments conducted on rodents under "standard laboratory conditions."

Did Rat Park undermine the foundations of modern psychiatry?

This question was on my mind at the time I welcomed a new crop of residents to a barbecue at my rented home. They had come from top medical schools all over the country and had just started at Stanford to specialize in psychiatry. I was also a resident, one year ahead of them. One of the students seemed particularly eager to skip the small talk. I shared what I had been reading, and the implications—which were nothing less than the undercutting of our specialty.

"If you want to understand addiction," I asked, "why study rats under 'standard laboratory conditions,' separated and confined in sterile, artificial environments? That's not how most people live!"

He was unperturbed, and what he said floored me.

"I'm not interested in studying happy, healthy rats, just like I'm not interested in studying happy, healthy humans. *Of course* addiction depends on social isolation in rats as it does in humans. *Of course* you can't get a rat to compulsively take a drug if they have other meaningful things to do. That's the point."

I realized he was right. Addiction and depression don't happen equally to the relationally well connected and the disconnected. If you want to study cancer, you have to give rats toxic chemicals or radiation until they get cancer. If you want them to act depressed, you isolate them. Perhaps, then, the main "toxic chemical" of mental health is social isolation.

So, if we're interested in experiencing the opposite of depression, we had better pay attention to our relational well-being.

AN UNNATURAL STATE

Relationships are critical to the health and flourishing of a gregarious species such as *Homo sapiens*. Like other primates, humans live and work in groups. Unlike other primates, we also have capacities to relate to others that go far beyond those of the rest of the animal kingdom. We have the ability to treat one another with fairness or injustice; we can show malice or love. Yet, it remains true, as Aristotle said, that "man is by nature a social animal."[3]

A team of researchers looked at how isolation affected physical health. By pooling the results of a series of studies that included a total of seventy-seven thousand people, the group found that loneliness increases the risk of death by 22 percent.[4] Being lonely seems to be as bad for your health as is obesity.[5]

Loneliness is even worse for your soul. In the course of this book, I've discussed various things that are good and bad for your mental health. Now we come to what may be the greatest single "toxin" for mental health.

I always knew that loneliness was a cause (and consequence) of depression, but I was astonished when I learned the magnitude of the effect.

Researchers in Switzerland looked at more than twelve thousand people in the general population to assess the relative impact of various aspects of social connection.[6] Most measures showed some impact. For example, people who answered *yes* to the question, "Do you ever miss having someone to talk to about really personal problems?" were 40 percent more likely to have major depression. However, a single item asking how often a respondent felt lonely (never, sometimes, quite often, very often) showed an impact that was off the charts. Those who answered "quite often" or "very often" were 897 percent more likely to have depression, and those who answered "sometimes" were 168 percent more likely. It was also interesting that objective time spent with others was *not* correlated with depression. This implies that it's not merely being physically present with other people, but *feeling* connected to them that matters. The Swiss study was a cross-sectional study, looking at data gathered at a single point of time or over a short period; other studies looking at the same measures over time found large but not gigantic effects.[7] It's also likely that depression itself blocks the feeling of connection with others. It seems like a vicious cycle: Feelings of loneliness cause depression, and depression causes feelings of loneliness.

Loneliness can be extremely painful. And like all pain, it's a signal to which we must respond. For most of our existence, humans wouldn't survive long outside of a tight-knit social group. Being alone meant certain death. As surely as cold drives us to shelter and hunger drives us to food, the pain of loneliness drives us to connect with others.

Unfortunately, in today's society, it isn't always easy to connect. Our communities, friendships, and families have been disintegrating for a long time now.

A LONELY ROAD

Depression robs a person of much that would otherwise be the foundation for relationships. It saps the energy needed to go out and be with others. The sadness and pain of social slights, miscommunication, and misunderstandings are magnified. Guilt-ridden ruminations whirl in the minds of the depressed before, during, and after even casual social inter-actions, making the stakes seem quite high (and thus exhausting). Worst of all, the feelings of warmth and connection with others are turned down to low or completely extinguished. Especially for those who believe that emo-tions define a relationship (rather than, for example, commitment), this may be the most devastating of all depressive symptoms.

Not wanting to spend time with others leads to a spiral of isolation—making the person feel even more depressed and even less interested in spending time with others.

To make matters worse, the past three decades have been catastrophic for American friendships. The number of people who have no friends at all doubled between 1990 to 2003, and then increased another sixfold from 2003 to 2021 (from 1 percent to 2 percent, to 12 percent). The number of well-connected people, who have a multitude of friends and hold the fabric of society together, dropped from 33 percent of the population in 1990 to 27 percent in 2003 to 13 percent in 2021. Also, the number of people reporting they have a best friend dropped 16 percent over the same period.[8]

In 1990, 75 percent of Americans were satisfied with the number of friends they had. This number remained stable through 2003 (73 percent).[9] By 2021, it had declined to 51 percent.[10]

Depressed or not, we're suffering relationally. We're lonely and isolated. Somehow we've lost the knack for friendship with one another.

And when it comes to family, the situation is even more dire.

PATEL'S BOMBSHELL

Grand Rounds at Stanford is a weekly event at which a scholar delivers a lecture to the entire psychiatry department. Normally, there are plenty of empty seats as the esteemed professors, residents, and medical students go on with their busy schedules. On this particular occasion, however, everybody seemed to have found the time to take in the presentation by Vikram Patel of Harvard, a world-renowned psychiatrist whose work focuses on global men-tal health. He had exciting new data to share. There was standing room only.

This would not be a typical lecture.

Typically, we would only see such a high level of participation when a famous biological psychiatrist was scheduled. Dr. Patel's topic was psychotherapy.

Typically, the research under discussion is based in the United States. In fact, psychology literature has been described by some as too WEIRD—Western, Educated, Industrialized, Rich, Democratic—to be broadly relevant to the human condition.[11] On this day, the treatment population under review was in rural India.

Typically, psychotherapy is practiced exclusively in a highly controlled setting, namely the therapist's office. This study, however, had been done in the wildly varied and uncertain conditions of the homes of Patel's patients.

Typically, psychotherapy is done in a population that believes in the diagnosis of clinical depression. Few people in rural India believed that "clinical depression" was the best explanation.

It was a perfect storm for failure, and we all knew it.

After describing the setup of the psychotherapy he had done, Dr. Patel clicked to the slide showing the results.

Surely that's a mistake, those familiar with the literature were no doubt thinking in unison. The impact of the treatment was astronomical!

Bruce Arnow—perhaps the most experienced psychotherapy researcher at Stanford—asked the question we all wanted to ask: "Vikram, how did you get these numbers? This is incredible!"

"We involve the family," Dr. Patel replied.

He said he found rather odd the view in the West that depression is an individual problem in the brain of one person, without consideration of the family. In his program, the community health workers involved spouses and parents, siblings and children, teaching them how to better understand depression and support the depressed person. Treatment involved changes not only in the thinking of the depressed person, but in the other family members as well.

Drawing on the strength of the family was what made this psychotherapy approach so successful. Family—what a powerful thing!

THE STATE OF THE FAMILY

The family is where we learn most of what we learn. It is difficult to overstate the importance of family relationships in our development. The family is where we first learn just about everything worth learning: justice, courage, kindness, fairness, hard work, and love. Early psychiatrists ascribed enormous significance to the role of the mother specifically, but clearly we are heavily influenced by both parents, as well as by other members of the family. For example, looking across twenty-nine studies and fourteen thousand participants, both parents influence a child's prosocial (e.g., kind, generous) behavior.[12]

Getting things right at home is pivotal to successful long-term outcomes. As discussed in an earlier chapter, a family that has successfully protected a child from adverse childhood experiences such as violence, abuse, or neglect has gone a long way toward helping that child grow up psychologically healthy. Beyond that, the family is also the place where values and attitudes are shaped. Depression can interrupt this connection; the depressed person may fail to play their role in the family as parent, sibling, or child. The family system adjusts and finds a new semi-stable equilibrium. A family has a certain inertia and gravity, and thus can either contribute to or protect against a depressive episode.

Unfortunately, the American family isn't doing very well lately. In the United States, the number of children growing up with two parents in the home has dropped from 88 percent in 1960 to 70 percent in 2022.[13] Marriage rates have dropped precipitously from 80 per 1,000 unmarried people in 1960 to 33.2 in 2019.[14] While the divorce rate seems to have peaked in 1980, about two thousand marriages end in divorce every day. And as often happens, all these indicators disproportionately affect the poor.

Here at the heart of human relationships (marriage and the family), human connection is visibly faltering. It's a sign of a bigger problem of weak relationships in our society, but society can only change if individuals change. So if relationships are a problem in your life, what can you do about it?

BUILD BRIDGES

A top subject that people talk about with their psychotherapists is relationships—friendships, family relationships, romantic relationships, and more. You may need professional help with your more problematic relationship conundrums, but meanwhile there are things you can do to build up your relationships. The key principle is to do small things that are within your power to do.

Call your mom

Yes, I'm serious. Call your mom if it's at all possible. If not her, then call another family member or close friend you haven't kept in touch with as well as you should. Now, if you're in active conflict with someone, he or she might not be the best candidate for this exercise right now. But I bet there's someone you've simply neglected, possibly because you've been busy. The other person might be lonely and missing you, just as you may be missing him or her. Get back in touch now.

Remember, your phone is good for more than tracking social media. It also happens to be an excellent tool for renewing relationships that matter to you. Send a nice text message to someone you haven't talked to in a while. Better yet, make it a phone call. Reassure the other person that you still care. Get caught up on the action in each other's lives. Provide encouragement when the other person is hurting.

Write a gratitude letter

One of the most potent, and simple, interventions in the history of psychology is expressing gratitude in the form of a letter. The following exercise, researched by psychologist Martin Seligman's group, produces positive feelings, not only at the moment, but even a month later.[15]

Think of a person who has helped you in some way, but whom you have not adequately thanked. Ideally, it will be someone you can see in person, not a friend who lives in another part of the world. Perhaps it's a mentor who has invested time in you. Or your sponsor in a recovery group. Maybe it's a parent. Write a letter expressing why you are grateful for that person.

Once you've completed the letter, ask to meet with the person—but don't explain why in advance. This should create some intrigue! When you're together, say that you'd like to read a letter you've written, and without interruption. Read the letter aloud, and then give it to the person to keep.

This simple exercise can spark powerful positive emotions and draw you closer to your friend or family member.

Perfect your reconciliation

In many cases, our relationships are not in active conflict or estrangement, but they're not perfectly reconciled either. For example, you may not have any deep-seated animosity toward a sibling, but there was a disagreement, both of you were stubborn about it, and still to this day the relationship isn't quite right. Reflect on your relationships and see whether some of them stick out as being impaired.

Usually we know when a relationship isn't right. We feel a coolness or a distance, even if someone watching our interaction with our friend wouldn't notice anything out of the ordinary. It's the lingering friction we need to deal with.

If a relationship is not harmonious, you may need to apologize for your part in upsetting the applecart. This may inspire the other person to apologize as well. And that may be all that is necessary to restore the relationship. But even if you apologize and the other person doesn't, you at least made an effort to heal the relationship. Just make sure you actually apologize for what you have said or done rather than using the "apology" as an opportunity to levy accusations. It's easy to approach conciliatory conversations in bad faith, so be careful how you practice this. In some cases, you may need professional help or intervention. We'll get to that a bit later.

Ask to get closer

If you are lonely and feel that you don't have enough friends, ask yourself, *Who are the people I want to be closer to? What can I do to be closer to those people?* Perhaps you have an acquaintance who you think could be a friend, or a friend with whom you'd like to be closer. Ask to get together and then share your thoughts with with him or her.

Some of these initial conversations may feel awkward at first. Yet when you take the initiative to move a relationship to the next level, the other person will usually appreciate it.

Keep it simple and low key, but ask for a regular time to get together, even if it's just for coffee once a week—or every other week. If the person isn't local, maybe it's a weekly phone call. Consistency goes a long way toward cultivating a friendship. You can build something quite remarkable with even just an hour a week with someone.

Join a group

This is the most straightforward solution, but it's the most awkward for many people. It's also one of the most potent interventions in the book. We are heavily influenced by our groups, and most of us have the luxury of picking groups we'd like to join.

Think of a group of people you want to become more like. Maybe it's people who are close to God; consider attending church (or joining a small group). Maybe it's people who are pursuing recovery from an addiction you share; consider joining a twelve-step group such as AA. Maybe you'd like to get better at a skill or hobby; look for a group or a class or a club. Perhaps you'd like to become more generous or helpful, or offer a skill that others need; joining a group of volunteers may be just right for you. If you can't find a group that already exists, maybe you're in a position to create a new one.

One key to group cohesion is consistency. Whatever you do, make it a regular part of your weekly or monthly routine. The friendships you form will influence you in deep ways. And you'll have the opportunity to get outside of yourself and share your knowledge, expertise, and perspective with others.

Get professional help

Sometimes relationships can be strained beyond the point where talking it out one-on-one will work. You may want to engage a professional counselor or mediator to help. For some people, it may be a pastor or priest. For others, it may be a special type of therapist.

If the conflict or misunderstanding is within your family, you'll probably want to seek out a family therapist. Family therapy can also help people who are not in conflict but just want to get closer.

Typically, when a person is recovering from depression, he or she is accustomed to being seen as the patient, or what we sometimes call *the identified patient*. A family may wrongly believe that their problems are purely because the identified patient has been so depressed. However, family therapy often frames the reality that the family, as an emergent entity, is not as flourishing as it could be. Family dynamics may need to change, to account for everyone's individual personality, strengths, and weaknesses. Sometimes, family therapy is a breath of fresh air for a person who has been in individual therapy for a long time.

Couples therapy can help romantic or marital partnerships resolve conflict and restore the intimacy, closeness, or depth of relationship that may have been lost. Or maybe it can help couples learn new aspects of growing together in a loving relationship.

In certain situations, particularly when there are financial or material stakes involved, a professional mediator can help partners or associates move toward reconciliation.

Whatever sort of help you seek, it's a major accomplishment to bring peace where there has been no peace. Initiating that conversation can be humbling, but also amazingly productive and rewarding. Pursuing reconciliation is a courageous step toward a life of flourishing.

LOVE GIVES

Love is the basis for human relationships. But what is the hallmark of love? For many, it is the happiness we can derive from it. Jesus had a radical view of love that can revolutionize and restore our relationships regardless of our system of faith. He said, "There is no greater love than to lay down one's life for one's friends."[16] The hallmark of love is self-sacrifice. It's about *giving*, not taking.

People in the throes of depression have trouble thinking beyond themselves. When they reach out to family and friends for help, they can seem needy and draining. Depressed people can feel that their relationships are about taking, not giving. Often this isn't true at all and is just a distorted view from their depression. But in those cases where there's a kernel of truth to it, it isn't selfishness. It's usually the result of their condition.

As you move further away from depression, you can begin to look more to the needs of others. You can be there for a spouse who is feeling defeated at work. You can notice, and respond, when a teenage child is developing feelings of self-loathing. You can comfort a friend whose parent is dying.

The paradox of self-sacrificial love is that, in giving it away—in putting the interests of others before your own—your life takes on a greater richness and purpose than it would if you remained passive or isolated, or pursued relationships for selfish gain.

STEPS TOWARD FLOURISHING

Living the good life means loving deeply. We pursue and maintain deep and intimate relationships with our family, friends, and community. We make time for those around us, and we show our love for them. We *learn by doing* what it means to love the people around us and how we must change to love them better.

13

HOPE: THE THING WITH FEATHERS

"Hope" is the thing with feathers—
That perches in the soul—
And sings the tune without the words—
And never stops—at all.
EMILY DICKINSON

Where there is no vision, the people perish.
PROVERBS 29:18, KJV

The story of humanity is a story of hopes and dreams—some that come to fruition, that pay off, that advance the lives of individuals, families, communities, and cultures to yet another pinnacle of human progress; others that are brought to ruin, to nothing, to the pit of depression.

Hope ascends and hopes are dashed. That is the human condition. It is a familiar pattern in our lives. We hope to have a challenging and rewarding career. We dream of a marriage built on trust and intimacy that doesn't lose its spark. We want our kids to grow up happy and to find fulfillment in their own hopes and dreams. All nice ideas, but no one has these things turn out the way they want all the time. Some of us have had our hopes dashed so brutally at times in the past that we're still reeling.

Is hope, then, merely optimistic self-delusion?

What part does hope play in living the good life?

Hope itself is a necessary motivation in the movement away from depression toward the life we want. It's the powerful magnet that draws us forward from the present into the unknown possibilities that lie ahead. We may need to purify our hopes. We may realize that what we once desired is but a shadow of something still greater. But we must be able to imagine a good and meaningful future for ourselves if we are to flourish.

CHANGING BARELY HOPEFUL'S MIND

As a psychiatrist, I'm concerned with the quality of hope in my patients. Hope is such a critical part of mental health, and it's something that is often impaired in depression.

Sometimes hopelessness has a basis in reality, such as when a person's life savings are stolen in a scam, a business goes bankrupt, or a long-standing relationship falls apart. We don't have to be struggling with depression for our view of the future to grow dark in situations like these.

Sometimes, though, the sense of hopelessness gets so bad that it drifts toward delusion. In depression, people can begin to imagine that the circumstances in their lives are unchangeable and irredeemable. They think that the ebbs and flows typical in most illnesses will not apply to them. That is, even if they've seen their depression go through phases when it was better, they don't think that applies to their future—it's all going to be bad. Their story simply feels like it's over, and there's nothing that can be done about it.

Whether we've been diagnosed with depression or not, hopelessness can be a challenge for all of us. It might even be considered a silent pandemic afflicting the human spirit in the twenty-first century. With ongoing conflicts, both interpersonal and international; with threats, real and imagined, all around us; with the uncertainty of the future looming ever larger, we live in a time when our hopes and dreams can feel small, constricted, or nonexistent. We should have a robust capacity for hope, but instead our hope muscle is atrophied. And if you think this kind of attitude doesn't affect outcomes for the future, think again.

To assess the role of hope in determining health and well-being outcomes in the future—that is, the *consequences* of hope—a team of researchers undertook a massive study of older adults in 2020.[1] What was fascinating is that, after accounting for all other factors, responses to four simple statements predicted how people would fare several years into the future.

1. "I feel it is impossible for me to reach the goals that I would like to strive for."
2. "I don't expect to get what I really want."
3. "The future seems hopeless to me and I can't believe that things are changing for the better."
4. "There's no use in really trying to get something I want, because I probably won't get it."

The researchers divided people into three equal groups, with low, medium, and high levels of hope. For the sake of illustration, imagine these groups as people named Barely Hopeful, Quite Hopeful, and Super Hopeful. One bit of good news at the outset was that even Barely Hopeful, the least hopeful of the trio, slightly disagreed with all four statements about hopelessness; that's why he's not called Totally Hopeless. Quite Hopeful and Super Hopeful were both more vigorous in their disagreement with the statements.

For our purposes, the most important finding is that the chance of escaping depression tracks closely with one's degree of hope. Compared to Barely Hopeful, Quite Hopeful was 26 percent less likely to become depressed, and Super Hopeful was 43 percent less likely. Perhaps even more surprising was that Super Hopeful was also 16 percent less likely to *die*, and 12 percent less likely to develop cancer, during the follow-up period.

What we do about our tendency to hope too little may say everything about what our future will look like. The solution is *not* to ignore the future and retreat into the present.

THE DANGER OF NOW

Popular psychology and spiritual paths often recommend staying in the "Now." Spiritual teacher Eckhart Tolle, in *The Power of Now*, tells us, "Realize deeply that the present moment is all you ever have. Make the Now the primary focus of your life."[2]

Tolle and others offer an extreme solution to the problems of the past and future: Cut them off. Don't worry about the future. Don't ruminate on the past. Live in the present moment.

I realize that these teachers are emphasizing self-empowerment in their idolizing of the present, but perhaps because of my clinical experience, I see the danger in this perspective.

Though recurrent rumination on past failures is common in moderate depression, when depression gets particularly bad, the ruminations sometimes fade into a fixed, restated belief about unworthiness. Like a virus that infects our memories and hopes, depression begins to rewrite both past and future to make them uniform. The Now becomes a trap.

On several occasions, I've seen patients I've treated for years relapse into depression and begin to rewrite our shared memories. These patients will often describe how long the depression has lasted and how bad things were at specific points in the past. Sometimes, with their permission, I share my treatment notes with them from those previous sessions. After seeing their own written answers to survey questions, and reading direct quotes I transcribed from past sessions, they usually relent. But only *usually*.

In the most serious cases, *Now* is all that depressed people have—and Now is horrifying for them. And herein lies a lesson for all of us. When the Now is corrupted, it cannot be helped by staying put. We have to do whatever we can to enter a better future.

In the film *Back to the Future*, Marty McFly uses a time machine powered by a "flux capacitor" to go back in time to make the future (his present) a better place. It's a great story that encourages us to think about the consequences of our actions. But consider this: As humans, we all have a built-in time machine. Your imagination is your flux capacitor. You can time-travel to a hoped-for future and then travel back to the present to work toward it, or imagine a future nightmare and identify how you are contributing to its development.

In extreme cases, the capacity for imagination itself is absent, and some degree of recovery or depression treatment is necessary before any progress can be made. For most of us, though, the future is something we can imagine, and the act of imagining a good future is a critical part of the flourishing life. It's also something we spend far too little time doing.

Like a group of miners trapped in a deep, dark pit, the human imagination can run ahead and try various passages of escape. If the imagination locates a way out of the mine, it can open the door and let light in, which will help the rest of the miners find their way out, though they may be far away and the light a dim, distant flicker. Often, the best way out of a terrible Now is to move toward a hopeful future.

As with faith, however, our hope is only as valid as its *object*. Having an abstract hope is no more reliable than trusting in the Now. The quality of what we're hoping *for* may determine the quality of our future.

IT DOESN'T TAKE MUCH

You may be concerned that you have a hard time imagining a wonderful future. Your church or your company may not have a shot at transforming the world for the better in the next few years. The thing I've observed is that it doesn't take much. A little bit of hope goes a very long way.

Many of my patients work for large tech companies such as Google, Facebook, Apple, and Intel, not to mention innumerable medium and small companies. I remember one in particular who came to me for help with social anxiety. Kevin, who was in his late twenties, came to his intake session straight from work, wearing a T-shirt, jeans, and sneakers—just a Patagonia sweater-vest short of the full Silicon Valley uniform.

Trying to get a job at one of the big tech companies is not unlike applying to Harvard. In fact, it might be tougher—Harvard's acceptance rate hovers around 5 percent, whereas Facebook's is rumored to be 3 percent.[3] People from all over the world compete to be allowed to code for companies in Silicon Valley. Kevin had done it. I asked about his work background and found that he came from the Midwest and had done very well at his former job before landing a spot at a top social media company. Kevin was among the tiny fraction of the tech *winners*, and he knew it.

So if that wasn't the root of his problem, I would have to dig deeper.

Sometimes what people call "social anxiety" is really job dissatisfaction in disguise. I asked Kevin how he liked his job.

"I love it."

The gusto with which he replied assured me he was telling the truth. But even if dissatisfaction wasn't the source of Kevin's social anxiety, I knew it might hold a clue. So I asked him to tell me more.

"I love working on helping to build the future of human connection,"

Kevin said, echoing his company's statements. (It's not about selling ads—it's about connecting people!) He *believed in* their vision and the future they were designing. It gave him *hope* for the future. As with any high-pressure job, he endured some hard things, but he not only tolerated his boss, the hours, the pressure, and the challenges—he *loved* it all. He came to me for help with a focused problem, but overall he was doing quite well because he believed he was contributing to solving one of the thorniest problems of human existence in one of the few places on earth (in his mind) likely to make a difference.

Many overworked people with a similar high-pressure job, cynical about the world and their role in it, would come to me with depression. Kevin was not depressed. His hope, among other things, protected him against depression. Over time, I was able to help him with his social anxiety, and he was able to go back to a job he loved, building a future he was excited about.

I chose this example because it shows how it doesn't take much for people to find something they believe makes the future worthwhile. For some, even the vision statement of a much-maligned corporation is enough to give great satisfaction to the psychological need for hope.

As you seek a worthwhile object for your hope, I encourage you to think hard about the inherent value of that object. But don't worry about whether you'll be able to find something worth giving yourself to. There are many options, big and small, and some will fit your makeup and capabilities. Seek out a vision that inspires you.

WRITING YOUR IDEAL FUTURE

Every once in a while, I read something in the scholarly literature—in psychology or a related discipline—that I have to go over a few times before I'll believe it. The reported impact of a tested treatment is so far beyond my expectations that I must read the article again to make sure I haven't misunderstood. Memorably, that happened one time with a research article about how to help underperforming students. The researchers had found a way to close the gender gap in student performance by 98 percent, and the ethnicity gap in the same area by 93 percent, using an exercise that took just a few hours to complete.[4]

How is that possible?

By getting the students "to reflect on their general, higher-order life goals"[5]—for example, "What do you hope to achieve in your life and what kind of person do you want to be?"[6]—and then to type out their ideal future (along with a plan to get there), using a detailed and structured guide. Then the researchers followed up to see how the exercise affected the subjects over the next several years. The experience was life-changing for many of the students, resulting in those 98 percent and 93 percent gains over the first two years that I found so incredible.

It's likely that this intervention had a remarkable and long-lasting impact because it inspired an epiphany among these students who were not doing well in school: *I can change my future by imagining it and setting goals.* That was an insight that thousands of hours of parenting, public schooling, TV, social media, and peer interactions apparently had not inspired. But writing—and imagining—did.

As we think about the role of hope in finding a better life for ourselves, this study offers a big takeaway: Imagining a good future, and taking time to plan for it, is a very important part of the present. You can do exactly what the test subjects did: Write down ways in which your life could be better in the future, and then devise ways in which you can change to make your desired outcome more likely.

This approach is also useful in other ways. If you're in a romantic relationship, spend time talking with your partner about what you'd like your future together to be like. If you're in your working years, write about what you want the future of your career to look like. Think, pray, meditate, discuss, and—without fail—*write* about the future.

Before I give you some guidance on how to do this, one word of caution: Imagining a distant future can be wonderful, but that imagined future is naturally ephemeral, so we must hold our predictions lightly. We don't know what will happen from one day to the next. Making plans about the foreseeable future is a good exercise, but it would be foolish to become arrogant or prideful about what we believe the future will hold.

Because the future, by its very nature, is uncertain, it isn't necessary to have a perfect plan—just some reasonable and attainable goals. Your plan may ultimately disappoint you, but perhaps something greater will emerge from that vision and you can adjust your hope accordingly. It will never be perfect, but what's important is to have a compelling, hope-filled vision of what you are building toward—a better life, better family, better community, better company, better outcomes.

PATHWAY TO THE FUTURE

The how-to for this chapter involves picturing an ideal future for yourself and for the world, and then describing a pathway to get there. For those who want to go into more depth, consider the Future Authoring module of the online Self Authoring program (www.selfauthoring.com).

Imagine your ideal future

Start by asking yourself what you want your future to look like in specific areas of your life. On your device or (better yet) with pen and paper, answer the following questions, along with any similar questions you think of on your own. As you're writing, imagine fulfilling your goals in a specific and not-too-distant future—say, five years, though you can choose a shorter or longer time period for this imaginative exercise. The point is not to answer these questions about an unspecified "someday." You want to be able to picture a desirable outcome within a specific, foreseeable future.

- What would be my ideal career?
- What are some hobbies or activities I would enjoy?
- What would the ideal family life be like for me?
- What would the best romantic life be like?
- What about an ideal spiritual or religious life?
- What about friendships?
- What would my ideal community or civic life look like?

You may have already thought about some of these things as you've read the preceding chapters. That's great. Build upon that, and get more specific as you answer these questions in writing.

Then prepare to put it all together.

Turn it into a story

Once you've written down your ideals in the different areas of your life, write a narrative of what your ideal life would look like if everything within your control went well. This doesn't have to be a great piece of writing, and it doesn't have to be long. Focus on creating an overall narrative that portrays what life will be like for you when you're pursuing the things you really want. Putting it in story form gives you an image of the future to pursue.

Create measurable goals

After you have thoroughly imagined—and put in writing—your desired future, break it down into steps to create a pathway to get there. Start with a handful of goals that are most important to you. What intermediate steps are required to achieve those individual goals? Also, how will you know if you're making progress toward those goals? The best goals will be measurable and have a timeline; with any goal, you want to be able to know whether or not you were successful.

Are you sensing greater clarity? Are you feeling the peace and excitement that come with clarity? Take those first steps. It could change your life.

It isn't the writing itself that makes the difference. What's so powerful is the mindset that the writing process unlocks. By imagining a desired future, you can map a pathway from your present situation to where you want to be.

You may have been held back in the past by weak motivation—lack of hope or vision. But now you're well on your way to the opposite of depression. This exercise is something you can do, even if all the imagining feels a little like science fiction.

ONCE UPON A ROCKET

On September 12, 1962, John F. Kennedy committed the United States to the goal of reaching the moon within the decade. He said, "We set sail on this new sea because there is new knowledge to be gained, and new rights to be won, and they must be won and used for the progress of all people."[7] The president's visionary words sparked another kind of hope—an organizing story that inspired countless people, from schoolchildren to engineers, to daydream, color, sketch, play, design, and build toward space.

Four years after Kennedy's famous address, another visionary announced a perhaps more famous and more ambitious mission—"to explore strange new worlds. To seek out new life and new civilizations. To boldly go where no man has gone before!" The visionary was Gene Roddenberry, the mission was that of the United Federation of Planets, and the commissioned ship was the starship USS *Enterprise*.

By the time I came along, the Star Trek franchise had relaunched as *The Next Generation*. I loved it. It was a wonderful show built on the optimism of the era from which it emerged and that it helped shape. It showed how a group of virtuous and adventurous individuals were able to overcome new challenges and threats. They lived by egalitarian rules, and anyone, whether black or white, Vulcan or Klingon, could rise up the ranks according to merit. Material needs had been eliminated with the advancement of technology. No one went hungry. Humanity wasn't fighting with itself; world peace had been accomplished. The mission now was about undertaking further exploration and spreading peace. The fantastical setting was part of the show's ability to stretch the imagination.

Envisioning outer space as a theater for the ongoing human saga, with science as our chief enterprise, continues to inspire many. Elon Musk, one of the richest men in the world, has invested heavily in pursuit of this vision.

I bring up *Star Trek* because it is a generally good and accessible example of the human capacity for hope. If you're inclined to say, "Well, yes, but it's science fiction," let me ask you: Do you have a vision of the future as inspiring as the bridge of the USS *Enterprise*? Can you define a mission more exciting than "to boldly go where no one has gone before"? For Christians who are looking ahead to life beyond the grave, what exactly do you think heaven or the Resurrection will be like? For those with an artistic or storytelling inclination, can you imagine a future more to be desired than *Star Trek*'s?

Science fiction can do for the human mind what prophecy does for the religious: offer a vision of a future worth striving for. Imagining an interstellar future for humanity is one example of a future that is better than most pessimistic alternatives (e.g., we all die because of global warming), not having an imagined future for our species at all, or giving up hope of making the planet a habitable, peaceful place—even temporarily.

Taking inspiration from science fiction, let's try another writing exercise to expand our capacity for hope.

WORLD BUILDING

You've already written about your ideal personal future. Now try to imagine an ideal future for something beyond yourself. Perhaps it's your family. Your community. Your church. Your company. The nonprofit where you volunteer. Your political party. Your nation.

Part of what has made Amazon so successful can be attributed to the company's "working backward method" of product development. The first thing they do when thinking of a new product is to write a press release for it.[8] The basic idea is that if we can't get excited about the press release for the product we want to create, then it's probably not worth creating the product.

I'm not asking you to write an actual press release, but I think it would be helpful for you to put in writing your imagined better future for a group or organization you care about.

With that organization in view, describe its role in a world that would be substantially better than the world we currently live in. Next, think through some ways that you could personally contribute to that hoped-for future. I realize that imagining something doesn't necessarily make it so, but expanding your imagination will open your mind to possibilities you might not have considered otherwise.

Perhaps you'd like to get even more creative here and write a short story about this imagined future. What are some things that are part of that future world? It could be a near-term or long-term story. What are some things we can work toward? What are some things we should avoid? What new possibilities can we explore?

Now think about the present. Are your current activities in line with what you want the future to be? Are you preparing for the world that's coming? Are you helping to bring it about? Are you preparing your family?

FUTURE NOW

Sometimes, predictions of a better future are exactly what we need to give us hope *now*. In the Judeo-Christian context, hope goes beyond an individual's imagination. The future involves more than simply one person's successful journey of self-discovery. In the Hebrew Scriptures, the pictures of hope center on God's glorious future of the family-become-nation Israel. In the Christian New Testament, hope focuses on God's plan for all people. When we're depressed, or just feeling down, the Bible's pictures of a beautiful future are like a rope lowered into the pit to pull us out. Here are a few of my personal favorites:

> They shall beat their swords into plowshares,
>   and their spears into pruning hooks;
> nation shall not lift up sword against nation,
>   neither shall they learn war anymore;
> but they shall sit every man under his vine and under his fig tree,
>   and no one shall make them afraid.
> MICAH 4:3-4

> Old men and old women shall again sit in the streets of Jerusalem, each with staff in hand because of great age. And the streets of the city shall be full of boys and girls playing in its streets.
> ZECHARIAH 8:4-5

> The ransomed of the LORD shall return
>   and come to Zion with singing;
> everlasting joy shall be upon their heads;
>   they shall obtain gladness and joy,
>   and sorrow and sighing shall flee away.
> ISAIAH 51:11

He will wipe away every tear from their eyes, and death shall be no more, neither shall there be mourning, nor crying, nor pain anymore, for the former things have passed away.

REVELATION 21:4

These pictures are images we can set our eyes on and work toward. We can meditate on these passages, or imagine how they might have been partially fulfilled. It also helps us think about what things are temporary and what are permanent. We can work for peace in the world, stable food supplies and secure property, long-lived elders, playful children, safe streets, unity among all races and nations, and comfort for those who mourn, eliminating causes of pain where we can.

This is how hope can be a virtue and not merely a feeling. Christians look forward to the happy ending, despite the current darkness. Fortunately, we are empowered by the Holy Spirit to live our lives in light of heaven's ultimate victory over sin and death.

STEPS TOWARD FLOURISHING

The opposite of depression is a world filled with hope, regardless of our circumstances. By envisioning our ideal future and working to bring it to fruition, we grow and develop and make the world a better place. We resist the temptation to despair, and focus our attention on moving forward wherever we can.

14

BEAUTY: THE ELEVATOR OF CONSCIOUSNESS

The defining feature of a major depression is loss of pleasure . . .
whose characteristic manifestation is an inability to appreciate sunsets.
ROBERT M. SAPOLSKY, *Why Zebras Don't Get Ulcers*

Ashley came to see me when she was in her forties. She was depressed, and I asked about her history. Through tears, she told me about being sexually abused by her sister when she was a child. Throughout her growing-up years, the shame was unbearable. Despair and self-loathing had consumed Ashley. She had begun thinking about suicide.

I asked whether she had ever attempted suicide. She told me about a time when she was twenty-one. While at home with her family, she found her father's revolver, loaded it, and sat on the edge of the bed, preparing to shoot herself. Before she could pull the trigger, she asked herself, *Are there any reasons not to do this?* In her mind, two reasons remained.

The first was a fear of hell. She thought suicide might earn her a place there—though, to be honest, she wasn't sure she was the kind of person who would escape it either way.

The second reason held more weight for her in the moment. It was her mother.

If Ashley shot herself there in the bedroom, her mother would likely be the one to discover the body. She imagined her mother finding her there and being heartbroken.

Then she imagined what her mother's first thought would be: *Oh no! The quilt is ruined!*

In Ashley's state of depression, her vision had dimmed to the point where she couldn't see her own spiritual beauty or believe that her mother would be able to see it. She couldn't imagine a beautiful future for herself. She couldn't see her own beauty, the beauty inherent in every human being. It was all invisible to her.

But the one thing she *could* see was the beauty of her grandmother's quilt beneath her on the bed. Even if she wouldn't be around to appreciate it, it should not be destroyed. She had sympathy for the quilt's heirloom significance and decided not to kill herself.

Most people have not experienced the level of trauma that Ashley endured. Yet, in our own way, we may be blind to the beauty all around us. Life feels flat. Nothing is special. Our spirits aren't lifted beyond whatever is offered by the ordinary activities of the day.

But sometimes, at least for most of us, I believe the veil of our mundane lives parts just a little bit and we catch glimpses of something more, something transcendent. It often comes through the beauty we find in the world and in others. But this sense of transcendence is another thing that can be lost in depression. And it's something we need to get back.

VISUAL CHANGES

I am continually astonished by the depth of understanding and precision of my patients in describing their depression. One common description is that the world looks gray. I had always assumed this was because the enjoyment of things was reduced. Recently, though, I discovered new research into visual perception of depression.

It turns out that people who are depressed have less ability to perceive visual contrast.[1] The brain seems unable to see black and white as distinct, instead blurring them into gray. Visual acuity is apparently diminished in much the same way as the differences between pleasurable and non-pleasurable activities, and the sharp distinctions between how a person feels now compared to how they anticipate feeling when engaging in an activity in the future. I suspect that homogeneity is part of the nature of depression. So when my patients talk about the world looking gray, it's not metaphorical; it's literal.

Ironically, the opposite happens with emotional reasoning. That is, people who are depressed tend to *think* in black-and-white terms. For example, depressed people often believe they are "totally worthless" rather than having at least *some* value. Therapists often encourage patients to not think in black-and-white but to shift to shades of gray. The changes are subtle, but they have profound meaning.

More recent work has shown that the physical differences are not limited to visual contrast. Another group of researchers tested the visual fields of depressed people.[2] This exam is part of routine screening by an optometrist. As the patient looks into a machine and stares at a central dot, little wiggling lines appear in various parts of the peripheral field. The patient is asked to press a button every time he or she sees one of the lines. In a carefully controlled test, people with depression did worse than people who were not depressed. The scientists went further and investigated the part of the eye that processes peripheral vision and found *physical* differences in the retina. Certain important layers were overly thin, and the thinning was worse in patients whose depressive symptoms were more severe.

In both literal and metaphorical ways, the world is gray and less distinct to people with depression. No activity feels better than any other. Nothing they see seems more or less bright or interesting than anything else.

SUICIDE PREVENTION SQUIRRELS

Nick was a high school student who came to see me for treatment of his depression. Like many of my patients, he said his ability to enjoy things was flat. He couldn't feel the ups and downs. He was seriously considering suicide. I treated him with accelerated TMS. In a telling way, we learned that the TMS was making a difference.

Patients receiving accelerated TMS have to be at the clinic for about ten hours a day for five days, but the treatments themselves last only ten minutes, leaving about fifty minutes of downtime every hour. Normally my depressed patients stay in their private rooms between sessions, but Nick decided, partway through his treatment, to go outside to an area with a walking loop through trees and a grassy space.

He came back feeling different.

"When I went for a walk," he recalled later, "I noticed pretty things. 'Oh, look at that tree!' I watched a squirrel playing. I watched the blossoming trees wave in the wind for a while. I have no idea when the last time was that I sat and watched something like that. But ever since then, I'm more conscious or aware, or those things are sticking out to me more. It almost feels like the saturation has been turned up."

I asked about whether his suicidal thoughts had changed.

Some patients conclude, for emotional reasons, that suicide is the only option. Rarely, someone will say it's a good option on rational grounds. Nick was among the latter; he had come to a "logical" belief that suicide was morally justifiable and appropriate in certain circumstances. After seeing the squirrels jump from branch to branch, however, those arguments didn't hold as much sway for him.

"It still makes logical sense to me," Nick said, "but the idea doesn't feel quite as compelling. The thought of suicide is still in my mind, but now there are other things going on as well."

There are other things going on is one of the strongest arguments against suicide, in both a physical and a psychological sense. Those things that are going on are things that make life worth living, even though they may be hard to see or completely invisible in the midst of depression.

G. K. Chesterton makes much the same point in a poem titled "A Ballade of Suicide."

> *To-morrow is the time I get my pay—*
> *My uncle's sword is hanging in the hall—*
> *I see a little cloud all pink and grey—*
> *Perhaps the rector's mother will not call–*
> *I fancy that I heard from Mr. Gall*
> *That mushrooms could be cooked another way—*
> *I never read the works of Juvenal—*

I think I will not hang myself to-day.[3]

Depression narrows a person's focus and constricts the world so that it seems nothing else is going on. Yet whether it's appreciation of a pink-and-gray cloud, uncertainty about a social connection, an unread book—or squirrels at play—the world is full of beautiful and interesting things.

Sometimes the only art that can break through depression is music.

THEN SINGS MY SOUL

Music is a fascinating art form for many reasons, and one that has a particular relationship with time. Paintings, sculptures, and photographs, for example, have a fixed physical existence. But a symphony, apart from the sheet music, exists only in performance—at a particular time and place with a particular audience. Only within the past 150 years have we been able to capture through recordings what before had always been ephemeral—a glorious memory without permanence.

Just as depression is a time traveler, modifying the past and present into a homogenous depressing unity, music can also travel through time, reporting accurately what we felt at a particular time in the past. A person in the throes of depression might feel as if everything has always been exactly as it is now; but when he or she hears an old song, a reminder of a time when things were happier and still felt hopeful, it exposes the lies told by depression. Depression's attempts to modify the past can be rebuffed when a powerful emotion from the past is evoked by music.

DEPRESSION VISIBLE FROM SPACE

It has long been held as common sense that having green space around us makes us happier, less depressed, and better connected. In line with this intuition, New York City planners in the 1850s approved a large park in the center of the city. It became known (uncreatively) as Central Park. Ever since its opening, the park has drawn visitors from far and wide, and it has become the most-filmed place on earth.[4]

I think we'd all prefer to live across the street from a park rather than a strip mall. We would all love to be able to walk out of our homes into a lovely, well-designed green space. Why? How does our proximity to nature affect our mental health?

One group of researchers compiled survey data about depression, anxiety, and stress in people from specific locations and compared it with remote-sensing satellite data from those same locations.[5] Using specialized onboard cameras to see which parts of the landscape had vegetation, the scientists were able to measure the relationship between mental health and living in a place surrounded by nature. They confirmed what we had always suspected: The concrete jungle isn't good for our state of mind. Perhaps more importantly, they observed an increasing correlation between natural surroundings and better mental health—that is, the more greenery, the less depression, anxiety, and stress. And it's not just a matter of comparing cities to rural areas; even within a city, the people in areas that were greener had better overall mental health than those in areas that were less green.

Want to relieve your depression, anxiety, and stress? Spend more time around trees and green spaces. If you don't live near any, go visit. Want better mental health for your grandchildren? Plant some trees. Encourage your city planners to make green spaces an integral part of their overall planning.

BEAUTY AND YOU

The application for this chapter is to become more aware of the beautiful and learn to walk away from what is ugly or banal. The general principle is to notice where beauty already exists and to actively support the creation of more beauty. Push back against the many trends in our modern world that are particularly hostile to beauty.

Notice beauty

Beauty is all around us. In some ways, it can be overwhelming—far more abundant than we have the time or attention to enjoy. Sadly, we often don't appreciate and absorb as much beauty as we easily could.

We can overcome our blindness to beauty by forming a habit of taking time to notice the beauty all around us in the course of our day. It might be natural beauty, something as large as a mountainous landscape or as tiny as an organism seen through a microscope. It could be created beauty, such as a work of architecture, a good book, or a funny comedy sketch. Or it could be something morally beautiful—an act of courage, generosity, or selflessness.

Before you go to bed at night, record some of the most beautiful things you've seen during the day. If you are practicing the "three good things" exercise from chapter 10, you can easily add your gratitude for scenes of beauty. Recalling the beauty you've seen during the day increases your capacity to *notice* and *appreciate* beauty in all its diversity.

Engage with beauty

As you become more aware of beauty, you will naturally want to seek out more. This might be as simple as going to a park, sitting on your back deck to watch birds at the feeder, or taking a walk around the block to appreciate the beauty in your neighborhood. It might include going to an art museum, or a concert, or a botanical garden. Go where the beauty is. For me, singing the songs at church on Sundays helps me transcend my day-to-day experience and helps me focus my mind on God, the creator of beauty.

Stop ruining beauty

Are there ways in which you've chosen ugliness—or simply the mundane—over beauty? We don't usually think of ourselves as culprits in making the world ugly, but maybe it's because we haven't taken the time to inspire, create, or pursue beauty in our surroundings. Truthfully, it's often easier to go with the flow—to settle for mindless TV instead of watching a classic movie or reading a good book; to place an online order or run to a big-box store rather than seeking out a local artisan or shop; to "interact" with family or friends on social media rather than getting together in person. If you think your community could use more parks, are you running for city council or voting for people who will build them?

In what ways have you made the world less beautiful in the last twenty-four hours by participating in systems that don't promote beauty? Write them down—not to make yourself feel guilty, but to nudge you toward the opposite of depression, toward beauty and a life of flourishing.

Create beauty

Creating beauty is not just for the artistically talented or aesthetically inclined. It's for all of us. Beauty can be found—and created—in every area of life, not just the arts. If creating beauty is too difficult right now in your current state of mind, try making something less ugly. Nearly everyone is capable of making their bed, straightening up their workspace, or putting dishes in the dishwasher. And most can do more than that: find a good book or watch a movie; take up a new hobby; invite someone for coffee and conversation; join a club or some other group; learn to paint.

In today's world, it's easy to think that only mass media stars can create something meaningful. But as author Andy Crouch reminds us in his book *Culture Making*, "We will have the greatest cultural effect where we already have cultural influence, where we have already cultivated a community that recognizes our ability to contribute something new."[6] If you play music, maybe it's only for the four people in your family, or forty people in a social club, or four hundred people in your church. You don't need an audience of forty million people for your creative efforts to matter. The world would be a much richer place if everyone participated in the creation of beauty.

STEPS TOWARD FLOURISHING

The opposite of depression is noticing the beauty that pervades our world. Flourishing means stopping to smell the roses—and maybe even planting some. It means avoiding spending time and money on things that are ugly, and investing our time instead in making things more beautiful for those around us and for our own enjoyment.

15

BLESSEDNESS: BEYOND FLOURISHING

Blessed are you who are poor, for yours is the kingdom of God.
Blessed are you who are hungry now, for you shall be satisfied.
Blessed are you who weep now, for you shall laugh.

LUKE 6:20-21

Sigmund Freud wrote to one of to his patients who felt destined to suffer because of her circumstances, "I do not doubt that it would be easier for fate to take away your suffering than it would for me. But you will see for yourself that much has been gained if we succeed in turning your hysterical misery into common unhappiness."[1] The most famous psychiatrist in history is saying that his reasonable aim was to deliver his patients from mental illness to the general unhappiness that is common to humanity.

Along those same lines, I often tell my patients, "There's always something you can do to make yourself a little less miserable." But that's not exactly a guarantee of abundant joy and happiness.

Sometimes our treatment efforts are successful. Some patients will take the blank slate provided by their medical or psychological therapy and write an incredible next chapter—far beyond what their psychotherapist or psychiatrist could have predicted.

When I had my appendix out, the surgeon made cuts and placed sutures, but he had no ability to heal me. That was something only my body could do. The doctor guided the healing via suture and knife, and he saved my life, but the miraculous ability of two wounded bits of flesh to connect and heal is far beyond the ability of modern medicine to bring about directly.

The same is true of medical and psychological treatments for depression. We can make people undepressed, but we cannot make them flourish.

That's why I have written *The Opposite of Depression*—to point you toward a life of flourishing that goes well beyond the state of the art in medicine. The life I am urging you toward is difficult to attain. But imagine for a moment that you have accomplished it.

You eat well. You follow the rhythms of creation in your waking and sleeping, work and rest. You exercise regularly, conducting the symphony of body and brain with ever greater mastery.

You grieve deeply when tragedy strikes, mourning with those who mourn. Your emotions are aligned with your higher values and expressed in appropriate ways. When a surprising emotion arises, you are aware and respectfully curious. Pleasure pervades your life, from the joy of the first moments of awakening to the gentle warm glow in your heart for no other reason than the fact that you're alive. You are focused at home and at work and attuned to your loved ones.

You evaluate thoughts that arise: Those that are unproductive or unsatisfactory are diverted, and those that are true, good, and beautiful are embraced. You regularly consult your Wise Advocate when faced with hard questions. You accomplish much but are never rushed; no one who wants to speak to you feels that you're "too busy." You feel guilty when you do the wrong thing, but not when you don't. You've considered your past and integrated your struggles into your ongoing story.

For you, life is deeply meaningful, and you find significance in the work you do. You volunteer your time to help others. You seek to know the truth, even when it upsets long-held beliefs about yourself or your view of the world. You hold fast to the things you've come to believe, even as public opinion shifts and pressures mount. You have deep and satisfying relationships. You care deeply about your family and sacrifice for them. You have close connections with your friends and grow with them toward becoming better people. You have a vision for your future, and a clear idea of how your daily activities contribute to bringing it about. You are struck by the profound beauty of the world and what lies beyond.

This is the life that I myself aspire to. I want this life for you too.

As a doctor, I will continue to work to get people undepressed. That is my professional commission. Beyond that, it is my sincere hope that my patients—and you—can move past the baseline toward ever increasing freedom, joy, and satisfaction. I'm certainly not there yet myself—and indeed it's a lifelong endeavor. And I look forward to one day being "laid off" by Jesus—for in heaven there will be no doctors, for all will be healed.

A SHIELD AGAINST THE SLINGS AND ARROWS OF OUTRAGEOUS FORTUNE

Life can be hard. As healthy as we eat, as much exercise as we get, as much community as we have, it doesn't stop conflict and tragedy. Even Aristotle, who valued the importance of virtue and the power of the mind as much as anyone, noted that "many changes occur in life, and all manner of chances, and the most prosperous may fall into great misfortunes . . . ; and one who has experienced such chances and has ended wretchedly no one calls happy."[2]

People sometimes turn to God for comfort when times are tough. But does that really help? Can people transcend misfortune by an awareness of God?

Some of my colleagues on the SoulPulse study (previously mentioned in chapters 6 and 10) decided to address the age-old question with data. They wanted to know how daily spiritual experiences affected people in everyday life. They had thousands of participants fill out dozens of surveys to provide a rich picture of daily life. No one had ever examined the fine-grained interaction of a person's daily spiritual experiences (e.g., feeling God's presence, feeling God's love, feeling thankful) with their stressors and emotions.[3] What they found was astonishing.

But before I describe the astonishing part, I'll first mention that the study confirmed some things the researchers were expecting. For example, they saw that as people reported having more stressors, they also reported having less flourishing and more depression.[4]

What happened to depression when people had more daily spiritual experiences? Stressors were *less able* to cause depression. As stressors increased, depression increased, but not nearly as much as for those in the control group. Feeling God's closeness lowered the ceiling on how bad things could be.

Something even more interesting happened to the indicators for flourishing. For those who were somewhat more aware of God than normal, flourishing decreased when stressors increased, but not as much as before; people who felt God's presence were more able to preserve their joy when trouble came.[5]

But the most interesting finding of the entire study was what happened when people were very aware of God: They turned their stress upside down![6] When things were going badly, they *flourished*. When things were going *even worse*, they *flourished even more*. Flourishing, against all expectations, *increased* with stress. When trouble came, those who were more aware of God remained joyful, even while allowing their joy to be mingled with some small sadness.

It seems that awareness of God confers a level of immunity to "the slings and arrows of outrageous fortune."[7] Daily spiritual experiences allowed people to rise above the typical rules.

I've tried to be as practical and useful in this book as I could be, and my last piece of advice to you is this: *Don't neglect your soul.* Find a way to transcend the iron laws of this difficult life by opening yourself to the love of God. If you already know God, get to know him better through daily spiritual experiences. If you don't know God, seek him out. Pray directly to God and ask for help even if you don't believe or don't fully believe. How to seek God is beyond the scope of this book, but it is one of the most important questions you could ask.

If you have a trusted friend or family member who has faith in God, you can ask for help. Or you can seek out a pastor or priest. If you'd like to make someone's day, go to a church and say to the pastor, "I'd like to know God better. Can you help me?" You could pick up a Bible and start reading it; sometimes people recommend starting with the Gospel of Luke or John. Or if you prefer, start with a book like Rick Warren's *The Purpose Driven Life.*

Allow me to close with a story about someone who, not so long ago, went beyond the opposite of depression. She transcended flourishing and achieved something even better: *blessedness*.

"MY JESUS"

Mabel lived in a state convalescent hospital, with some of the toughest circumstances one could imagine. She was blind and nearly deaf, and cancer had eaten away much of her face. New nurses on the ward were assigned to care for Mabel—because if they could do *that*, they would be prepared to handle *anything*.

That was more or less Mabel's life. For twenty-five years.

One day, she began receiving a visitor, a kindly young man named Tom, who decided to keep Mabel company and perhaps relieve her distress in some small way.

After a while, Tom realized that, apart from his visits, Mabel was utterly alone day after day after day, in the prison and darkness of her many disabilities. So Tom asked her, "Mabel, what do you think about when you lie here?"

Her reply was quick and certain: "I think about my Jesus."

Tom was amazed. He knew he would have a hard time thinking about Jesus for even five minutes. He wanted to learn Mabel's secret, so before asking his next question, he took out a pad of paper and a pen to record her answer.

"*What* do you think about Jesus?"

Here's what Mabel told him:

I think about how good he's been to me. He's been awfully good to me in my life, you know. . . . I'm one of those kind who's mostly satisfied. . . . Lots of folks wouldn't care much for what I think. Lots of folks would think I'm kind of old-fashioned. But I don't care. I'd rather have Jesus. He's all the world to me.[8]

Mabel had almost none of the aspects of the flourishing life we have talked about.

In previous chapters, we discussed the importance of a good diet. Mabel was stuck with whatever the cafeteria fed her.

We discussed the importance of exercise. Mabel couldn't leave her chair.

We discussed the importance of getting regular sunlight. Mabel was blind.

We discussed the importance of friendship and community. Mabel was alone, except for Jesus.

We discussed the importance of seeking out beauty in the world. How could Mabel do that?

She didn't have many of the things that lead to flourishing in this life, but she had Jesus, and thus she was able to transcend the plane of human suffering and experience what the Bible calls "the peace of God, which surpasses all understanding, [and] will guard your hearts and your minds in Christ Jesus."[9] Though her body was failing her, she had something better: *blessedness.*

Mabel had learned to live in a state of blessedness while still on this earth. But most of us are not as aware of the realm of God as Mabel was.

But what's stopping us? We scheme and strive and labor for a better life, and that's all well and good. But we often forget that there is a realm of blessedness available to us that transcends—and may even redeem—the circumstances of our lives.

My hope for you is that you would be free of depression and weariness. My hope is that you will press on toward a flourishing life. But my greatest hope is that you will remain ever thirsty for something beyond flourishing.

May you one day achieve blessedness.

Notes

INTRODUCTION

1. Adapted from the parable of the farmer scattering seed in Matthew 13:3-8.

CHAPTER 1: DEPRESSION'S SURPRISING GIFT

1. National Institute of Mental Health, "Major Depression," updated January 2022, https://www.nimh.nih.gov/health/statistics/major-depression.
2. Alize J. Ferrari et al., "Global, Regional, and National Burden of 12 Mental Disorders in 204 Countries and Territories, 1990–2019: A Systematic Analysis for the Global Burden of Disease Study 2019," *Lancet Psychiatry* 9, no. 2 (February 2022): 137–150, https://doi.org/10.1016/S2215-0366(21)00395-3.
3. Ferrari et al., "Global, Regional, and National Burden"; Joshua A. Salomon et al., "Disability Weights for the Global Burden of Disease 2013 Study," *Lancet Global Health* 3, no. 11 (November 2015): E712–E723, https://doi.org/10.1016/S2214 -109X(15)00069-8.
4. Job 4:1-21.
5. Samantha L. Cohen et al., "A Visual and Narrative Timeline of US FDA Milestones for Transcranial Magnetic Stimulation (TMS) Devices," *Brain Stimulation Journal* 15, no. 1 (January 2022): 73–75, https://doi.org/10.1016/j.brs.2021.11.010.
6. The formal name of the condition is *major depressive disorder* (MDD), and it is descriptive of a person who is both functionally and indisputably disordered. I will sometimes refer to MDD as a "disease" or "brain disease" because I believe those terms are useful when emphasizing the aspects of MDD that are physical and in the brain. But I'm not reducing MDD to *merely* a disease. It is also the result of psychological qualities and can be caused by social and spiritual factors.
7. Leo Tolstoy, *Anna Karenina*, trans. David Magarshack (New York: Signet Classics, 1961), 5.
8. Adapted from American Psychiatric Association, *Diagnostic and Statistical Manual of Mental Disorders*, 5th ed. [DSM-5] (Washington, DC: American Psychiatric Association Publishing, 2013), 125.

CHAPTER 2: MOOD: FEELINGS AND EMOTIONS

1. Francis Crick, *The Astonishing Hypothesis: The Scientific Search for the Soul* (New York: Charles Scribner's Sons, 1994), 3.
2. Jeffrey M. Schwartz and Rebecca Gladding, *You Are Not Your Brain: The 4-Step Solution for Changing Bad Habits, Ending Unhealthy Thinking, and Taking Control of Your Life* (New York: Avery, 2011), 21–23.
3. Ecclesiastes 7:2-4.
4. Ran R. Hassin et al., "Subliminal Exposure to National Flags Affects Political Thought and Behavior," *Proceedings of the National Academy of Sciences of the United States of America* 104, no. 50 (December 11, 2007): 19757–19761, https://www.pnas.org/doi/epdf/10.1073/pnas.0704679104.
5. Matthew 17:17; Luke 22:44; John 2:14-16; 11:33-35.
6. Matthew D. Lieberman et al., "Putting Feelings into Words: Affect Labeling Disrupts Amygdala Activity in Response to Affective Stimuli," *Psychological Science* 18, no. 5 (May 2007): 421–428, https://doi.org/10.1111/j.1467-9280.2007.01916.x.
7. Joanna Moncrieff et al., "The Serotonin Theory of Depression: A Systematic Umbrella Review of the Evidence," *Molecular Psychiatry* (July 20, 2022), https://doi.org/10.1038/s41380-022-01661-0.
8. Kerry J. Ressler and Helen S. Mayberg, "Targeting Abnormal Neural Circuits in Mood and Anxiety Disorders: From the Laboratory to the Clinic," *Nature Neuroscience* 10 (September 2007): 1116–1124, https://doi.org/10.1038/nn1944.
9. Pekka Jylhä et al., "Do Antidepressants Change Personality?—A Five-Year Observational Study," *Journal of Affective Disorders* 142, nos. 1–3 (December 2012): 200–207, https://doi.org/10.1016/J.JAD.2012.04.026.
10. It should be noted that, for most people taking the medication, emotional flattening is not a reported side effect. This may be because it is truly absent or because the change is so minor or gradual that it escapes notice. Some people describe a reduction in peak emotions while taking an SSRI: Their happiness isn't quite as high as it used to be. But for someone coming out of extreme depression, that's usually a small price to pay. For others, the effect really does feel like a flatness. This experience is rare, but it might also be underappreciated. Because depression itself causes emotional flattening, if the consequence or side effect of the SSRI is a less-severe emotional narrowing, it might be a net positive. But it's still an impairment.
11. Molly J. Crockett et al., "Serotonin Selectively Influences Moral Judgment and Behavior through Effects on Harm Aversion," *Proceedings of the National Academy of Sciences of the United States of America* 107, no. 40 (October 5, 2010): 17433–17438, https://doi.org/10.1073/pnas.1009396107.
12. Genesis 6:6; Exodus 20:5; Deuteronomy 9:22; Judges 2:18; Jeremiah 31:3.
13. For a few examples, see Hebrews 12:2; John 11:35; Matthew 9:36.
14. Ecclesiastes 3:1, 4.
15. Gilbert K. Chesterton, *Orthodoxy* (New York: Dodd, Mead, 1908), 294–296.

CHAPTER 3: PLEASURE: THE PATHWAY OF ENJOYMENT

1. Richard Dawkins, "Preface to First Edition," *The Selfish Gene*, 40th anniv. ed. (Oxford, UK: Oxford University Press, 2016), xxix.

2. Friedrich Nietzsche, *Beyond Good and Evil: Prelude to a Philosophy of the Future* (1886), eds. Rolf-Peter Horstmann and Judith Norman, trans. Judith Norman (Cambridge: Cambridge University Press, 2002), 15. Italics in the original.

3. Aristotle, *The Nicomachean Ethics*, trans. Harris Rackham (Ware, Hertfordshire, UK: Wordsworth, 1996), 37. *The Nicomachean Ethics* was written circa 340 BCE.

4. For a sampling of these, see https://scholar.google.com/scholar?as_ylo=2022&q =%22trolley+problem%22&hl=en&as_sdt=0,44.

5. N. T. Wright, *After You Believe: Why Christian Character Matters* (San Francisco: HarperOne, 2010), 33.

6. Aristotle, *Nicomachean Ethics*, book 2, chapter 3, paragraph 1, trans. W. D. Ross, Internet Classics Archive, https://123philosophy.files.wordpress.com/2019/08 /aristotle-nicomachean-ethics.pdf.

7. Wright, *After You Believe*, 78.

8. Corey L. M. Keyes, "The Mental Health Continuum: From Languishing to Flourishing in Life," *Journal of Health and Social Behavior* 43, no. 2 (June 2002): 207–222, https://doi.org/10.2307/3090197.

9. Keyes, "The Mental Health Continuum," 207.

10. Marijke Schotanus-Dijkstra et al., "What Factors Are Associated with Flourishing? Results from a Large Representative National Sample," *Journal of Happiness Studies* 17, no. 4 (August 2016): 1351–1370, https://doi.org/10.1007/s10902 -015-9647-3. "Flourishing is defined as having high levels of both hedonic well-being and eudaimonic well-being. . . . Hedonic well-being comprises subjective or emotional well-being which, in turn, consists of the components happiness, life-satisfaction and a positive–negative affect balance. Psychological well-being and social well-being are part of eudaimonic well-being and include a wide variety of components such as meaning, engagement, purpose in life, positive relations and personal growth. Flourishers seem to have excellent mental and physical health and are more resilient to vulnerabilities and challenges in life than non-flourishers."

11. Matthew 5:3-12.

12. Matthew 5:6.

13. "The Westminster Shorter Catechism," 1647, A Puritan's Mind website, accessed May 31, 2023, https://www.apuritansmind.com/westminster-standards/shorter -catechism/.

CHAPTER 4: TRAUMA: BROKEN, MENDED, STRONGER

1. "Haunting Pictures of Londoners Sheltering in the Underground during World War II, 1940–1941," Rare Historical Photos website, accessed May 31, 2023, https:// rarehistoricalphotos.com/london-blitz-underground-photos/.

2. Raymond Eliot Lee, *The London Journal of General Raymond E. Lee, 1940–1941*, ed. James Leutze (Boston: Little, Brown, 1971), 25, 59.

3. Vincent J. Felitti et al., "Relationship of Childhood Abuse and Household Dysfunction to Many of the Leading Causes of Death in Adults," *American Journal of Preventive Medicine* 14, no. 4 (May 1998): 245–258, https://doi.org/10.1016/s0749-3797 (98)00017-8.

4. Bessel A. van der Kolk, *The Body Keeps the Score: Brain, Mind, and Body in the Healing of Trauma* (New York: Penguin, 2014), 96–97.

5. Michelle Kelly-Irving et al., "Childhood Adversity as a Risk for Cancer: Findings from the 1958 British Birth Cohort Study," *BMC Public Health* 13 (2013): 767, https://doi.org/10.1186/1471-2458-13-767.

6. "We Can Prevent Childhood Adversity," Violence Prevention, Centers for Disease Control and Prevention, March 2, 2022, https://www.cdc.gov/violenceprevention/communicationresources/infographics/preventchildhoodadversity.html.

7. In a study conducted in 2009, life expectancy for people with six or more ACEs was nearly twenty years less than for people with no ACEs (60.6 years vs. 79.1 years). See David W. Brown et al., "Adverse Childhood Experiences and the Risk of Premature Mortality," *American Journal of Preventive Medicine* 37, no. 5 (November 2009): 389–396, https://doi.org/10.1016/j.amepre.2009.06.021; and "Life Expectancy for Countries, 2009," Infoplease, updated September 9, 2022, https://www.infoplease.com/world/health-and-social-statistics/life-expectancy-countries-2009.

8. Robert M. Sapolsky, *Why Zebras Don't Get Ulcers*, 3rd ed. (New York: Henry Holt, 2004), 6.

9. Klaus Kuch and B. J. Cox, "Symptoms of PTSD in 124 Survivors of the Holocaust," *American Journal of Psychiatry* 149, no. 3 (March 1992): 337–340, https://doi.org/10.1176/ajp.149.3.337.

10. Risë B. Goldstein et al., "The Epidemiology of DSM-5 Post-traumatic Stress Disorder in the United States: Results from the National Epidemiologic Survey on Alcohol and Related Conditions-III," *Social Psychiatry and Psychiatric Epidemiology* 51, no. 8 (August 2016): 1137–1148, https://doi.org/10.1007/s00127-016-1208-5.

11. Craig J. Bryan et al., "Happiness, Meaning in Life, and PTSD Symptoms among National Guard Personnel: A Multilevel Analysis," *Journal of Happiness Studies* 21, no. 4 (2020): 1251–1264, https://doi.org/10.1007/s10902-019-00129-3.

12. An important note about this study is that depression was not directly measured. Instead, the key measure was presence or absence of happiness, which we have already established is not necessarily the opposite of depression. But I suspect that similar effects would be found with depression as well. Also, when I say "PTSD symptoms," it should be noted that the participants were graded according to the PCL-5 (a self-reported measure of the presence and severity of PTSD symptoms), and the overall group averages were below threshold for likely occurrence of PTSD. This work should be replicated in a group that has confirmed PTSD, not just some symptoms of PTSD.

13. You can check out the growth in use of the word by going to the Google Books Ngram Viewer and typing in *trauma*.

14. American Psychiatric Association, *Diagnostic and Statistical Manual of Mental Disorders*, 5th ed. [DSM-5] (Washington, DC: American Psychiatric Association Publishing, 2013), 271.

15. DSM-5, 286, 290.

16. See Greg Lukianoff and Jonathan Haidt, *The Coddling of the American Mind: How Good Intentions and Bad Ideas Are Setting Up a Generation for Failure* (New York: Penguin, 2018).

17. See Jean M. Twenge, *iGen: Why Today's Super-Connected Kids Are Growing Up Less Rebellious, More Tolerant, Less Happy—and Completely Unprepared for Adulthood: And What That Means for the Rest of Us* (New York: Atria Books, 2018).

18. Martin E. P. Seligman, "Learned Helplessness," *Annual Review of Medicine* 23 (February 1972): 407–412, https://doi.org/10.1146/annurev.me.23.020172.002203.
19. Sapolsky, *Why Zebras Don't Get Ulcers*, 392.
20. J. Brockhurst et al., "Stress Inoculation Modeled in Mice," *Translational Psychiatry* 5, no. 3 (March 31, 2015): e537, https://doi.org/10.1038/tp.2015.34.
21. M. D. Seery, E. A. Holman, and R. C. Silver, "Whatever Does Not Kill Us: Cumulative Lifetime Adversity, Vulnerability, and Resilience," *Journal of Personality and Social Psychology* 99, no. 6 (December 2010): 1025–1041, https://doi.org /10.1037/a0021344.
22. Jeffrey Guina et al., "Benzodiazepines for PTSD: A Systematic Review and Meta-Analysis," *Journal of Psychiatric Practice* 21, no. 4 (July 2015): 281–303, https://doi .org/10.1097/PRA.0000000000000091.
23. Eleanor Roosevelt, *You Learn by Living: Eleven Keys for a More Fulfilling Life* (Louisville, KY: Westminster John Knox, 1960), 29.
24. Bill P., Todd W., and Sara S., *Drop the Rock: Removing Character Defects, Steps Six and Seven*, 2nd ed. (Center City, MN: Hazelden, 2005), x–xii. According to Bill P., the original story comes from "an old intergroup newsletter" and was later popularized in a 1976 AA convention talk by Sandy B.
25. Fred Luskin, *Forgive for Good: A Proven Prescription for Health and Happiness* (New York: HarperCollins, 2002), 118.
26. Martina A. Waltman et al., "The Effects of a Forgiveness Intervention on Patients with Coronary Artery Disease," *Psychology & Health* 24, no. 1 (January 2009): 11–27, https://doi.org/10.1080/08870440801975127.
27. For a variety of resources compiled or written by psychologist Everett L. Worthington, see http://www.evworthington-forgiveness.com/diy-workbooks.

CHAPTER 5: CONSCIENCE: THE BURDEN OF GUILT

1. Much work and intense argument have gone into defining the words *guilt* and *shame* differently from how they are commonly used. One typical definition sees guilt as, "I've *done* something bad," whereas shame is, "I *am* bad." Others connect guilt to wrongdoing or trespass, whereas shame is more connected to violations of social norms (e.g., accidentally wearing mismatched socks may induce shame but wouldn't commonly be something to feel guilty about). My patients often use the terms somewhat interchangeably. In my own use, I don't insist on there being a big difference between the two words. I'll use *guilt* in this section, meaning closest to "I've done something bad" but also recognizing that repeatedly and habitually doing something bad has implications about actually *being* bad, so it also includes shades of that definition of *shame*.
2. Luke 22:19-20.
3. Jonathan Haidt, *The Righteous Mind: Why Good People Are Divided by Politics and Religion* (New York: Pantheon, 2012), 70. Italics in the original.
4. Haidt, *The Righteous Mind*, 91.
5. Paul Bloom, *Just Babies: The Origins of Good and Evil* (New York: Broadway, 2013), 7.
6. William Shakespeare, *Macbeth*, act 5, scene 1.
7. Adapted from Alcoholics Anonymous, *Twelve Steps and Twelve Traditions* (New York: Alcoholics Anonymous World Services, Inc., 1952), https://www.aa.org/twelve-steps -twelve-traditions.

8. Isaiah 6:5.

9. 1 Timothy 1:15.

10. *Merriam-Webster*, s.v. "ruminate (*v.*)," accessed May 9, 2023, https://www.merriam -webster.com/dictionary/ruminate.

11. Susan Nolen-Hoeksema, Blair E. Wisco, and Sonja Lyubomirsky, "Rethinking Rumination," *Perspectives on Psychological Science* 3, no. 5 (September 2008): 400–424, https://doi.org/10.1111/j.1745-6924.2008.00088.x.

12. Revelation 12:10.

CHAPTER 6: ATTENTION: CHOOSING WHERE TO FOCUS

1. Thomas H. Maugh II, "Physicists Catch a Paradox in a Jar," *Los Angeles Times*, March 17, 1990, https://www.latimes.com/archives/la-xpm-1990-03-17-mn-216 -story.html.

2. There are several interpretations of what is happening in this experiment. The idea that observations change the physical world is called the Copenhagen interpretation and holds at least a plurality among other options. Though it's weird, it's the least weird option. For example, some suggest that every time we observe something, we split off an entirely new physical universe, creating an alternate reality where alternative options occur.

3. Maugh, "Physicists Catch a Paradox in a Jar."

4. "Facebook Average Revenue Per User (ARPU) as of 1st Quarter 2023, by Region," Statista, accessed May 31, 2023, https://www.statista.com/statistics/251328 /facebooks-average-revenue-per-user-by-region/; "Average Daily Time Spent on Selected Social Networks by Adults in the United States from 2017 to 2022, by Platform," Statista, accessed March 1, 2023, https://www.statista.com/statistics /324267/us-adults-daily-facebook-minutes/. These numbers pertain to US users.

5. Roy F. Baumeister, Bradley R. E. Wright, and David Carreon, "Self-Control 'In the Wild': Experience Sampling Study of Trait and State Self-Regulation," *Self and Identity* 18, no. 5 (June 2019): 494–528, https://doi.org/10.1080/15298868.2018 .1478324.

6. Vinoth K. Ranganathan et al., "From Mental Power to Muscle Power—Gaining Strength by Using the Mind," *Neuropsychologia* 42, no. 7 (2004): 944–956, https:// doi.org/10.1016/j.neuropsychologia.2003.11.018.

7. Samuel C. Scholefield et al., "The Effectiveness of Mental Imagery for Improving Strength in an Asymptomatic Population," *Physical Therapy Reviews* 20, no. 2 (2015): 86–97, https://doi.org/10.1179/1743288X15Y.0000000013; Wan X. Yao et al., "Kinesthetic Imagery Training of Forceful Muscle Contractions Increases Brain Signal and Muscle Strength," *Frontiers in Human Neuroscience* 26, no. 7 (September 2013): 561, https://doi.org/10.3389/fnhum.2013.00561.

8. Now, to be fair—and before you non-exercisers get too excited—the greatest changes came from thinking *and* moving. So actual exercise is still better.

9. Eleanor A. Maguire, Katherine Woollett, and Hugo J. Spiers, "London Taxi Drivers and Bus Drivers: A Structural MRI and Neuropsychological Analysis," *Hippocampus* 16, no. 12 (December 2006): 1091–1101, https://doi.org/10.1002/hipo.20233.

10. Peter Schwenkreis et al., "Assessment of Sensorimotor Cortical Representation Asymmetries and Motor Skills in Violin Players," *European Journal of Neuroscience* 26,

no. 11 (December 2007): 3291–3302, https://doi.org/10.1111/j.1460-9568.2007
.05894.x.

11. Nicolò F. Bernardi et al., "Mental Practice Promotes Motor Anticipation: Evidence
from Skilled Music Performance," *Frontiers in Human Neuroscience* 7 (August 20,
2013): article 451, https://doi.org/10.3389/fnhum.2013.00451; Serene Lim and
Louis G. Lippman, "Mental Practice and Memorization of Piano Music," *Journal
of General Psychology* 118, no. 1 (January 1991): 21–30, https://doi.org/10.1080
/00221309.1991.9711130; David Eldred-Evans et al., "Using the Mind as a
Simulator: A Randomized Controlled Trial of Mental Training," *Journal of Surgical
Education* 70, no. 4 (July–August 2013): 544–551, https://doi.org/10.1016/j.jsurg
.2013.04.003.

12. Will Durant, *The Story of Philosophy: The Lives and Opinions of the Great Philosophers
of the Western World* (1926; reprint, New York: Simon & Schuster, 2012), 61. Durant
is summarizing some of Aristotle's thought from his *Nicomachean Ethics*.

13. Adapted from personal teachings of Jeffrey Schwartz. An instructional video by Dr.
Schwartz can be found here: "Mindful Breathing Exercises [Jeffrey Schwartz]," video,
6:58, accessed May 10, 2023, https://www.youtube.com/watch?v=oH1H3eC_KFE.

14. Genesis 2:7.

15. Wendy Hasenkamp et al., "Mind Wandering and Attention during Focused
Meditation: A Fine-Grained Temporal Analysis of Fluctuating Cognitive States,"
NeuroImage 59, no. 1 (January 2, 2012): 750–760, https://doi.org/10.1016/j
.neuroimage.2011.07.008.

16. The brain state centered on the dorsolateral prefrontal cortex was called the "executive
network" in the Hasenkamp study cited above. Others may attribute that task to
other resting-state networks, including the task-positive network, the dorsal attention
network, or the frontoparietal network. The methods of analysis and nomenclature
have evolved somewhat since 2011, but the key insights stand.

17. The classic text for this is *The Practice of the Presence of God*, based on the teachings of
Brother Lawrence, a seventeenth-century Carmelite monk, and still in print through
several sources.

18. Lao-tzu in *Tao Tě Ching*, ch. 10, trans. R. B. Blakney, accessed May 31, 2023,
https://terebess.hu/english/tao/blakney.html#Kap10. The *Tao Tě Ching* dates to
approximately 500 BC and probably contains contributions from multiple people.

19. 1 Thessalonians 5:17.

CHAPTER 7: FOOD: WHAT'S ON YOUR PLATE?

1. Christian Otte et al., "Major Depressive Disorder," *Nature Reviews Disease Primers* 2,
article 16065 (September 15, 2016), https://doi.org/10.1038/nrdp.2016.65.

2. Thomaz F. S. Bastiaanssen et al., "Gutted! Unraveling the Role of the Microbiome
in Major Depressive Disorder," *Harvard Review of Psychiatry* 28, no. 1 (January/
February 2020): 26–39, https://doi.org/10.1097/HRP.0000000000000243.

3. P. Zheng et al., "Gut Microbiome Remodeling Induces Depressive-like Behaviors
through a Pathway Mediated by the Host's Metabolism," *Molecular Psychiatry* 21,
no. 6 (June 2016): 786–796, https://doi.org/10.1038/mp.2016.44.

4. Jonathan Flint and Kenneth S. Kendler, "The Genetics of Major Depression,"
Neuron 81, no. 3 (February 5, 2014): 484–503, https://doi.org/10.1016/j.neuron
.2014.01.027.

5. Jun S. Lai et al., "A Systematic Review and Meta-Analysis of Dietary Patterns and Depression in Community-Dwelling Adults," *American Journal of Clinical Nutrition* 99, no. 1 (January 2014): 181–197, https://doi.org/10.3945/ajcn.113 .069880.

6. The formula is: 21 million depressed people x 16 percent = 3.36 million. This assumes a steady state; the reduction would be mostly accomplished in the first year after the dietary change via prevention, but it wouldn't be 3.36 million in the first year. Because there would be a minority of chronically depressed people in that 21 million who would not be affected, it would take some time to see the full benefits from this hypothetical.

7. I recommend trying to get your nutrients from foods rather than from supplements, mostly because food is complex and supplements are simple. Nonetheless, if you must take supplements, those that have the best evidence for helping with depression are S-adenosylmethionine (SAMe), methylfolate, omega-3, and vitamin D (though another enormous study showed no benefit from vitamin D in *preventing* depression). See also Jerome Sarris et al., "Adjunctive Nutraceuticals for Depression: A Systematic Review and Meta-Analyses," *American Journal of Psychiatry* 173, no. 6 (June 1, 2016): 575–587, https://doi.org/10.1176/appi.ajp.2016.15091228.

8. Recent opinions are swinging away from any amount of alcohol consumption being good for you; carefully controlled observational studies seem to point at risks of even small amounts of alcohol. However, I am not aware of good, randomized evidence at this time, so I will leave the original recommendations, which have been tested, in place.

9. Ramón Estruch et al., "Primary Prevention of Cardiovascular Disease with a Mediterranean Diet Supplemented with Extra-Virgin Olive Oil or Nuts," *New England Journal of Medicine* 378, no. 25 (June 21, 2018): e34, https://doi.org /10.1056/NEJMoa1800389.

10. F. Barzi et al., "Mediterranean Diet and All-Causes Mortality after Myocardial Infarction: Results from the GISSI-Prevenzione Trial, *European Journal of Clinical Nutrition* 57 (2003): 604–611, https://doi.org/10.1038/sj.ejcn.1601575.

11. David G. Loughrey et al., "The Impact of the Mediterranean Diet on the Cognitive Functioning of Healthy Older Adults: A Systematic Review and Meta-Analysis," *Advances in Nutrition* 8, no. 4 (July 2017): 571–586, https://doi.org/10.3945/an .117.015495.

12. Cécilia Samieri et al., "The Association between Dietary Patterns at Midlife and Health in Aging: An Observational Study," *Annals of Internal Medicine* 159, no. 9 (November 5, 2013): 584–591, https://doi.org/10.7326/0003-4819-159-9 -201311050-00004.

13. Felice N. Jacka et al., "A Randomised Controlled Trial of Dietary Improvement for Adults with Major Depression (the 'SMILES' Trial)," *BMC Medicine* 15 (2017): article 23, https://doi.org/10.1186/s12916-017-0791-y.

14. "Obesity and Overweight," National Center for Health Statistics, Centers for Disease Control and Prevention, January 5, 2023, https://www.cdc.gov/nchs/fastats/obesity -overweight.htm.

15. "$71 Billion US Weight Loss Market Pivots to Survive Pandemic," Research and Markets, June 8, 2020, https://www.researchandmarkets.com/issues/us-weight-loss -market-pivots.

16. Luke 7:34.
17. Matthew 9:15.
18. Larissa Galastri Baraldi et al., "Consumption of Ultra-Processed Foods and Associated Sociodemographic Factors in the USA between 2007 and 2012: Evidence from a Nationally Representative Cross-Sectional Study," *BMJ Open* 8, no. 3 (March 9, 2018): e020574, https://doi.org/10.1136/bmjopen-2017-020574.
19. Kevin D. Hall et al., "Ultra-Processed Diets Cause Excess Calorie Intake and Weight Gain: An Inpatient Randomized Controlled Trial of *Ad Libitum* Food Intake," *Cell Metabolism* 30, no. 1 (July 2, 2019): 67–77.e3, https://doi.org/10.1016/j.cmet.2019.05.008.
20. James W. Wheless, "History of the Ketogenic Diet," *Epilepsia* 49, no. 8 (November 2008): 3–5, https://doi.org/10.1111/j.1528-1167.2008.01821.x.
21. Albert Danan et al., "The Ketogenic Diet for Refractory Mental Illness: A Retrospective Analysis of 31 Inpatients," *Frontiers in Psychiatry* 13, article 951376 (July 6, 2022): 1–11, https://doi.org/10.3389/fpsyt.2022.951376.

CHAPTER 8: SLEEP: MIND AND BODY AT REST

1. Quoted in D. T. Maxx, "The Secrets of Sleep," *National Geographic*, April 30, 2010, https://www.nationalgeographic.com/magazine/article/sleep.
2. Long Zhai, Yi Zhang, and Dongfeng Zhang, "Sedentary Behaviour and the Risk of Depression: A Meta-Analysis," *British Journal of Sports Medicine* 49, no. 11 (2015): 705–709, https://doi.org/10.1136/bjsports-2014-093613.
3. Yu Jin Lee et al., "Insufficient Sleep and Suicidality in Adolescents," *Sleep* 35, no. 4 (April 2012): 455–460, https://doi.org/10.5665/sleep.1722.
4. Yu Jin Lee et al., "Insufficient Sleep."
5. Roy F. Baumeister, Bradley R. E. Wright, and David Carreon, "Self-Control 'In the Wild': Experience Sampling Study of Trait and State Self-Regulation," *Self and Identity* 18, no. 5 (June 22, 2018): 494–528, https://doi.org/10.1080/15298868.2018.1478324.
6. 1 Kings 19:4-5.
7. 1 Kings 19:7.
8. Ursula Debarnot et al., "Sleep Contribution to Motor Memory Consolidation: A Motor Imagery Study," *Sleep* 32, no. 12 (December 2009): 1559–1565, https://doi.org/10.1093/sleep/32.12.1559.
9. Jeffrey M. Ellenbogen et al., "Interfering with Theories of Sleep and Memory: Sleep, Declarative Memory, and Associative Interference," *Current Biology* 16, no. 13 (July 11, 2006): 1290–1294, https://doi.org/10.1016/J.CUB.2006.05.024.
10. Jeffrey J. Iliff et al., "A Paravascular Pathway Facilitates CSF Flow through the Brain Parenchyma and the Clearance of Interstitial Solutes, Including Amyloid β," *Science Translational Medicine* 4, no. 147 (August 15, 2012): 147ra111, https://doi.org/10.1126/scitranslmed.3003748.
11. Sigmund Freud, *The Interpretation of Dreams*, trans. James Strachey (New York: Avon, 1965), 647.
12. Freud, *Interpretation of Dreams*, 215.
13. Genesis 1:14.
14. The Nobel Assembly at Karolinska Institutet, press release, October 2, 2017, https://www.nobelprize.org/prizes/medicine/2017/press-release/.
15. Nobel Assembly press release.

16. Marc D. Ruben et al., "A Database of Tissue-Specific Rhythmically Expressed Human Genes Has Potential Applications in Circadian Medicine," *Science Translational Medicine* 10, no. 458 (September 12, 2018): eaat8806, https://doi.org/10.1126/scitranslmed.aat8806.

17. Philip D. Campbell, Ann M. Miller, and Mary E. Woesner, "Bright Light Therapy: Seasonal Affective Disorder and Beyond," *Einstein Journal of Biology and Medicine* 32 (2017): E13–E25, https://www.ncbi.nlm.nih.gov/pmc/articles/PMC6746555/.

18. Damien Leger et al., "Sleep Disorders in Children with Blindness," *Annals of Neurology* 46, no. 4 (October 1999): 648–651, https://doi.org/10.1002/1531-8249 (199910)46:4<648::aid-ana14>3.0.co;2-x.

19. Ketema N. Paul, Talib B. Saafir, and Gianluca Tosini, "The Role of Retinal Photoreceptors in the Regulation of Circadian Rhythms," *Reviews in Endocrine and Metabolic Disorders* 10 (September 2009): 271–278, https://doi.org/10.1007/s11154-009-9120-x.

20. Gregg D. Jacobs, *Say Good Night to Insomnia: The Six-Week Solution* (New York: Henry Holt, 1998).

21. Gregg D. Jacobs et al., "Cognitive Behavior Therapy and Pharmacotherapy for Insomnia: A Randomized Controlled Trial and Direct Comparison," *Archives of Internal Medicine* 164, no. 17 (September 27, 2004): 1888–1896, https://doi.org/10.1001/archinte.164.17.1888.

22. There are some conditions, particularly bipolar disorder, where such sleep restriction needs to be carefully weighed against risks. Please speak to your doctor before trying this if you have bipolar disorder.

23. R. Nagare, B. Plitnick, and M. G. Figueiro, "Does the iPad Night Shift Mode Reduce Melatonin Suppression?," *Lighting Research & Technology* 51, no. 3 (2019): 373–383, https://doi.org/10.1177/1477153517748189.

24. Landon Hester et al., "Evening Wear of Blue-Blocking Glasses for Sleep and Mood Disorders: A Systematic Review," *Chronobiology International* 38, no. 10 (2021): 1375–1383, https://doi.org/10.1080/07420528.2021.1930029.

25. Dalia Al-Karawi and Luqman Jubair, "Bright Light Therapy for Nonseasonal Depression: Meta-Analysis of Clinical Trials," *Journal of Affective Disorders* 198 (July 2016): 64–71, https://doi.org/10.1016/J.JAD.2016.03.016.

26. The app can be downloaded here: https://mobile.va.gov/app/cbt-i-coach. See also Eric Kuhn et al., "A Pilot Randomized Controlled Trial of the Insomnia Coach Mobile App to Assess Its Feasibility, Acceptability, and Potential Efficacy," *Behavior Therapy* 53, no. 3 (May 2022): 440–457, https://doi.org/10.1016/J.BETH.2021.11.003.

27. For a list of trained, certified clinicians trained by Dr. Gregg Jacobs, visit https://www.cbtforinsomnia.com/clinicians-recently-trained-by-dr-jacobs/.

28. *Tao Tê Ching*, trans. R. B. Blakney (New York: Signet Classics, 1995), 105. *Tao Tê Ching* dates to approximately 500 BC and probably contains contributions from multiple people.

29. John Ortberg, "Ruthlessly Eliminate Hurry," *Christianity Today*, July 4, 2002, https://www.christianitytoday.com/pastors/2002/july-online-only/cln20704.html.

CHAPTER 9: EXERCISE: GET MOVING

1. *Merriam-Webster*, s.v. "lassitude (n.)," accessed May 31, 2023, https://www.merriam-webster.com/dictionary/lassitude.

2. St. Benedict, *The Rule of St. Benedict in English*, ed. Timothy Fry (Collegeville, MN: Liturgical Press, 1982), 69.

3. John 15:13, NLT.

4. C. S. Lewis, *The Screwtape Letters* (1942; reprint, New York: HarperCollins, 2001), 37.

5. 1 Corinthians 9:24-27.

6. Sammi R. Chekroud et al., "Association between Physical Exercise and Mental Health in 1.2 Million Individuals in the USA between 2011 and 2015: A Cross-Sectional Study," *Lancet Psychiatry* 5, no. 9 (September 8, 2018): 739–746, https://doi.org/10.1016/S2215-0366(18)30227-X.

7. Siri Kvam et al., "Exercise as a Treatment for Depression: A Meta-Analysis," *Journal of Affective Disorders* 202 (September 15, 2016): 67–86, https://doi.org/10.1016/j.jad.2016.03.063. Note that while exercise did work as augmentation to medication, the effect size was smaller. Treatment-resistant depression may be harder to address.

8. Samuel B. Harvey et al., "Exercise and the Prevention of Depression: Results of the HUNT Cohort Study," *American Journal of Psychiatry* 175, no. 1 (January 1, 2018): 28–36, https://doi.org/10.1176/appi.ajp.2017.16111223.

9. Centers for Disease Control and Prevention, "How Much Physical Activity Do Adults Need?," updated June 2, 2022, https://www.cdc.gov/physicalactivity/basics/adults/index.htm.

10. Zhiguo Jiang et al., "Strengthened Functional Connectivity in the Brain during Muscle Fatigue," *NeuroImage* 60, no. 1 (March 2012): 728–737, https://doi.org/10.1016/j.neuroimage.2011.12.013.

11. Yolanda Borrega-Mouquinho et al., "Effects of High-Intensity Interval Training and Moderate-Intensity Training on Stress, Depression, Anxiety, and Resilience in Healthy Adults during Coronavirus Disease 2019 Confinement: A Randomized Controlled Trial," *Frontiers in Psychology* 12 (February 24, 2021): 643069, https://doi.org/10.3389/fpsyg.2021.643069.

12. Chekroud et al., "Physical Exercise and Mental Health."

CHAPTER 10: MEANING: A *WHY* TO LIVE FOR

1. Irvin D. Yalom, *Existential Psychotherapy* (New York: Basic Books, 1980), 422.

2. Tait D. Shanafelt et al., "Changes in Burnout and Satisfaction with Work-Life Integration in Physicians during the First 2 Years of the COVID-19 Pandemic," *Mayo Clinic Proceedings* 97, no. 12 (December 2022): 2248–2258, https://doi.org/10.1016/j.mayocp.2022.09.002.

3. Nikitha K. Menon et al., "Association of Physician Burnout with Suicidal Ideation and Medical Errors," *JAMA Network Open* 3, no. 12 (2020): e2028780, https://doi.org/10.1001/jamanetworkopen.2020.28780.

4. Hippocrates, *Of the Epidemics*, book 1, sec. 2, para. 5, trans. Francis Adams, http://classics.mit.edu/Hippocrates/epidemics.1.i.html.

5. Quoted in Ashlee Vance, "This Tech Bubble Is Different," *Bloomberg Businessweek*, April 14, 2011, https://www.bloomberg.com/news/articles/2011-04-14/this-tech-bubble-is-different.

6. Viktor Frankl, *Man's Search for Meaning* (Boston: Beacon Press, 1959/2006), 99.

7. Randy Cohen, Chirag Bavishi, and Alan Rozanski, "Purpose in Life and Its Relationship to All-Cause Mortality and Cardiovascular Events: A Meta-Analysis,"

Psychosomatic Medicine 78, no. 2 (2016): 122–133, https://doi.org/10.1097/PSY .0000000000000274.

8. Jaime Kucinskas, Bradley R. E. Wright, and Stuart Riepl, "The Interplay between Meaning and Sacred Awareness in Everyday Life: Evidence from a Daily Smartphone Study," *International Journal for the Psychology of Religion* 28, no. 2 (2018): 71–88, https://doi.org/10.1080/10508619.2017.1419050.

9. M. E. P. Seligman et al., "Positive Psychology Progress: Empirical Validation of Interventions," *American Psychologist* 60, no. 5 (2005): 410–421, https://doi.org /10.1037/0003-066X.60.5.410.

10. Adam M. Grant et al., "Impact and the Art of Motivation Maintenance: The Effects of Contact with Beneficiaries on Persistence Behavior," *Organizational Behavior and Human Decision Processes* 103, no. 1 (May 2007): 53–67, https://doi.org/10.1016/J .OBHDP.2006.05.004.

CHAPTER 11: TRUTH: IT WILL SET YOU FREE

1. In its early days, cognitive therapy was a stand-alone therapy, focusing on cognition, or thoughts, rather than behavior. However, enough alignments were found with behavioral therapies that the streams were eventually combined into cognitive-behavioral therapy (CBT). Consequently, today there are not many purely cognitive therapists in practice; CBT is much more common. In this section, I refer to "cognitive therapy" to emphasize dealing with *beliefs*, not as something distinct from CBT, which would have no disagreements with the content of this section.

2. Of course, in reality, any solution would involve much more complex activity in the brain. This is used for illustration purposes only.

3. David D. Burns, *Strategies for Therapeutic Success: My 50 Most Effective Techniques* (self-published, 2006), 412.

4. John 5:6, NIV.

5. D. L. Norris, "The Effects of Mirror Confrontation on Self-Estimation of Body Dimensions in Anorexia Nervosa, Bulimia and Two Control Groups," *Psychological Medicine* 14, no. 4 (1984): 835–842, https://doi.org/10.1017/S0033291700019802.

6. Neir Eshel et al., "Global Connectivity and Local Excitability Changes Underlie Antidepressant Effects of Repetitive Transcranial Magnetic Stimulation," *Neuropsychopharmacology* 45, no. 6 (May 2020): 1018–1025, https://doi.org /10.1038/s41386-020-0633-z.

7. Adapted from Gilbert K. Chesterton, *Orthodoxy* (New York: Dodd, Mead, 1908), 58. Chesterton's original sentence is, "There is a thought that stops thought. That is the only thought that ought to be stopped."

8. Adapted from the *Oxford Advanced Learner's Dictionary*, s.v. "determinism (*n.*)," accessed May 12, 2023, https://www.oxfordlearnersdictionaries.com/definition /english/determinism.

9. *Oxford Advanced Learner's Dictionary*, s.v. "subjectivism (*n.*)," accessed May 12, 2023, https://www.oxfordlearnersdictionaries.com/definition/english/subjectivism.

10. Free will is philosophically and theologically complex. I believe the experience of making a choice has at least something real or true in it. Thomas Aquinas's argument is concise and describes at a minimum what must be happening: "Man has free-will:

otherwise counsels, exhortations, commands, prohibitions, rewards, and punishments would be in vain." Thomas Aquinas, *The Summa Theologiae of Thomas Aquinas*, second ed., trans. Fathers of the English Dominican Province (online ed., copyright 2017), question 83, https://www.newadvent.org/summa/1083.htm. I believe these things to be at least partly real and important. As Eleonore Stump, reflecting on Aquinas, says: "An act is free if and only if the ultimate cause of that act is the agent's own will and intellect." See Eleonore Stump, *Aquinas* (London: Routledge, 2003), 304.

11. Sigmund Freud, *Introductory Lectures on Psycho-Analysis*, trans. Joan Riviere (London: George Allen & Unwin, 1922), 87–88.

12. Karl Marx, *Selected Writings in Sociology and Social Philosophy*, trans. T. B. Bottomore (New York: McGraw-Hill, 1956), 24.

13. For more on this useful tool, see David D. Burns, *The Feeling Good Handbook*, rev. ed. (New York: Penguin, 1999), 73–96. For an online copy of the Daily Mood Log (but without the instructions), see https://content.randomhouse.com/assets /9780767923897/pdfs/Daily%20Mood%20Log.pdf.

14. Examples of negative emotions would include sadness, anxiety, guilt, shame, inferiority, loneliness, embarrassment, hopelessness, despair, frustration, anger—and many others.

15. Art Kleiner, Jeffrey Schwartz, and Josie Thomson, *The Wise Advocate: The Inner Voice of Strategic Leadership* (New York: Columbia University Press, 2019), 5.

16. If you're Christian, this doesn't have to be merely a thought exercise. You can rely on the wisdom and insight of the Holy Spirit, whom the Bible describes as "the Advocate" or "the Helper" (see John 14:16, 26).

17. David D. Burns, *Feeling Good: The New Mood Therapy* (New York: Avon, 1980), xviii–xix.

CHAPTER 12: RELATIONSHIPS: THE POWER OF TOGETHER

1. Bruce K. Alexander et al., "Effect of Early and Later Colony Housing on Oral Ingestion of Morphine in Rats," *Pharmacology Biochemistry and Behavior* 15, no. 4 (October 1981): 571–576, https://doi.org/10.1016/0091-3057(81)90211-2.

2. Similar studies have since confirmed that animals in standard laboratory conditions are primed for addictive-like and depressive-like behaviors. The more the conditions are relieved, the less the animals act like hopeless addicts. For example, see Kenneth J. Thiel et al., "Environmental Enrichment Counters Cocaine Abstinence-Induced Stress and Brain Reactivity to Cocaine Cues but Fails to Prevent the Incubation Effect," *Addiction Biology* 17, no. 2 (March 2012): 365–377, https://doi.org/10.1111 /j.1369-1600.2011.00358.x.

3. Aristotle, *Politics*, book 1, section 1253a. This statement is sometimes translated "man is a political animal," based on Aristotle's concern with the city-state as a model of community. The scope and scale of something like an American presidential election is absolutely not what he had in mind, which is why I selected the translation I did. Nonetheless, his main contention is the same as mine: It is part of the very nature of our humanity to be members of a community.

4. Laura Alejandra Rico-Uribe et al., "Association of Loneliness with All-Cause Mortality: A Meta-Analysis," *PLoS ONE* 13, no. 1 (2018): e0190033, https://doi.org/10.1371 /journal.pone.0190033.

5. Katherine M. Flegal et al., "Association of All-Cause Mortality with Overweight and Obesity Using Standard Body Mass Index Categories: A Systematic Review and Meta-Analysis," *Journal of the American Medical Association* 309, no. 1 (January 2, 2013): 71–82, https://doi.org/10.1001/jama.2012.113905.

6. Steven D. Barger, Nadine Messerli-Bürgy, and Jürgen Barth, "Social Relationship Correlates of Major Depressive Disorder and Depressive Symptoms in Switzerland: Nationally Representative Cross Sectional Study," *BMC Public Health* 14, no. 1 (2014): article 273, https://doi.org/10.1186/1471-2458-14-273.

7. Evren Erzen and Özkan Çikrikci, "The Effect of Loneliness on Depression: A Meta-Analysis," *International Journal of Social Psychiatry* 64, no. 5 (August 2018): 427–435, https://doi.org/10.1177/0020764018776349.

8. Daniel A. Cox, "The State of American Friendship: Change, Challenges, and Loss," Survey Center on American Life, June 8, 2021, https://www.americansurveycenter.org/research/the-state-of-american-friendship-change-challenges-and-loss/.

9. Joseph Carroll, "Americans Satisfied with Number of Friends, Closeness of Friendships," Gallup, March 5, 2004, https://news.gallup.com/poll/10891/americans-satisfied-number-friends-closeness-friendships.aspx.

10. May 2021 American Perspectives Survey results, cited in Cox, "State of American Friendship."

11. Joseph Henrich, Steven J. Heine, and Ara Norenzayan, "The Weirdest People in the World?" *Behavioral and Brain Sciences* 33, issue 2–3 (2010), https://doi.org/10.1017/S0140525X0999152X.

12. Lisa van der Storm et al., "Maternal and Paternal Parenting and Child Prosocial Behavior: A Meta-Analysis Using a Structural Equation Modeling Design," *Marriage and Family Review* 58, no. 1 (2022): 1–37, https://doi.org/10.1080/01494929.2021.1927931.

13. "Historical Living Arrangements of Children," United States Census Bureau, November 2022, https://www.census.gov/data/tables/time-series/demo/families/children.html.

14. Wendy Wang, "The U.S. Divorce Rate Has Hit a 50-Year Low," Institute for Family Studies, November 10, 2020, https://ifstudies.org/blog/the-us-divorce-rate-has-hit-a-50-year-low.

15. M. E. P. Seligman et al., "Positive Psychology Progress: Empirical Validation of Interventions," *American Psychologist* 60, no. 5 (2005): 410–421, https://doi.org/10.1037/0003-066X.60.5.410.

16. John 15:13, NLT.

CHAPTER 13: HOPE: THE THING WITH FEATHERS

1. Katelyn N. G. Long et al., "The Role of Hope in Subsequent Health and Well-Being for Older Adults: An Outcome-Wide Longitudinal Approach," *Global Epidemiology* 2 (2020): 100018, https://doi.org/10.1016/j.gloepi.2020.100018.

2. Eckhart Tolle, *The Power of Now* (Sydney: Hodder Australia, 2004), 35.

3. Aidan F. Langston, "Harvard Accepts Record-Low 5.2 Percent of Applicants for Class of 2020," April 1, 2016, *The Harvard Crimson*, https://www.thecrimson.com/article/2016/4/1/admissions-low-2020/; and Abhishek Som, "How to Get Software Engineering Jobs at Facebook," Interview Kickstart, August 23, 2021, https://www.interviewkickstart.com/blog/facebook-software-engineer-jobs.

4. Michaéla C. Schippers, Ad W. A. Scheepers, and Jordan B. Peterson, "A Scalable Goal-Setting Intervention Closes Both the Gender and Ethnic Minority Achievement Gap," *Palgrave Communications* 1 (2015): article 15014, https://doi.org/10.1057/palcomms.2015.14; D. Morisano et al., "Setting, Elaborating, and Reflecting on Personal Goals Improves Academic Performance," *Journal of Applied Psychology* 95, no. 2 (2010): 255–264, https://doi.org/10.1037/a0018478.

5. Schippers, Scheepers, and Peterson, "A Scalable Goal-Setting Intervention."

6. "Future Authoring," Self Authoring website, https://selfauthoring.com/future-authoring.

7. John F. Kennedy, address at Rice University on the nation's space effort, Houston, Texas, September 12, 1962, https://www.jfklibrary.org/archives/other-resources/john-f-kennedy-speeches/rice-university-19620912.

8. See "Working Backwards (the Amazon Method)" at https://www.productplan.com/glossary/working-backward-amazon-method/.

CHAPTER 14: BEAUTY: THE ELEVATOR OF CONSCIOUSNESS

1. Johnson Fam et al., "Visual Contrast Sensitivity in Major Depressive Disorder," *Journal of Psychosomatic Research* 75, no. 1 (July 2013): 83–86, https://doi.org/10.1016/j.jpsychores.2013.03.008.

2. Kyoung In Jung et al., "Attenuated Visual Function in Patients with Major Depressive Disorder," *Journal of Clinical Medicine* 9, no. 6 (2020): 1951, https://doi.org/10.3390/jcm9061951.

3. Gilbert K. Chesterton, "A Ballade of Suicide" (1915), The Society of G. K. Chesterton website, https://www.chesterton.org/a-ballade-of-suicide/.

4. Barbara Davidson, "The World's Most Popular Movie Locations," NetCredit, February 28, 2021, https://www.netcredit.com/blog/most-filmed-location-every-country/.

5. Kirsten M. M. Beyer et al., "Exposure to Neighborhood Green Space and Mental Health: Evidence from the Survey of the Health of Wisconsin," *International Journal of Environmental Research and Public Health* 11, no. 3 (March 21, 2014): 3453–3472, https://doi.org/10.3390/ijerph110303453.

6. Andy Crouch, *Culture Making: Recovering Our Creative Calling* (Downers Grove, IL: IVP Books, 2008), 235.

CHAPTER 15: BLESSEDNESS: BEYOND FLOURISHING

1. Sigmund Freud and Josef Breuer, *Studies in Hysteria*, trans. Nicola Luckhurst (New York: Penguin, 2004), 306.

2. Aristotle, *Nichomachean Ethics*, trans. W. D. Ross (Kitchener, ON: Batoche Books, 1999), 14.

3. I helped with the initial structure of the overall data gathering but did not work on this particular analysis. See Blake Victor Kent et al., "Do Daily Spiritual Experiences Moderate the Effect of Stressors on Psychological Well-Being? A Smartphone-Based Experience Sampling Study of Depressive Symptoms and Flourishing," *International Journal for the Psychology of Religion* 31, no. 2 (2020): 57–78, https://doi.org/10.1080/10508619.2020.1777766.

4. I'll use their terminology for this section, but the population assessed did not have major depressive disorder, so the term is somewhat misleading.

5. Note that this analysis was true for both "theistic" experiences like prayer and "non-theistic" experiences like meditation. I'm defining "somewhat" as one standard deviation above their usual, or in their personal 68th percentile. In other words, if we asked a person ten different times about their spiritual experiences, "somewhat" more aware of God than normal is the "third place" experience, better than seven other experiences but not quite the best.

6. Two standard deviations above their usual, or in their personal 95th percentile. If we asked a person twenty different times about their spiritual experiences, "very aware" is the "first place" experience, better than nineteen other experiences.

7. William Shakespeare, *Hamlet*, act 3, scene 1.

8. John Ortberg, *The Life You've Always Wanted: Spiritual Disciplines for Ordinary People* (Grand Rapids: Zondervan, 2009), 21–24. Ortberg is quoting his friend Tom Schmidt.

9. Philippians 4:7.

About the Author

Dr. David M. Carreon is a psychiatrist and cofounder of Acacia Mental Health, a clinic in Silicon Valley working to transform mental health care. He studied and served at Stanford, where he earned his MD, completed a psychiatry residency, and worked as a professor. He is a leading clinician in the treatment of major depressive disorder, achieving success in some of the most challenging cases using an approach that combines the latest technologies and the oldest truths. His research has focused on human agency and on new ways to restore freedom through treating depression. He loves teaching; going on dates with his wife, Abigail; and excessively long brunch conversations.

Tyndale | REFRESH

Think Well. Live Well. Be Well.

Experience the flourishing of your mind, body, and soul with Tyndale Refresh.